Mad for
GLORY

Mad for GLORY

A Heart of Darkness in the War of 1812

ROBERT BOOTH

Tilbury House Publishers

Thomaston, Maine

Tilbury House Publishers
12 Starr Street, Thomaston, Maine 04861
800-582-1899 • www.tilburyhouse.com

First hardcover edition November 2015
ISBN 978-0-88448-357-1
eBook ISBN 978-0-88448-416-5

Library of Congress Control Number: 2015952705

Text designed by Janet Robbins, North Wind Design and Production
Cover designed by Jon Friedman, Frame25 Productions

Printed in the USA by the Maple Press, York, PA.

15 16 17 18 19 20 MAP 5 4 3 2 1

Show me a hero, and I'll write you a tragedy.

—F. Scott Fitzgerald, from the notebooks, 1945

This life mask of David Porter was made in 1825, eleven years after he lost the USS *Essex* in the bloodiest naval fight of the War of 1812. His face still bore a large right-cheek scar earned not in battle, but in the streets of Baltimore during his escape from a mob. *(Fenimore Art Museum, Cooperstown, New York; gift of Stephen C. Clark, N0215.1961; photograph by Richard Walker)*

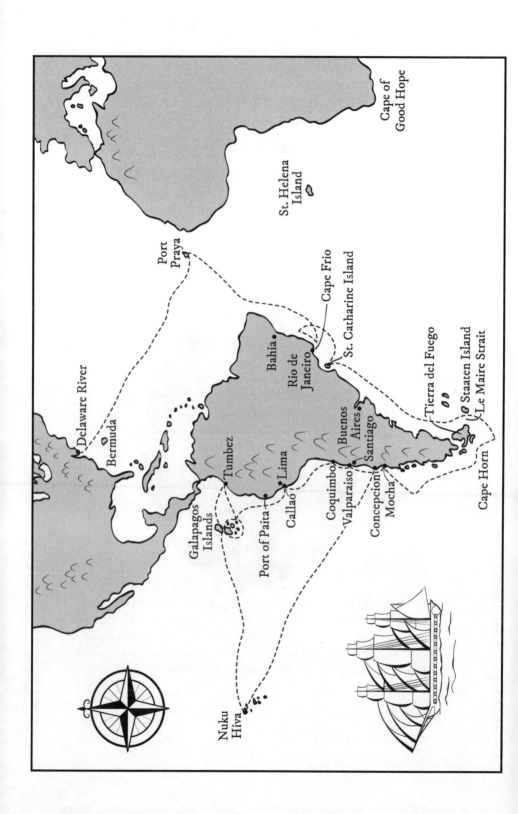

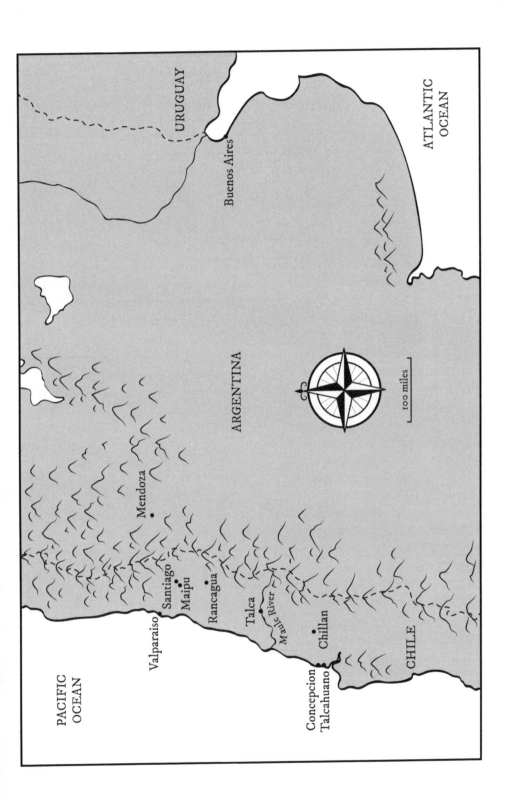

PACIFIC
OCEAN

URUGUAY

Buenos Aires

ATLANTIC
OCEAN

ARGENTINA

100 miles

Mendoza

Valparaiso
Santiago
Maipu
Rancagua
Talca
Maule River
Concepcion
Talcahuano
Chillan

CHILE

In memory of my father

Robert A. Booth
1922–2000

Pacific navigator, famous handicapper

Contents

Prologue 1

1. Captain Porter 5
2. Consul General Poinsett 13
3. Against the Gods 21
4. Off the Chart 33
5. Revolution in Chile 42
6. A New America 52
7. Americans at War 63
8. A-whaling 78
9. Opotee in Nooaheevah 95
10. Taipi 114
11. Rendezvous 126
12. Victory 140
13. Consequences 158
14. Rancagua 175
15. Reverberations 185
16. Minute Guns 203

Sources   224
Index   237
About the Author 245

Prologue

On the afternoon of March 13, 1813, while running past a desolate stretch of Chilean shoreline, the square-rigged U.S. frigate *Essex* has the misfortune of losing her main topsail yard. Her captain, David Porter, intent on making an impressive entrance at the port of Valparaiso, orders his battleship hove-to.

That night, after repairs are made, the *Essex* rides at anchor in the gentle swells of the western ocean and Captain Porter sleeps soundly, dreaming of the British whalers that he has come so far to capture, a fleet of them, slow and awkward and full of oil, easy prey for a mighty battleship. Waking in the dark, striking a match, he is convinced that the moment has arrived. He wakes his lieutenant and gives orders, and by sunrise 300 men are at their battle stations and the *Essex* is bowling along under full sail.

Taking up his spyglass, Porter searches the horizon in the morning brightness, seeing only the azure line and low clouds in the distance. Confident, he keeps his vigil by the hour, until his men start muttering and his officers are exchanging glances. Finally, betrayed by his dreams and the empty sea, the scar-faced little captain gives it up and sets the *Essex* on a course for the coast under English colors. The mariners soon spot fishing vessels and know that they are close to their destination, but when a signal is sent aloft to summon a pilot, the local skippers stay away.

The *Essex* sails on, trending northeasterly. In the distance are a couple of huts and some cattle on a coast "skirted by a black and gloomy rock, against the perpendicular sides of which the sea beats with fury." Farther inland, the country appears "dreary beyond description: yellow and barren hills, cut by torrents into deep ravines." This stark foreground to the blank immensity of the Andes is far from Porter's long-held fantasy of "handsome villages and well-cultivated hills" beside a beautiful blue Pacific.

Rounding the next barren bluff, the Point of Angels, Porter seeks some sign of the elusive port of the Valley of Paradise. He scans a long sandy beach, then a mule-train zigzagging its way down a hill, then "in an instant afterwards, the whole town—shipping with their colors flying, and the forts—burst out, as it were, from behind the rocks": Valparaiso at last.

But Porter sails too close to the cliffs, and the frigate's sails luff as she suddenly decelerates. With a rush of paranoid dread, he realizes that his error has left them helpless "under the guns of a battery prepared to fire into us." Seconds pass in silence as the *Essex* glides slowly on, until a breeze fills her topgallants and starts her back on her way. Evidently the English flag is a sufficient shield, for she sails unmolested toward an "animated" scene in the harbor, which includes a deep-riding American brig with her yards and topmasts struck, and a big "clumsy-looking" English vessel that Porter imagines to be "a whaler repairing her damages after her passage around Cape Horn." Then he spots several large Spanish merchant ships preparing to depart, perhaps for Peru; if they recognize him, they might inform the English up the coast.

Porter roars at his lieutenant, John Downes, to put the helm down and send the *Essex* back out to sea, and in four windy hours they are thirty miles away, staring at another vista of "sun-burnt hills" dotted with cattle. Upon reflection, however, Porter realizes that this too is wrong. Callao, some 1,400 nautical miles north—the port for Lima, the Spanish viceroy's royal capital—is the more dangerous port, so he reverses course for Valparaiso, and when the *Essex* reenters the bay she is flying her true colors, the Stars and Stripes.

Porter knows that the Spanish officials will not be happy. He has brought a new war with him, that of the upstart United States against Spain's ally Great Britain; he is endangering the peace of Chile, a quiet country slumbering by the ocean. But he needs provisions for his 300 men and for the dozens of British sailors whom he is holding prisoner down below, some in irons.

Porter has brought his ship around Cape Horn unauthorized, bent on a private mission of wealth and glory. Ignorant of conditions in the Pacific world, he has no idea that Chile is in revolt, that its people will regard him as a savior, and that he is about to encounter the only other American official in the Pacific, Joel Roberts Poinsett, U.S. consul general for Southern Spanish America.

Chile's fateful gravity has drawn Porter and Poinsett into the presence of three other remarkable figures: José Miguel Carrera, the heroic leader of the revolution, seeking support for his embattled government; José Fernando de Abascal, the Spanish viceroy at Lima and virtual monarch of western South America, sworn to crush the rebellion; and Captain James Hillyar of the Royal Navy, sent out on pain of death to win Chile for Britain. As these men and forces converge, the longtime peace of the somnolent Pacific will be shattered, and systems and cultures will collapse under the massive violence imported from the Atlantic world.

But none of that is apparent as the *Essex* approaches Valparaiso. Captain Porter, thirty-three, and Consul Poinsett, thirty-four, have traveled thousands of miles by very different routes to come face to face here. Porter has embarked upon the longest, strangest cruise in naval history; Poinsett is deeply involved in creating a new nation. The self-reliance of these men is impressive and typically American. No other country could have produced (or empowered) people so certain of their ability as individuals to effect change on a massive scale.

Porter is a ruthless buccaneer and Poinsett a romantic idealist, but each considers himself a patriot and an agent of destiny. The Pacific is not a theater of the larger war nor even understood to be an area of American strategic interest, yet these two young men, a navy captain and an ambassador, both operating well beyond the chain of command, will become the godfathers of all subsequent United States imperialism and nation-building.

Chapter One

Captain Porter

In his Baltimore boyhood, David Porter Jr., small and skinny, was his mother's favorite, much given to playing pirate and reading about the freebooters of the Spanish Main and the more recent explorers of the Pacific. Despite his interest in books, he was not destined for college or the countinghouse, and so received only a grammar-school education. From their hilltop home, where his sea-captain father had set up a marine signal tower, David could see the tall ships coming up the Chesapeake and imagine their adventures on all the seas of the world.*

That pleasant dream ended in 1796 when he was thrown into the hardships of merchant seafaring at the age of sixteen. He worked as a deckhand for his father, a pugnacious former navy man and privateer of the Revolution, aboard a small trading schooner manned by five other crewmen. On his first voyage to the Caribbean—the West Indies of rum, sugar, and molasses—the boy participated in a horrifying battle with an armed cutter of the British Royal Navy. The Americans, without weapons, resorted to throwing knives and belaying pins at their opponents, who fired guns and

---

* The Porters were not, as has been claimed elsewhere, a Boston family. David's father came from Delaware, and his mother was the daughter of an immigrant. David Porter was born February 1, 1780, in Medford, Massachusetts, near Boston, the son of David Porter (1754–1808), a Delawarean then privateering out of Boston, and Margaret Henry (1755–1801), born in Boston, the daughter of a blacksmith from Scotland.

cannon into the vessel, killing two of David's new friends. In three later voyages, he met with more gunfire and brief imprisonment. He concluded that the world was harsh and violent, to be met with greater violence, and he developed a hatred of the English that convinced Captain Porter to enroll his scrawny son as a midshipman in the navy.

Porter had grown up in a post-revolutionary country facing westward. While the nations of Europe engaged in a war for world domination beginning in 1793, the United States had enjoyed an exemption. Neutral America was free to pursue its own prosperity and growth at the expense of Native Americans but otherwise without interference. People poured through the western valleys into the new lands of Ohio, Kentucky, and Tennessee, clearing wilderness and planting farms. At sea, things were not so gratifying: for a few years in the 1790s, Yankee shipping was subject to predation by the navies of the two main combatants, England and France.

As a world player with no part in the world war, America found that its neutrality had serious consequences abroad. Both Napoleon Bonaparte—leader of a November 1799 coup that had made him first consul of Revolutionary France—and the English under King George attempted to draw America into the conflict as an ally and to block its ability to render assistance to the enemy. President Thomas Jefferson, happy to purchase the Louisiana Territory from the French in 1803, was unwilling to encourage alliances or build up an oceangoing navy. His main goal was to preserve America as the land of peace and plenty and to foster the populating of the western lands.

There was one exception to Jefferson's strategy of peaceful neutrality, and that was the limited war with the Barbary States of North Africa. It began in 1801 and was conducted by the navy to make the seas safe for American merchant shipping in the Mediterranean. During this conflict, as in the recent naval quasi-war with France, young David Porter stood out. Most of his fellow middies had been raised in well-to-do families with some degree of gentility and refinement, and they had none of his experience of the harsh realities of seafaring. Their tendency to hesitate and reflect found no analogue in Porter's rash temperament. He showed great courage under fire and was wounded in action at sea and on the shore.

He was on board the frigate *Philadelphia* with Captain William Bainbridge when she ran aground at Tripoli and had to be surrendered, with all of her men given up and incarcerated for more than a year. Cheerful amid the general dismay and depression of imprisonment, Porter was much admired for teaching navigation to the boys and for improving his own abilities. From officers who were much better educated than he, Porter learned French, drawing, and elegant handwriting, crowned by a highly stylized signature that would ornament all of his future correspondence.

Lieutenant Porter emerged from his early years in the navy as a fierce fighter with a short fuse, a good seaman and leader of men, intrepid and decisive. His superiors liked him, peers feared him, and men followed him proudly. Away from war zones, he worked hard to meet the navy's expectations of an officer and a gentleman. Sometimes, though, trouble seemed to follow him. Returning briefly to his hometown of Baltimore, he was sent by the navy on a nighttime foray into the sailor's district of Fell's Point to recruit—or, more accurately, to impress—young men into the service. Things went wrong, and Porter killed a popular tavern keeper while trying to fight his way out of a mob. With his face torn open, he ran to the docks, leaped into a boat, and rowed off into the darkness.

Navy officials protected their headstrong young officer, although his temper remained a liability. Back in the Mediterranean, on a Sunday in a crowded harbor, Porter, then commanding a small cruiser, ordered his men to kidnap a mouthy British seaman. He had the man strung up in the rigging for a barbaric public flogging, an action that nearly started a battle, if not a war.

Later, while on Mediterranean joint maneuvers with the Royal Navy, he reined in his Anglophobia sufficiently to cultivate a friendship with an older British captain at Gibraltar, James Hillyar, and his kindly wife and sweet children. "Visiting them frequently," Porter, for the first time in years, experienced the pleasures of domesticity. For the Hillyars, Porter wrote, "I entertained the greatest respect; and among the American officers generally no officer of the British navy was so great a favorite as Captain Hillyar."

After 1806, when Britain achieved uncontested dominance of the seas, America's ship owners lost their protected monopoly of the world's freight. In the absence of any blue-water American navy, England and France were both free to implement policies inimical to American shippers. London promoted British maritime commerce and employed the Royal Navy, with a thousand vessels of war, to carry out a policy of harassment toward Americans.

Returning to America in 1807 after a long spell overseas, Porter, twenty-seven, fell in with a group of Manhattan writers who adopted him as their much-admired "Sindbad." Their leader, Washington Irving, who would go on to become first among American authors, was then publishing the satiric magazine *Salmagundi* and had just bestowed the name of Gotham upon New York. In barrooms and on rambles into the countryside with these new friends, Porter found himself flattered as the man of action and experience, able to hold his own in their quick-witted company. His companions validated his efforts at self-improvement and encouraged him to write a book about his naval adventures in the tradition of Captain Cook and the buccaneers—a thing no American seaman had yet done.

Duty soon called Lieutenant Porter away from New York. Recommitting to the navy, whose numbers had been reduced in time of peace, he evidently felt that marriage would help him to advance in his career. Impulsively, he pursued Evelina Anderson, seventeen, the daughter of a well-connected hotelier of Chester, Pennsylvania, near Philadelphia. Courting her against her family's wishes, he finally won over her parents and took his prize. Soon after the wedding, Porter was promoted to the rank of commander and assigned to run the naval station at New Orleans, a desk job in a seamy city on the edge of the newly acquired Louisiana Territory. Porter's widowed father went with the couple. Overstating his scientific qualifications, Porter persuaded the secretary of the navy to sponsor an exploring expedition on the way to New Orleans. They traveled 800 miles over hills and down rivers in the spirit of Meriwether Lewis and William Clark—whose already famous expedition into the Louisiana Purchase had departed in 1804—but, as it happened, without any of the results.

At New Orleans, Porter's father died of sunstroke and the senior Porter's friend George Farragut lost his wife to yellow fever. Commander Porter stepped in to adopt the suddenly motherless ten-year-old James Glasgow Farragut, renaming the boy David after himself and turning him into a naval midshipman who would be his constant companion for years to come.

Porter had little patience with bureaucracy and was happiest when chasing smugglers along the coast of West Florida, now Alabama. His capture of some notorious privateers earned him federal bonus money and a large reward allegedly posted by merchants in Havana. The former would prove very difficult to cash in, and the latter would become an elusive obsession; both would feed his resentment of the navy secretary.

He left New Orleans as soon as he could, in 1809. Excited by reports from the Lewis and Clark Expedition, and perhaps aware of American adventurer William Shaler's published description of California and the weakness of its Spanish defenses, Commander Porter thought he knew how to make himself most useful to the United States: by realizing his dreams of exploring the Pacific.

Since Captain Cook's voyages in the 1760s, the Pacific Ocean had called to mariners and entrepreneurs intent on discovering the possibilities of a new world. By the 1780s, British and American merchants were sending ships to the Pacific Northwest to trade with the Aleut, Tlingit, Chinook, and other Native peoples for glossy otter pelts. These beautiful furs, taken west across the ocean, turned out to have great value in China and spurred lucrative businesses run primarily from Boston and London.

At the same time, the whale-oil barons of the Massachusetts island town of Nantucket were sending ships and men into the Pacific—the South Sea that Spain considered its own. Their relentless pursuit of sperm whales, largest and most oil-rich of the cetaceans, yielded immense profits. Not to be outdone in seafaring or moneymaking, London merchants had their own strategy for the Pacific: they enticed large numbers of Nantucketers to relocate to England and serve on British whaleships.* Spain, Russia, Britain, and the United States all made claims on the Pacific coast of North America, but none had yet explored and mapped it thoroughly, inventoried its resources, or colonized its territory. With the European world preoccupied by war, Porter saw a great opportunity for America to fulfill its manifest destiny and for himself to become a national hero.

He submitted a fulsome proposal to Secretary of the Navy Paul Hamilton and to former President Jefferson requesting that he be given a couple of ships and some men and supplies to visit the west coast and secure American territory there. To his astonishment, they had no interest. Denied his Pacific fantasy, Porter informed Secretary Hamilton that he intended to leave the navy if he was not given a promotion. Hamilton counseled patience and held out the prospect of Porter's commanding

---

* Whale oil, and especially sperm-whale oil, was a superior source of lighting, but it was in no way essential to British manufacturing, claims to the contrary notwithstanding.

one of the navy's twelve real battleships. He assured Porter that a war was coming soon.

England, dominating the high seas in its war with France, had continued to exercise its treaty right to detain American ships and inspect them for contraband and to impress any English-born sailors found on board. The French were far more damaging to American interests: Napoleon, who controlled all the ports of Continental Europe, engaged in wholesale impoundment of American vessels and their cargoes, leaving the owners without any hope of recovery. Consequently, Federalist ship owners—residing mainly in New York and New England—had many reasons to hate the French, while Jefferson and his successor as president as of 1809, James Madison, heads of the pro-French Democratic-Republican Party, inflamed the public by exaggerating the extent of British impressment of American sailors.

At that time the United States had a population of about seven million, of whom one million were enslaved. Other than neutrality, the government had no foreign policy and no overseas ambitions, but change was coming out of the West, where several new territories had been claimed, reaching across the Mississippi all the way to the disputed Oregon frontier. Clearly, the country was destined to become enormous both in geography and in population, with ceaseless waves of pioneers peopling the regions soon to become new states.

In 1811, Henry Clay of Kentucky, avatar of this western future, became speaker of the U.S. House of Representatives and began pushing hard for Congress to drop neutrality and declare war on Britain. He and his adherents in the Democratic-Republican Party aimed to drive the British out of North America—to take Canada and the Great Lakes regions—and to push the Native American peoples, clients of the British, across the Mississippi. Under a banner of "Free Trade and Sailors' Rights," the war party's operatives agitated in the seaports, hoping to extend their political base into enough of the old states to win a resolution in Congress.

War was indeed on its way, and Commander Porter, still arguing for a captaincy, agreed to take on the eleven-year-old *Essex* despite his deep dissatisfaction with the vessel and with a perceived lack of respect from the Navy Department. He felt that the *Essex* was not fast enough and had the wrong armament—too many carronades, good only for close-in smashing, and too few long guns for engaging a distant opponent. He demanded a transfer to a different vessel and even wrote a confidant that the navy secretary was an incompetent drunkard who owed him a small fortune.

Porter finally won his coveted promotion to captain despite a notorious gaffe in New York. While preparing the *Essex* for sea, he allowed his men to tar and feather a patriotic fellow sailor and throw him into the street for the crime of being born in England and thus unable to swear an oath against his home country. The public outcry in Manhattan was loud enough to disturb Porter's superiors—"I do exceedingly regret that an officer of your high rank and intelligence should have permitted the proceeding in question," wrote Secretary Hamilton—but they could not afford to lose him. The lack of experienced naval commanders was one of the many indicators that the country was unprepared for the war it was rushing into.

Privately, Porter was fanatical about many aspects of the upcoming conflict. The war planners, he thought, were crazy to want to invade Canada—it was not "the most noble and dignified" way to oppose Britannia, which he considered vulnerable on the very waves she claimed to rule. He imagined oceans lit up by the fires of burning British merchantmen, and American naval vessels falling like wolves upon hapless fleets while somehow the Royal Navy missed the action. Despite the irrational quality of this vision, Porter believed fervently that the undersized U.S. Navy could do more damage to imperial Britain by interfering with its vital maritime trade than by harassing its vastly superior navy or sending armies across a border.

And he was furious at the role to be played by American privateers. Consumed by his hallucination of a free-ranging, unstoppable navy, he could not abide the thought of a large private force consisting of hundreds of well-armed vessels of all sizes, widely dispersed and preying at will on the enemy's shipping. "I detest the idea of trusting to our privateers for the destruction of British commerce," he wrote to a friend. "Are we to become a nation of buccaneers, a nest of villains, a detestable set of pirates? When a general system of piracy is countenanced by our government, when the whole maritime defense of a nation consists of buccaneers, farewell national honor, farewell national pride!"

But no matter how much he might wish it otherwise, the enormous, well-protected, worldwide commerce of the British Empire could not be significantly affected by a tiny navy, and a privateer fleet was the only means of expanding American sea power. Porter's red-hot temper and his ungovernable jealousy continued to blind him. He was certain that he was right, and anyone who disagreed with him was stupid or a traitor, including the navy secretary: "I shall persevere," he declared. "It is noble to struggle against the gods."

Chapter Two

Consul General Poinsett

W hen Commander Porter had been departing New Orleans in 1809,
Joel Roberts Poinsett, Esq., had been leaving France after a stay of
several years in Europe. A young gentleman of independent means, possessed
of elegant manners and martial dignity, Poinsett was nearly unique among
Americans of his time. He had spent most of his adult life in foreign countries, without any affiliations or obligations, living out the remarkable conceit
of a self-invented patrician military officer and roving amateur diplomat.

Poinsett's journey had begun early. When only thirteen, he had
been sent north by his wealthy and ambitious Charleston parents to be
educated in Connecticut by the famous traveler and author Reverend Timothy Dwight, soon to become president of Yale.* Three years later, Poinsett
boarded a ship for London, his mother's native city, and there he studied at
his uncle's private school before going on to Edinburgh, Scotland, to begin
college and follow his father into the medical profession.

But continuous intensive study laid him low, and after recuperating
in Lisbon, he returned to England with a plan to satisfy his strong sense of
patriotism and his desire for personal glory. A career as a soldier—no doubt
culminating as a general of armies—would assure him of adventure and

---

* Joel Poinsett received his early classical education from the excellent James Hamden Thomson of Charleston, a graduate of Princeton and a native of Abington, Massachusetts.

activity as well as responsibility commensurate with his ego. Subsequently he received private instruction in military science and engineering, but once again he fell ill. He retreated to Charleston for the first time since boyhood, hoping to join the peacetime army, but instead his father arranged for him to read the law. Chafing against the drudgery of legal studies, Poinsett finally persuaded Doctor Poinsett, by then a widower, to send his only surviving son on another voyage across the Atlantic in 1801 to make the grand tour of the capitals of Europe.

So ended the first phase of the remarkable career of Joel Roberts Poinsett, during which his foreign travels and mastery of several languages and subjects, from law to medicine to warfare, made him the talk of Charleston. What was he preparing for? Where would it end? He made no answer; he had become a gentleman and a scholar, true, but that was merely a prelude to his next role, in which he would realize the fantasy of living heroically in Europe, challenging himself to have grand adventures and see amazing sights, to discuss policy with statesmen and princes, to attend the salons of deep thinkers and great writers, to be the first to represent his country in remote and exotic places. Long before the days of Richard Burton and T. E. Lawrence, this rather frail young American decided to risk everything in order to see what one man, alone in the world, could learn—and perhaps achieve. He would spend most of the next eight years abroad, and father and son would never meet again.

In Paris, Poinsett studied the arts of statecraft, war, and the wielding of power as exemplified by Napoleon, self-made emperor of France and general of its ever-victorious armies. French civilization was superior in many ways; as an American patriot, Poinsett intended to observe what made it great and what he could take away to apply at home, both to advance his own career and to improve the government and military of his country.

After a few months he took to the field, hiking from Switzerland through Savoy and Italy, visiting counts and philosophers. Armed only with letters of introduction, he beguiled his way into rarefied settings where rank and privilege had always prevailed but where all were willing to set aside their biases in order to host a real American. To them, Poinsett personified the intelligence and vigor of the New World; from them, he gathered an appreciation of the art, manners, culture, and conversation of the Old. Returning to France, he went on to march with republican militiamen in Switzerland and to visit Robert Livingston, the American minister to France. He and Livingston spent a few weeks near Geneva as guests of the crumbling old financier Jacques Necker, whose dismissal as France's minister of finance by King Louis XVI in 1789 had provoked the storming of the Bastille. By the time of Poinsett's visit, Necker was living his final days in lofty exile with his doting daughter, Napoleon's nemesis, the famous author Madame de Staël.

Having absorbed a great deal of Napoleonic lore and added substantially to his knowledge of American policy and diplomacy, Poinsett departed for Austria, footing it through Bavaria to Vienna, where he found a place at the imperial court. Learning there of the death of his father, he sailed for America and arrived just as his only sister Susan contracted a fatal illness. With her death he inherited a large fortune. He traveled in Canada and in the American Northeast, then spent a few months in Charleston as an aide to Governor Charles Pinckney, who made him a major in the state militia.

In 1807, with his impersonation now perfected by a South Carolina uniform as gaudy as a costume from an operetta, Poinsett returned to Europe and this time introduced himself in Saint Petersburg, the capital of Russia, where he was received by the new czar, Alexander. A strapping fellow Poinsett's own age, Alexander happily granted a place at court to this new man from across the seas. Poised, gallant, and multilingual, Colonel Poinsett, by all appearances an officer of the American army, soon became a popular member of the glittering inner circle of nobles and military men at the palace, many of them Russian but others from all over Europe, driven into exile by Bonaparte and hoping for vengeance. Alexander, allied with Britain against the French, spoke with Poinsett about American political principles and came away impressed. "Were I not an emperor," he averred, "I would certainly be a republican!"

Alexander offered his American military friend a high post in the Russian army, but Poinsett wavered. In all of his wanderings, he had remained certain that the United States was the true hope of the world; now, fearing a loss of his identity, he declined Alexander's offer of command but accepted his invitation to conduct a fact-finding mission to the frontiers of the empire as his personal representative. Accompanied by an English friend, his manservant Sam, and an eight-man Cossack bodyguard, Poinsett entered a large carriage and began a journey over hundreds of miles through the forests south to Moscow, and then hundreds more across the steppes to the Volga, then down toward the Caspian city of Astrachan, the mart and resort of all the westward-trending caravans of Asia.

Heading southeast into the nomadic territories of Persia, Poinsett risked his life several times and witnessed many sights previously unseen by American eyes. Finally he turned toward the setting sun and reentered the war-torn frontiers of his own ancestral Europe. Bored by a Russian army siege in Armenia, he traversed the mountains to the Black Sea and then rode steadily across the steppes and through the forests back to the palace at Saint Petersburg. Only three of his eight companions survived the trip, and Poinsett himself, after reporting to the czar, decided to head for the healing waters of the hot springs at Teplitz. There he met the Prussian monarchs in exile, stunned at the defeat of their army by Napoleon and happy to enjoy the diversion of Poinsett's thrilling tales. The queen described her shame at having had to beg Napoleon for an armistice, and the king observed that, while "he could not have expected to terminate a disastrous war by an advantageous peace," still he had expected assistance from his ally the czar, who, after suffering initial defeats by French forces, had changed sides and accepted Napoleon's gift of a piece of Prussia.

Poinsett returned to Paris and eagerly followed news of the brilliant French campaign against Austria, ending in the capture of Vienna and in Bonaparte's marriage to its princess. He read about the British haplessly fighting Napoleon in Spain, and he correctly predicted their defeat—although they would regroup and renew their invasion later. He studied military science with a special focus on cavalry tactics, and he took private fencing lessons from one of Napoleon's generals, the amused survivor of a botched assassination attempt by the emperor himself.

Full of Europe, Poinsett returned to the United States in 1809 to seek a place in the upper echelons of the military at Washington, D.C. His rather high appraisal of self-worth was not misplaced. Through his Charleston friend Thomas Sumter Jr., the new ambassador to Brazil, he was re-introduced to Treasury Secretary Albert Gallatin, President Madison's closest advisor. To Gallatin's surprise, Poinsett passed along to him a proposal from Czar Alexander for a Russian-American partnership in the Pacific Northwest to fend off the British Canadians. Madison met with Poinsett but decided not to pursue it; he was more interested in the American Southeast. Poinsett made a strong impression, however. No other American could match his knowledge of the current state of Europe, and John Quincy Adams, the first American minister to Russia, would report that the czarina had suggested that the elegant Colonel Poinsett be made an ambassador.

President Madison and his cabinet had begun looking seriously at ongoing revolutionary events in Spanish America. Madison, only dimly aware of the extent of these independence movements, had no great desire to challenge Spain except in the Floridas—the big Florida peninsula in the east, and the coastal regions of what are now Mississippi and Alabama in the west. He had decided that these places, adjoining American states and territories, needed to be acquired before the British or French could do so. His opportunity came in June 1810 when word arrived that Francisco Miranda and others at Caracas had called for all of Spanish America to follow them into rebellion against Spain. Rather than wait for an insurrection in West Florida, Madison planned to annex by proclamation.

In the course of these maneuverings, Madison and Gallatin conferred about the news from South America. Creoles, the native-born descendants of Spanish settlers, had declared independence in Buenos Aires and in Mexico City, as in Caracas. American merchant shippers were already engaged in a large business at Caracas and Buenos Aires, at Rio in Brazil, at Veracruz in Mexico, and in many other Caribbean ports, including Havana. With Spanish America starting to fracture, the United States, with its maritime commerce imperiled, remained a noncombatant in the world war, while Great Britain, in particular, began to militarize in the western hemisphere.

Britain, building its empire through conquest and alliance, had made Brazil a client state by rescuing the Portuguese royal family from Napoleon. Rio de Janeiro was the new imperial capital of King Joao and his wife, Carlotta, sister of the imprisoned king of Spain, and Britain's large naval base at Rio ensured its domination of the South Atlantic. Madison agreed with Gallatin that it was time to start monitoring events from the inside. They tasked Secretary of State Robert Smith with hiring three men to serve as spies. Foremost was Smith's old friend Captain William Shaler, author, mariner, and smuggler on the coast of Chile, who was given the Mexican assignment, while Robert Lowry of Baltimore was assigned the post in Caracas. They sailed in June 1810. When the candidate for the Buenos Aires job reneged, Secretary Gallatin thought of the ambitious fellow from Charleston.*

By mid-August 1810, Gallatin reported to President Madison, "I have found a gentleman who appears to me peculiarly fitted in every respect for the undertaking [in Buenos Aires]. It is Mr. Poinsett of South Carolina,

---

* Maltby Gelston of New York, son of the collector of customs there, was their first choice.

with whose intellect, information, and standing you are already acquainted." Poinsett's mastery of French and Spanish would serve him well in a polyglot setting. Moreover, he combined independent wealth with committed patriotism; "his object being reputation and not money, there is no fear of his thinking of monopolies and private speculations instead of applying his whole time and faculties to the public objects."

Gallatin noted that Poinsett wished for a military appointment at home, and had agreed to this mission out of a sense of patriotic duty, not preference. His absence in South America, he hoped, might "not be prejudicial to any promotion" into a top army position if the United States should engage in a war. Given "the difficulty of obtaining agents perfectly qualified and willing to go," Gallatin persuaded Madison to expand Poinsett's responsibilities to include Peru and Chile, on the Pacific side of the continent.

The new secret agent sailed for Rio in October 1810 and arrived at Buenos Aires in February 1811. There, he did his job exceedingly well, spying and fomenting amid the imperial designs of Europeans and the rebel aspirations of the Creoles. His hosts in Argentina had been the first to establish an independent state, having overthrown the Spanish viceroy's rule in May 1810. For eight months Poinsett worked with this rebel government, rulers of the huge United Provinces—modern Paraguay, Uruguay, Bolivia, and Argentina—to advance American interests and block the British. As a secret agent, he regularly filed exemplary reports on commerce, politics, geography, and demographics, but it was as a provocateur that he truly excelled.

England, long at war, had the ability, by diplomacy or by force, to devour much of the faltering Spanish empire in the western hemisphere. The English, however, were not popular with the people in general or the rebel leaders in particular. A few years before, British troops had invaded Buenos Aires only to be defeated—a matter that could not easily be forgotten by either side and one that Poinsett constantly exploited, contrasting America's peaceful commerce with Britain's warmaking. More recently London, despite claims of friendship toward the rebels, had made an alliance with the royalist junto in Spain. Consistency and honesty meant little to the English ministers of state as they pursued their larger goal, which was outright victory in this interminable, winner-take-all world war.

The Buenos Aires junto—the independent government's executive council, which pretended loyalty to the Spanish king, Fernando, so as not to invite an invasion—had no love for the British, and welcomed Poinsett as the secret representative of the still-neutral United States. So well did he do his work, so thoroughly did he compromise relations between the junto and the British, that the name of Poinsett was known and reviled in London as well as in Madrid and Rio de Janeiro. When the moment came for public recognition, he convinced the junto to acknowledge him before receiving any British officials. He advised on regulations for maritime commerce that gave Americans the exact same rights and privileges as the British, and he convinced the junto to outlaw the impressment of sailors by Britain's Royal Navy—an outcome that infuriated his opponents.

In late May 1811, Roberts Poinsett received a letter from the new secretary of state, James Monroe, appointing him consul general of the United States for Buenos Aires, Chile, and Peru. The promotion made a huge difference: Poinsett emerged from the shadows and assumed the status of an ambassador—without a staff, embassies, or stations, but with enormous prestige. Secretary Monroe assured him that "the disposition shown by most of the Spanish provinces to separate from Europe and to erect themselves into independent states excites great interest here. As inhabitants of the same hemisphere, as neighbors, the United States cannot be unfeeling spectators of so important a movement."

Consul General Poinsett saw his role in the broadest terms, anticipating the moment that the United States became a combatant in the ongoing world war. And when that should come to pass, Poinsett had advised President Madison, he expected the United States to intervene on behalf of any deserving rebel state with both material support and recognition of sovereignty.

The Madison administration, without a formal position on South America and its independence movements, had not yet recognized the nationhood of Buenos Aires and its United Provinces. In the hope of forcing these issues, Poinsett urged Secretary Monroe to adopt a policy encouraging Creole revolution throughout the continent. In a letter dated October 24, 1811, he outlined his ideas and relayed his concern that the United Provinces could not defend itself from the likely assaults of European empires—it needed support from regional allies and the United States itself. Poinsett admitted that he had taken his own advice and counseled the Buenos Aires junto to form "an alliance of all Spanish America" and to "solicit the aid and protection of the United States and make one great simultaneous movement of the whole continent" toward independence. If the Creoles won their freedom in southern Spanish America, Poinsett wanted to be sure that the United States, and not Britain, would become their champion. With that in mind, he had decided that he had done all he could in Buenos Aires, and that the rumors of upheaval coming from Chile suggested that it was time to extend his mission to the Pacific.

Soon after posting the letter, Poinsett hired a carriage and guides and began a 600-mile crossing of the Patagonian pampas to the western outpost of Mendoza and then the high passes of the Andes. If Secretary Monroe and President Madison were surprised at Poinsett's aggressive tone or his decision to head west, there is no record of it. Evidently they did not try to respond, knowing that he was carrying out the duties they had agreed to and was now beyond their reach. In fact, Consul General Poinsett would receive no official communications during his entire tenure in Chile.

Although Poinsett knew he was risking his career, he believed in the mission and in his ability to thwart the British on the Pacific side. It was an audacious thought—to set himself against the resources of a well-established world empire with large naval bases, highly effective diplomats, and a willingness to arm and assist rebels. But Roberts Poinsett had seen Napoleon in Paris, and he knew what one man could do.

Chapter Three

Against the Gods

I n June 1812, despite London's efforts to prevent war and over the opposition of the New England states and the Federalist Party, Congress, with President Madison's assent, declared war on Great Britain. America had a standing army of 6,000 men and a navy comprising just seventeen deepwater vessels.

The United States was now a combatant nation in the world war, aligned, in effect, with Napoleon and his allies against the British. The timing could not have been worse, as Napoleon chose that moment to begin his doomed invasion of Russia, which, within a year, would put him on the defensive everywhere in Europe and leave London free to deploy its military resources to other theaters, such as North America, where its navy was capable of enforcing an unbreakable blockade and where its armies, made up of veterans of Wellington's victorious forces in Europe, could easily defeat untested American soldiers.

America was no match for imperial Britain. The nation was only half-formed. Most of the inhabited sections ended well east of the Mississippi River. Florida and Texas belonged to Spain, and California and the Pacific Northwest were up for grabs among Britain, Spain, and Russia. The states were not united, and the regions did not agree. New England was so strongly anti-war that there was talk of secession in seaport taverns, and Massachusetts refused to allow federal forces to operate within its boundaries. Nevertheless, with commercial shipping at a wartime standstill, many New

England vessel owners joined those of New York, Philadelphia, Baltimore, and New Orleans in converting the best of their merchant vessels into privateers. Licensed by the government as warships and upgraded with a few cannon on deck and swivel guns on the rails, these privateers were sent out to capture British merchant vessels and cargoes to be sold in American ports.

Much hope and very little money or materiel went into this new conflict. All of the rosy assumptions would prove incorrect. Those who thought a war would give the United States a chance to take Canada from Britain had not reckoned on the Canadians' fighting spirit nor on a British invasion of American coastal cities. Such unthinkable developments would become realities, and America's leaders had no plan to turn things around and save the country.

The army performed poorly in the early going, but the U.S. Navy excelled. Porter's initial cruise in the thirty-two-gun *Essex*, among the smallest of the navy's twelve frigates, was a success as he led his 300 men in capturing several British merchant vessels and an obscure Royal Navy ship, the *Alert*. It was the first naval victory of the war for the United States, and Porter would have won real fame had it not been for the U.S.S. *Constitution* and her men and master, Captain Isaac Hull, who, one week after Porter's victory, vanquished the British battleship *Guerriere* in spectacular style. The hero's laurels went to Hull, leaving Porter to look to the next cruise for his chance at glory.

In September 1812, at his riverside estate, Green Bank, on the Delaware below Philadelphia, Captain David Porter raged around the house, terrifying his family and servants. He was furious that the navy's vessels were no longer allowed to freelance; instead, the ships had been organized into three squadrons under Commodores Stephen Decatur, John Rodgers, and William Bainbridge, each in command of two frigates and a smaller vessel. Bainbridge, commanding the *Constitution*, forty-four guns, was to be accompanied by Porter in the *Essex* and James Lawrence in the new sloop of war *Hornet*, mounting twenty-eight guns. *Constitution* and *Hornet* were to sail from Boston, and Porter was to sail from the Delaware and join them at sea. But when? Although he had long been ready to sail, he could not get the Navy Department's clearance for departure. It was almost as if the naval high command had lost its will to fight as bad news came in from the west and north: the largest American army had surrendered at Detroit, and another army had been repulsed in Canada.

For the first time since 1783, war was the central fact of America—a war being fought on American soil and along its borders and shores, threatening to place America back under the control of the English king and to undo the gains of twenty years of expansion, settlement, and generally positive relations with the Creeks, Cherokees, and other big Indian nations. America was losing the war, and its frontier was soaked in blood. With the British inciting many of the Native American tribes, southerners and westerners were given an excuse to slaughter Indians and take their lands, but many in the east and north were already thinking that Congress and President Madison had made a colossal blunder. Having forfeited all support in New England, Madison was in trouble. The war hawks, however, wanted to keep fighting, even after the big defeats out west and the British naval blockade of North and South America, and even though Napoleon had lost his main army in Russia and might soon lose his hold on Europe, leaving Britain the undisputed champion of the world.

Porter, ravenous for combat, took out his anger on his men, who were confined on board the *Essex*, moored within sight of his residence. Weeks passed. Overcrowded and heartily sick of themselves, the sailors smuggled booze on board and stayed drunk, which did not solve their basic problem. Their stir-crazy warden stared out at the river's stillness and at the frigate, inert and skeletal, seeming to grow larger and darker and more immobile, a prison ship moored a few miles from the pleasures of Philadelphia.

Porter's antipathy for Secretary of the Navy Hamilton led him to suspect the secretary of incompetence, timidity, even cowardice, and he was not completely wrong. Hamilton had argued in Madison's cabinet for keeping naval vessels in port until springtime rather than risking losses, but President Madison had rejected his advice and dropped him from the council of war. Unaware of this, Porter slatted around in his rooms, smoldering with wild thoughts, exploding at his wife, writing red-hot letters to a friend alleging that "the neglect of the Department is unpardonable: three days after my arrival, I would have sailed with three months' provisions [but] I have yet received no orders" and no approval of his proposal for "a first campaign" against British commerce. With paranoia striking deep, Porter had more than one enemy in this war.

Marooned in his house, consumed with loathing, he persuaded himself that the navy secretary was a traitor. If so, Porter concluded that he was not bound by his orders and restrictions and might use his own "discretion," as he put it, in carrying on his part of the war.

If his own high sense of honor had earned him only disrespect, he

David Porter (1780–1843), captain of the U.S. frigate *Essex*, began his fighting career as a teen-aged midshipman. Valued for his bravery under fire and his ferocious intensity, he was contemptuous of his Navy Department superiors and dangerously ambitious. *(from* Analectic Magazine, *Philadelphia, 1814; D. Edwin engraving from* Wood painting*)*

thought, he might as well act less honorably and more in his own interests, like everyone else, and especially like the privateers he had scorned. It was still possible to "carry into execution the plan that once gave so much pleasure to the Secretary," but which had later been dropped. Porter took it up again, secretly, with the intention of making his fortune. Noting the arrival of more British warships on the blockading stations, he foresaw disaster for the navy in the Atlantic theater. The secretary, he predicted, would keep them holed up in the harbors until winter—a prospect that justified "a change in our Department, or we never can expect to do anything except on our own responsibility. . . ." Going rogue, however, was not an approved option for a U.S. Navy captain.

Finally he received from Bainbridge a set of orders that Hamilton confirmed shortly after. In elation and relief, Porter wrote in a letter that "in two or three days I sail on a long, a very long cruise; our destination and intended movements I am not at liberty to divulge—perhaps a more important cruise was never undertaken by the vessels of any nation, and I have vanity to believe that my plan for the 'first campaign' produced it—it may be many months before you hear of my arrival in the U.S., and if you hear of me at all I hope the accounts may not be unfavorable."*

Whatever Porter's hopes, Bainbridge was the author of the squadron's final plan, which involved getting away from the coast and the Royal Navy in order to have the best chance of capturing British merchant vessels.

Bainbridge and Lawrence cleared Boston on October 26 and headed east to rendezvous with the *Essex* at Porto Praya in the Cape Verde islands, off Africa. Failing that, Porter was to meet them at specified islands off the coast of Brazil on certain dates; then, if still apart, he was to proceed easterly to St. Helena off South Africa to prey on English merchantmen returning from India.

It was a good plan, but it was not what Porter had in mind.

On October 28, Porter bade farewell to his pregnant wife Evelina and their toddlers, William and Elizabeth. Resplendent in the bright uniform and gold epaulets of a captain, he strode across the lawn of Green Bank, accompanied by David Glasgow Farragut, eleven years old and wearing the outfit of a midshipman. A pulling boat took them out to the frigate *Essex*.

The sailors, informed that this cruise would be a long one, had been allowed to make extra purchases with part of their first-cruise prize money. Like most navy crews, this one had been recruited mainly from among drydocked merchant seamen looking for a berth. Of the 319 men, 31 were marines under twenty-two-year-old Lieutenant John Marshall Gamble, and most of the rest had the ratings of boy, landsman, seaman, ordinary seaman, or supernumerary. There were a boatswain and his mates, a gunner and his mates, and seven each of quartermasters and quarter gunners. There was a

---

* The exact meaning of this confidential letter is not known, but its implication is that Porter had already mentioned some distinctive plan to U.S. Navy purser Samuel Hambleton, his friend and fellow Marylander. Perhaps the "first campaign" was a proposal for an extended cruise against British merchant shipping, in which the U.S. naval vessels would provision themselves off the spoils of their captures and range beyond the North Atlantic. Porter may even (as he later claimed) have mentioned to his superiors the idea of a cruise into the Pacific, but clearly this had not been endorsed, as proved by the orders that Bainbridge had sent to Porter, with approval by the navy secretary, calling for him to go to the coast of Africa, then to the coast of Brazil, and then to St. Helena to intercept British traffic from the Orient. Later, after Porter's cruise had ended, Bainbridge invited his old friend up to Boston for a drinking bout, saying that he preferred to drown him rather than hang him—almost certainly a jocular reference to the penalty for Porter's having disobeyed orders and gone off by himself.

master at arms, an armorer, a sailmaker, a steward and cook, a carpenter, a coxswain, a cooper, and a captain's clerk, Melancthon W. Bostwick. Porter was assisted by First Lieutenant John Downes, Second Lieutenant James P. Wilmer, Third Lieutenant James Wilson, acting Fourth and Fifth Lieutenants William Finch and the very near-sighted Stephen Decatur McKnight, sixteen, chaplain-teacher David P. Adams, purser John R. Shaw, surgeon Robert Miller, and sailing master John Glover Cowell, twenty-five, who had two mates. The twelve midshipmen, ranging in age from eleven to twenty-one, were the special responsibility of the captain, and one or two might be promoted to the rank of acting lieutenant during the cruise.

Cowell, from the north-of-Boston port of Marblehead, was the rare navy man who had spent time in the Pacific—three years in his teens on board a Boston ship engaged in the otter-pelt trade with the Pacific coast, the islands of Oceania, and, ultimately, China. The son of a privateer of the Revolution—as was Porter—Cowell had seen the *Essex* being built in 1799 across the harbor from Marblehead at Salem, a world-famous seaport and the seat of the county of Essex.* Married with two children, well-traveled in Europe, Cowell was as eager for promotion as Porter himself had been; ambition drew the two men together. Cowell had come late to the navy, signing up as a sailing master in 1809 after his career as a merchant sea captain had been blocked by Jefferson's embargo on overseas trade and then by the French assault on American shipping. On board the *Essex*, he was chief navigator, supervisor of sail trimming, accountant for provisions, and keeper of the log and charts. He was also a petty officer, which meant that he was subject to the command of much younger commissioned officers. Cowell, however, was not to be trifled with; he looked like the salty deck-boss he had been, strong and sturdy, wearing his long, dark hair in a pigtail, sporting a gold hoop in his left ear. He had the unswerving loyalty of his six fellow Marbleheaders, among Porter's best crewmen, including Joseph Thomas, captain of the maintop,† who was chief, aloft, for the setting and taking in of the ship's many sails. Captain Porter encouraged Cowell and assigned him competent master's mates, but there was no guarantee of promotion. Cow-

---

* The entire cost of construction of the *Essex*, about $70,000, had been borne by Salem's anti-French Federalist merchants, fabulously wealthy from their trade in Asia and quite willing to bankroll a new battleship for the navy, which, in 1799, was engaged in a quasi-war with France.

† The Marblehead crewmen on board the *Essex*, other than Cowell and Thomas, were carpenter Benjamin Wadden, seamen Enoch Milay and Thomas Russell, and ordinary seamen Samuel Dinsmore and William Sinclair.

ell had written to the navy secretary that "the many mortifications incident to the situation of [Sailing] Master loudly demand that I should aspire to a more dignified situation." Porter understood and valued those aspirations, but even more, he valued Cowell's experience in the Pacific.

Unlike most commanders, Porter cared about his men and tried to create a supportive community on board what was in many ways a prison. Porter was entirely responsible for meeting the basic needs of those who were giving up their liberties and most of their rights in order to live en masse and under surveillance, dependent on the captain and officers for the quality of their lives and often for life itself.

He overloaded the *Essex* with stores and did not skimp on anti-scurvy fruit, vegetables, and lime juice. Disease, he knew, was the enemy; he dreaded an outbreak of sickness that could spread like fire through a ship at sea. Porter had three doctors on board, each a trained surgeon. He had dumped nine "incurables," although a tenth, William Klaer, suffering from severe liver problems, had accidentally stayed on. Others passed muster despite sprains, ulcerated legs, and syphilis. Like any other vessel of its day, the *Essex* was a vast sink of microbial infection, with dozens of latent diseases, Western and Asian, afflicting the men. It was up to Porter to create and enforce the conditions that would prevent a ship-wide epidemic from which there was no escape.

Sick or well, the men of the *Essex* poured out their hearts in farewell letters to loved ones. The letters were put in a sack belonging to the shorebound pilot, who delivered them, in secret, to Porter. He opened them all to see if somehow his men had "become possessed of a knowledge of our destination." Although the answer was no, he had all of the letters destroyed.

They sailed on a fresh north wind with all flags flying and the great vessel riding extremely low in the water. Crowds formed along the river and on the sand hills of Cape Henlopen as the 850-ton frigate made her majestic way toward the horizon. The *Essex* was a splendid, enormous machine, unlike anything found on land: stem to stern, top to bottom, she was a symphony of moving parts and wind-powered complexity, requiring the best efforts of about 250 seamen (not counting the marines and other specialists in her crew manifest) to make her go. At 141 feet along the gun deck, she was about as long as a large merchant ship, but she was built on an entirely different scale of strength and amplitude, with massive timbers and thick planks that gave her hull a fortress-like character. She seemed immense as she passed by the cheering onlookers under full sail at nine knots or more;

on three towering masts and her extended bowsprit, she carried sixteen major sails and more than a mile of heavy cordage in her rigging. As impressive as she was, the *Essex* measured just thirty-seven feet in beam across the spar deck and was the smallest frigate in the American fleet—the *Constitution* was double her tonnage. She had other virtues, though, including speed and stoutness, that would make her as seaworthy as any warship afloat; and on her maiden voyage in 1800 under Captain Edward Preble she had been the first U.S. Navy vessel to cross the Indian Ocean.

Within twenty-four hours of clearing the Delaware, the mighty *Essex* was fighting for her life off the shoals of Chincoteague in a roaring gale. Staggering seaward, she plunged and rolled in thirty-foot ocean swells, shipping enormous quantities of water. Porter did not need to butt heads with a hurricane. He could have jibed around and run before the wind back to the safety of the river, but retreat was unthinkable to David Porter. Risking everything, he drove his men and ship into the storm, and succeeded in forcing the *Essex* past the danger of the coast and out to the open sea.

When the storm blew by, Porter assembled his soaked, shaken, seasick crew and gave them a speech. He thanked them for their good service and refrained, as usual, from any mention of God's providence in the matter. Porter was neither sentimental nor religious. Next, he excoriated them for their drunken, slovenly behavior while waiting in the Delaware. He assured them that they deserved severe punishment; however, in view of their now-spoiled provisions and soaked bedding and clothes, he granted a general pardon and promised a cruise full of adventure and rewards for all who did their duty, and three dozen lashes for those who did not. He acknowledged that their rations would be limited, but consoled them with the prospect of a full daily share of first-rate rum. Porter then set forth the rules for cleanliness and health, starting with ship-wide fumigation by pouring vinegar on red-hot cannonballs first thing every morning.

The navy had no standing orders as to sanitation, and some captains gave it no heed. Not Porter, who had once spent nineteen months in prison and had seen the miseries of the typical sleeping quarters, or berth deck, a permanently dark space less than six feet high where 300 men in their hammocks would foul the air with their breathing as they struggled to sleep. By contrast, Porter had hammocks slung on the gun deck as well as the berth deck, which gave the men more space and cleaner air and allowed the gun crews to sleep near their long friends, just in case—the gunports were kept open to the breeze, and the men got a good night's sleep and awoke refreshed. Porter was different, too, in having an officer command the berth deck and attend to health and cleanliness, and he was unique in allowing his men, starting at four o'clock every afternoon, to enjoy two hours of leisure during which the whole ship was "a scene of noisy merriment."

Following a southeasterly track, the *Essex* sailed for Africa flying an English flag; in waters devoid of Americans, there was no need to call attention to a U.S. naval presence among the trading vessels of various nations. Like Americans themselves, American naval vessels looked like their English counterparts, and their officers had no trouble working up an English accent.

One morning about three weeks into the cruise, they spied a vessel on the horizon, but she proved to be a Portuguese merchant brig, and they let her pass. Portugal was allied with Britain against the French but was not an enemy of the United States. In fact, the Portuguese solicited American trade in Continental ports, island colonies, and in the huge, rich Portuguese territory of Brazil. In spite of internal divisions, shaky finances, an overextended military, and relocation of the royal court to Rio de Janeiro, Portugal remained an imperial power in the world.

Soon after spotting the Portuguese brig, the *Essex* gave chase once again, in heavy winds, and this time the men were thrilled to see a distant battleship. To the beat of drums they ran to their stations and jumped into the rigging to reef the topsails and prepare for action, but they were hit by a squall. When it cleared, "the chase" was under press of sail, escaping into the darkness. Porter decided that she had been the U.S. sloop of war *Wasp*, which had sailed from the Delaware a few days before the *Essex*.

One day, while rolling along in mid-ocean, the *Essex* came to a stop as Cowell ordered her foresails backed, and the masthead lookout cried, "Sail-o!"

"Where away?" called Lieutenant Downes, "and what does she look like?"

"'Tis Neptune's own boat!" came the answer from aloft. "The god of the seas! He wishes permission to come aboard with his train!"

The midshipmen looked on in astonishment as the king of the sea made his appearance. William Feltus, a young New Yorker, watched Neptune and his wife Amphitrite roll across the quarter deck in the divine car—two chairs on an old gun carriage—drawn by "four men, some with their shirts off and their bodies painted, and others with their trousers cut off above the knees and their legs painted and their faces painted in this manner, accompanied by his barbers with their razors made of an iron hoop, and constables, and band of music." Neptune "dismounted with his wife and spoke to the Captain for permission to shave such as had not crossed the Line before, officers excepted, provided they would pay with some rum." All of the eligible non-crossers were sent below. On the spar deck the god and his barbers stood in a rowboat filled with salt water, armed with rusty straightedges and buckets of slush and pitch. They bawled for their victims; and slowly, one at a time, at the pace of a death march, crewman after crewman was presented and subjected to the full Neptunian treatment, including "the rough ministrations of lesser gods when the deities themselves collapsed in inebriated satisfaction."

At sunrise three days later, the men sighted the island of San Nicolas in the Cape Verde archipelago, off the Guinea coast of Africa. Consulting the charts closely, Porter ran down among the islands, passing between Isla de May and San Jago and standing in to Porto Praya, the first rendezvous site for the squadron. Porter stayed on for five days, touring the old buildings and recording his impressions of the sweltering island with its crumbling fort, mangy dogs, and ragtag inhabitants. He gave his men shore leave and let them bring live pigs and goat kids on board. The *Constitution* and *Hornet* were not to be found, so Porter gave orders to depart. The main deck of the *Essex* resembled a corral as she headed west toward the coast of Brazil, but the friendly beasts needed too much water in the tropical heat, so Porter had them slaughtered for food, despite the protests of those who had their pigs drinking rum instead.

At a cry on December 11 the crew ran to the weather rail to observe a distant vessel. Through his glass, Porter thought he saw a Royal Navy brig of war. Using British signals captured from the *Alert*, he tried to decoy her downwind, but her captain held steady. At sunset, she hoisted British colors, and after dark she made her night signals, fearing no danger. Porter shaped his course to intercept, and by nine he had come up close enough to sink her with his carronades.

He called to her commander to haul up his courses and heave to windward to be boarded. Instead, the other vessel began maneuvering for battle, and Porter responded with musketry. Muzzles flashed in the darkness, and bullets tore into the stranger. One man fell dead, several screamed from their wounds, and the captain surrendered the ten-gun packet *Nocton* from Falmouth, England. Porter took $55,000 in government funds but no private property. The $55,000 would buy him enough provisions in South America to sustain a long campaign at sea.

Lieutenant Finch took command of the *Nocton* with a small prize crew of Americans, including the sick man, William Klaer. Finch, with many prisoners, was to sail for an American port. Porter kept thirteen of the strongest British seamen on board the *Essex,* and he wrote a note advising the navy secretary to take the well-built *Nocton* into the navy as a cruiser.

Next day, Porter made out the Pyramid, a high peak of the rendezvous island of Fernando da Noronha. It was another stop at the end of the world. Fruitful, tropical, and well-fortified, the isle supported a few exiled Portuguese and a gang of naked enslaved Africans whom Porter perceived as happy: "[A]s clothing is not in use here, as hunger may be gratified without labour, and as there is an appearance of cheerfulness, those that are not in chains may be supposed, in some measure, reconciled to a state as good, perhaps, as any they had formerly been accustomed to."

The *Essex* glided into the harbor disguised as a large Rio-bound Londoner, and Downes went ashore, returning a couple of hours later with news of the departure of two British naval vessels the week before. Porter understood these ships to have been Bainbridge and Lawrence. Once again he had failed to connect. There was also a letter for Porter, which he read eagerly. Between the lines was a message in invisible ink, which closed, "Go off Cape Frio to the northward of Rio Janeiro and keep a look-out for me."

Porter hoisted up the boat and "made sail to the southward." Off steamy Pernambuco, he made his men wear winter woolens as punishment for some forbidden clothes-selling at Porto Praya. Sailing under English colors, the *Essex* "lay to under easy sail" off Frio, looking for British traffic but finding only Portuguese. Near the entrance to Rio harbor they captured the British merchant schooner *Elizabeth,* whose captain claimed that three heavily laden merchantmen had departed the night before in convoy with an armed schooner.

Seeing a great chance, Porter put Midshipman Clarke and nine men on board the leaky *Elizabeth* and sent her in for repairs and then on for the United States. Wishing the teenager well, Porter then took off after the convoy. On the morning of December 30, sailing before fair winds, he discovered that his main topmast was about to collapse in an avalanche of wood, cordage, and canvas. Hot after his prey, he sent men aloft to secure the topgallant mast to the mainmast and set out the great wings of the studding sails to lower the pressure on the upper rigging. A heavy head sea strained the masts "excessively" and caused some light spars to fall overboard, but Porter pressed on, calculating that his quarry could go no faster than five knots while he went seven, and that shortly he would catch them, topmast or no topmast. Below, on deck, his men stood in the shadow of imminent disaster.

Early on New Year's Day 1813, the lookout spotted the convoy and the chase began, but soon the distant sails "proved to be nothing but small clouds rising from the horizon." When a Portuguese shipmaster indicated that the *Constitution* and the *Hornet*, Porter's long-lost partners, were cruising off the Bahia coast, he decided to forego the rendezvous and keep up his pursuit of the unseen and perhaps imaginary convoy.

With a mizzen topmast as shaky as the main topmast, Porter took advantage of calm seas to make repairs. Eighty feet above the deck, the tall topmasts were removed and lowered, and soon they were back up and fastened with new trestletrees. The *Essex* sailed on, seeking the phantom convoy, encountering Portuguese and Spanish vessels, the latter with troops for the royalists of Montevideo at war with the *independencias* of Buenos Aires. Finally, having gone far from the coast and well past the date of the planned rendezvous, Porter headed back toward Cape Frio.

Many chances for rendezvous had been missed. Bainbridge and Lawrence, *Constitution* and *Hornet*, had done all they could to find Porter at the appointed places and times. After scoring victories over British opponents, they sailed for home, giving up hopes for the ghost ship *Essex*, which had seemingly been swallowed by the wide waters of the South Atlantic.

Chapter Four

Off the Chart

Porter and the men of the *Essex* had been out of touch with Americans since October. Low on wood, water, and provisions, he made for Santa Catarina, hundreds of miles south and far from the British warships at Rio. The *Essex* arrived there in the squalls and rain of January 19, having made no effort to cruise where Bainbridge had last been seen.

As usual, Downes and a boat crew went ashore, visiting first at the island fortress, where Downes negotiated the matter of a proper salute. In the morning, after losing both wind and tide, Porter propelled his vessel toward the harbor by means of an anchor sling using drag ropes and 300-man muscle power. By breakfast, the *Essex*'s thirteen-gun salute was returned by the fort. He found a beachfront pool of fresh water and quickly filled many casks, and he distributed some prize money, enabling officers and men to purchase hogs, fowls, plantains, yams, bananas, onions, eggs, and other good things that were conveyed from shore by Portuguese boatmen.

Next day, Porter heard rumors that the British blockade of South America had been strengthened and that the seventy-four-gun *Montagu* had sailed from Rio. He visited the port's elderly military commander. Like so much of the Portuguese empire, the old man's fort was crumbling away, overgrown by trees and bushes and manned by a garrison of "about twenty half-naked soldiers." Porter noticed that the guns were honeycombed with age and mounted on rotten carriages. Surprisingly, there was a small church with a crowbar hung as a bell to call the men to services. Santa Catarina was both a penal colony and the Portuguese whaling capital of the South

Atlantic; one cape down from the fort was a village of about 500 men forced to go whaling at sea in small boats and along the shore in season when the whales came in to calve. The greasy village had stores and boilers for the whale oil, which ultimately was "deposited in an immense tank, formed for the purpose in the rock, and [was] from thence transported to Portugal and elsewhere."

Whaling was a big business for the Portuguese, but in some British and American seaports, whaling was among the biggest of all businesses and had continued despite the war. As Porter well knew, most of the whale-men of the Pacific, whether on British or American vessels, hailed from the Massachusetts island of Nantucket. As he also knew, American whalers and merchantmen, along with their British counterparts, had long engaged in a very active and profitable smuggling trade along the western shore of Span-ish America. Spain claimed the entire coast and forbade foreign commerce of any sort, but the Spanish viceroys did not have the resources to fend off the Anglo-Americans, whom they tended to see as a single rapacious species.

If anything, the Americans were the more dangerous breed. Their vessels came more often, and sometimes they came with a political agenda. The far-faring Yankees insisted on their rights to trade with any willing part-ner and proselytized for independence and republican government.* The Anglo-American sperm-whale fishery had prospered beyond the ship own-ers' wildest projections. By 1800, one hundred whaleships—sixty of them British-owned, the rest from Nantucket—were making the trip to the prime grounds in the Pacific, and the numbers and profitability increased every year, as Nantucket captains and Nantucket crews manned British and Amer-ican whaleships equally. Most expatriate whalemen residing in Britain con-sidered their exile a temporary condition caused by careless and brutal gov-ernments, and they hoped to return at last to their home in the sea.

January 21 was stormy at Santa Catarina. Lieutenant Wilmer went in by boat to wait on the governor, taking with him purser John Shaw, Doc-tor Richard Hoffman, Marine Lieutenant Gamble, and Gamble's protégé William M. Feltus, the fourteen-year-old midshipman son of an Episcopal minister. The boat did not return by the end of the day nor in the evening. Two hours after midnight, Wilmer and Gamble, soaked and naked, got on board the *Essex* and came to Porter's cabin to tell their tale. After they had gone ashore and purchased provisions, their overloaded boat had capsized

---

* See, for example, the 1803 voyage of American merchants Richard J. Cleveland and William Shaler, up the western coast of South America and on to California, smuggling goods and distributing copies of the U. S. Constitution.

returning, and all hands had drifted for four hours, holding fast until landing on a small island. All had survived; much could be salvaged.

For two days on the waterfront, Purser Shaw tried to scrounge a small supply of beef, bread, flour, and rum. On board the *Essex*, the beef proved to be spoiled, so the sailors threw it overboard, "and shortly afterwards an enormous shark, at least 25 feet in length, rose alongside with a quarter of a bullock in his mouth." Porter was aghast: the man-eater was as large as a young whale. "It would be impossible," he wrote, "to describe the horror that the voracious animal excited," as it churned the waters where men had been swimming the evening before.

The shark proved to be a mariner's omen. The master of a recent arrival reported that the mighty *Montagu* had captured a twenty-two-gun American corvette and was pursuing her consort, a frigate. Three more British warships had taken some American privateers, he said, and others were on their way; but Americans had captured a convoy of British Indiamen and a packet with a great deal of specie on board—likely, thought Porter, a reference to his own capture of the *Nocton*.

Judging from these rumors, Porter suspected that the *Montagu* had made a prize of the sloop-of-war *Hornet* and that Bainbridge and the *Constitution* were on the run. He decided to clear out. That night, January 25, he freed five prisoners, gave up on two runaway crewmembers, and made all sail for the open ocean—but not before being overtaken by death. While laying out on the yard to unfurl the mainsail, seaman Samuel Gross fell to the deck and suffered terrible injuries. Gross, one of the best and most popular sailors on board, died a few hours later, and the long-declining Edward Sweeney, sixty-four, ship's livestock tender, also expired. Santa Catarina seemed a good place to leave behind.

Porter was still short on provisions. He had blown his various rendezvous and knew nothing certain about the fate of Lawrence and Bainbridge. He left a letter for his colleagues, closing, "Should we not meet by the first of April, be assured that, by pursuing my own course, I shall have been actuated by views to the good of the service, and that there will have been an absolute necessity for my doing so." Once at sea, Porter made the move that he had been considering all along. He headed south toward Cape Horn, bound for the Pacific.

Since boyhood, Porter had been reading, thinking, and fantasizing about the Pacific and the great fame and greater riches that awaited those who saw its possibilities—adventurers like old Lord Anson, chief of the English intruders in Spanish waters. Seventy years before, in 1741, with Spain and England at war, Commodore Anson had rounded Cape Horn and staggered into the western ocean with only his flagship *Centurion* and two others. Despite a fatal outbreak of scurvy among his men, he had managed to sack several ports in Chile and Peru before heading home across the Pacific. In the Indian Ocean he had captured the largest Spanish galleon of the Manila treasure fleet. In London, laden with a fabulous fortune in silver and gold, he had received a hero's welcome, elevation to the peerage, and appointment as high admiral of the Royal Navy.

Lord Anson seemed a living presence to Porter: rival, provocation, and inspiration. The Pacific still sparkled with the promise of riches, and it was clear to Porter, if to no one else, that the nation's future lay in the far west. His boyhood imaginings remained vivid, his Pacific dream as powerful as ever. The blindness and stupidity of superiors could not diminish his belief in the power of one vessel pursuing a fateful opportunity.

Somehow, during many years of global conflict, no one had thought to make the Pacific a war zone. Hunters who had no thought of being hunted, the fabulously lucrative British sperm-whaling fleet plied their bloody trade. Porter's idea was to make them his prey in the ocean of peace. It seemed brilliant. At minimal risk to the *Essex*, he could pillage his way north through the whalers, then escape into the farther oceans of the setting sun. Porter alone, it seemed, could see a world for the taking. If his superiors couldn't see it, they had no need to know.

With 300-plus loyal and unwitting men, Porter made the decision to leave it all behind: America, the navy, the chain of command, and the Atlantic world of war, history, knowledge, and civilization. Already well south of the last seaport of the continent, he put the *Essex* on a due southerly course, and his men started talking. During two more days on the same heading, the mystery deepened. Some made a guess and gathered their woolens. By day three, Porter could no longer conceal his intentions, and he called the whole crew to the spar deck. Before their expectant faces, under the straining towers of canvas, he made a brief speech.

"Sailors and Marines! A large increase in the enemy's force compels us to abandon a coast that will neither afford us security nor supplies; nor are there any inducements for a longer continuance there! We will, therefore, proceed to annoy them where we are least expected!

"What was never performed by a single ship, *we will attempt!*

"The Pacific Ocean affords us many friendly ports! The unprotected British commerce on the coasts of Chile, Peru, and Mexico will give you an abundant supply of wealth; and the girls of the Sandwich Islands shall reward you for your sufferings during the passage around Cape Horn!"

The sailors roared their approval, all in favor of getting rich and enjoying orgies in the Pacific. Although they had not signed up for *this* cruise, and they were not sure what Porter meant by attempting what no ship had ever performed, they trusted their fiery leader with their lives.

Having read about the islands of Terra del Fuego, Porter stood clear of the treacherous coastline. He had to, because he had no sea chart or coastal chart, only a very small-scale map, an emblem of his extreme recklessness and self-destructive tendencies. As they entered the colder latitudes near Le Maire Strait, the atmosphere grew hazy and the wind blew hard. The men would need to be at their best, alert and strong and steeled to their duty, and so, just as he faced the most difficult feat of navigation in the world, Porter was terrified when a dozen sailors fell ill. An outbreak of scurvy would force him to turn back with a prostrated crew. Porter had done all he could to prevent it by fumigation, sanitation, and diet. In taking on his last provisions, he had acquired plenty of fresh fruit and onions, and he had distributed daily doses of vinegar to every man. Porter and his officers speculated with Doctor Hoffman; perhaps it was only cholera morbus, from bad food, or painter's colic, from lead in the rum. The specter loomed over the *Essex* for a day and a night, but the sailors' affliction did not spread.*

On they plunged into ever-higher seas and colder winds, sailing a course well east of any land, but then, in horror, they saw evidence that they could not be on the open sea: a flock of storm-buffeted geese, masses of floating seaweed, a wicked rip in the current, each a fatal sign of a lee shore. Porter posted men, reefed topsails, and strained his gaze into the storm. Suddenly, snarling white breakers appeared, and then headlands, low and dark, less than a mile away. Porter instantly changed course hard to the eastward, but thirty-foot waves met them head-on, burying the deck and jolting the vessel so hard that they thought she would come apart. The whole ocean, he wrote, "from the violence of the current, appeared in a foam of breakers, and nothing but the apprehension of immediate destruction could have induced me to have ventured through it."

---

*   They had probably become sick with the change of diet from salt junk (preserved beef) to one with added fresh fruits and vegetables.

Jolted by cresting waves and with no room to jibe, they could only try to tack the ship onto a different course. Orders were screamed into the roar of the gale; men scrambled up the ratlines and fought their way out onto the main yard to unfurl the huge mainsail. The helm was put down, the *Essex* swung crashing through the seas, and, with a sound like the crack of doom, the sail filled and the frigate leaped forward on the other side of the wind.

Porter had the topgallant yards sent down and the jib and spanker set to get driving close-hauled, but then the jib exploded in tatters, leaving the *Essex* unable to point. With night coming on, with "a tremendous sea and the wind directly on shore," and with "no prospect of saving the ship but by carrying a heavy press of sail to keep off the lee shore," Porter bet everything on setting more sails, and the men responded with their lives to their leader's commands. *Essex*, carrying far too much canvas, powered her way west-northwest, defying disaster from moment to moment, seemingly an extension of Porter's will, speeding and groaning across the wind even as huge waves pushed her toward shore. Porter fixed his gaze on the topmasts, strained to the utmost and likely to let go at any moment, which would have knocked the *Essex* off the wind and instantly wrecked her, killing every man on board. He kept up his vigil in the gale, and the *Essex* held course for nearly an hour until suddenly it was over; the wind and seas died away, sperm whales appeared alongside, puffing and gamboling, and "at half past seven, to our unspeakable joy, the land was discovered ahead" about a mile distant. They had entered the safety of Le Maire Strait.

Porter was amazed at his good fortune. Navigating without a chart, mistaken in his position, he had come through the breakers only by virtue of his crew's superb seamanship, the incredible strength of the vessel's spars, and a large amount of sheer luck. Had he been north of Cape St. Vincent as he had supposed, "it would have required our utmost exertions, under the heaviest press of canvas, to have kept the ship from going on shore; and the loss of a single spar, or the splitting of a topsail"—the snapping of a topmast—"would have sealed our destruction." Destruction would also have befallen them had he been able to hold his original course, which was certain to have "entangled us in the night with the rocks and breakers," for he "could not have seen the danger 100 yards from the ship." He had nearly lost his vessel and drowned all of his men; he could not have come closer without actually doing it. Yet they had pulled through, and his crew gave him all the credit and loved their captain more than ever.

Shaken, probably imbibing freely in his cabin, he wrote the story twice in his journal, once while it was occurring and once while reflecting on it, processing the trauma as if he needed to keep telling himself that he had actually survived. "Thanks to the excellent qualities of the ship," he wrote, "we received no material injury, although we were pitching our forecastle under [the waves]."

Verging on the Pacific and all it meant to him, Porter felt little of the elation that he had anticipated. He knew—unlike his men—that the *Essex* had just become the first U.S. Navy vessel to enter the Pacific, which would put his name in the history books, but his satisfaction was undercut by obsessive thoughts about ravening scurvy and murderous storms and, for the last time, about reversing course and perhaps sparing himself a hanging. Even in his journal—which he was writing for publication, should he survive—he admitted that, "I was departing from the letter of my instructions, and in prosecution of a plan which might not prove successful or meet the approbation of my commanding officer, or the Navy Department; and, however justifiable my conduct may be, the apprehensions of censure could not otherwise than produce their effect on my mind."

His scheme was his own; he had not shared it with anyone. In truth, his rogue mission could be excused by only one outcome: extraordinary results against the British. Porter knew that any degree of failure would likely end his naval career and might well result in prosecution for the treasonous act of running off with a battleship in the middle of a war.

After a few days of westering into the Pacific, the *Essex* headed north in fair weather. One pleasant morning the sky suddenly turned dark, the wind freshened, and once again they encountered a gale out of the west, strong enough to appall "the stoutest heart on board" with "a fury far exceeding anything we had yet experienced, bringing with it such a tremendous sea as to threaten us every moment with destruction." The frigate tossed so violently that no one was able to cross the deck, and Porter, badly hurt from several falls, retreated to his cabin. John Cowell and the chief officer, Lieutenant John Downes, were left to manage the ship and rally the men.

The *Essex* saved them once again. After three days of the most severe abuse, she had not "received any considerable injury; and we began to hope, from her buoyancy, and other good qualities, we should be enabled to weather the gale." By March 5, finally beyond the influence of Cape Horn, they enjoyed fine breezes from the south. Wide-spanned albatrosses glided along on the wind. In the distance, above the shoreline, shone the white summits of the Andes. The men looked around at their new world and its great ocean, and praised the Lord.

In this crisis as in all others, Porter remained a stoic, without a God to watch over and preserve him. In his journal, as, presumably, in his conversation, he neither invoked a deity nor expressed any of the pious beliefs typical of the times. He was alone and unsponsored, and when he prevailed, he had only himself and his excellent vessel to thank.

The island of Mocha was their first stop in the Pacific. Twenty miles off the coast, it stood alone, rising from seas often full of sperm whales, chief among them the notorious Mocha Dick, an albino bull fully seventy feet long and famous for smashing whaleboats. For two decades the whalers of Britain and America had arrived at the island hoping for the glory of "subduing the monarch of the seas," and one day, many years later, the furious whale would be fictionally matched with a godless captain in Herman Melville's *Moby-Dick*.

After a brief spell ashore, Porter sailed for the island of Santa Maria, hoping to get news about the enemy before proceeding to Talcahuano on the Bay of Concepcion, but the wind started to roar in the rigging. Without a chart, Cowell was unable to find a safe passage along the lee shore, so the *Essex* hauled off seaward under double-reefed topsails, and soon the crew had to take in more canvas to keep from losing the main topmast.

"Pitching very deep, and straining considerably," the frigate flew before the storm all night, and by morning she had passed well north of the Bay of Concepcion. Having overshot it, Porter decided to get provisions farther on at Valparaiso—a fateful difference, for ten American whalers were awaiting a savior at Talcahuano. The captain of the *Essex* was unaware of this splendid chance to be a hero. The unarmed whaleships were laden with oil, millions of dollars' worth, with which to light the streets and buildings of wartime America; without a convoy, their Quaker pacifist captains and crews stood little chance of getting past the British blockade in the Atlantic and arriving safely home.

Sailing onward through a dungeon bank of fog, Porter stood on the quarterdeck, fantasizing. War bringer and admiral of the South Sea, he could not be stopped. He would wipe out the enemy's commerce, capture their oil and men, and transform their vessels into his own fleet of warships. Ghosting northward in the obscurity somewhere close to the Bay of Valparaiso, the men of the *Essex* suddenly realized that they were not alone; the quiet sea came to life, exhaling the breath of its depths as a great shoal of sperm whales plunged and surged along by the invisible hundreds. In a sea full of whales, where were the whaleships? Perhaps they were out there, killing—busy British whalers, full of oil. He would, he thought, become as wealthy as Lord Anson; and he would return to New York at the head of a flotilla that would make him a legend.

It was this secret and self-assigned mission, this fantasy of wealth and glory, that carried the renegade Porter into Valparaiso.

Chapter Five

Revolution in Chile

After receiving President Madison's appointment as consul general to Southern Spanish American Republics, Roberts Poinsett set out in November 1811 to cross the pampas and the high passes of the Andes on his way to Chile. Descending from the mountains into the lush summer abundance of the Aconcagua Valley, he thought he had arrived in another world. Riding into the capital city of Santiago, he was greeted by the inhabitants as if he were the answer to their prayers—an avatar of independence descending via the Andes from los Estados Unidos, the nearly legendary republic of America.

Poinsett was surprised by everything he saw: the European character of the center city, its beautiful river setting, the marching troops, the fervor of the people, and the popularity of the head of the revolutionary state, José Miguel Carrera. And Poinsett was surprised to find himself without rivals; apart from a scattering of business agents and merchants, London was unrepresented in the capital.

He knew that his mission in Chile would be very different from that in Buenos Aires. This world on the far side of the Andes was walled off and subject to its own cultural and political influences. As he studied the complex and potentially explosive situation of a country in revolt and verging on warfare, Poinsett, the visionary individualist, came to see his own image reflected in the charismatic Carrera, twenty-six, the undisputed leader of the revolutionary junto.

Part of Carrera's singularity, Poinsett realized, was his distance from the other revolutionaries and their infighting. Like Poinsett himself, he had spent most of his young manhood abroad in Europe, growing up in the Spanish army. Far from the quiet of his home colony, he had engaged in the business of warfare and had risen through the ranks to cavalry major, and he had witnessed the fall of the inept Bourbon kings and the rise of the strong Spanish republican faction for which he had fought against Napoleon. Returning to Chile in July 1811, the idealistic Carrera "had no knowledge of my country, as I was a newcomer." Immediately he had been enlisted in a conspiracy, along with his brothers Luis (Lucho) and Juan José, militia captains, to overthrow the government of "inept men" who were "enemies of the cause." The chief conspirators had been the fomenters of the original uprising in June 1810, the leaders of the powerful Larrain family of Santiago, who, inspired by events in Buenos Aires, had made a grab for power primarily to place their own people in offices that had been held for centuries by Spanish bureaucrats.

In his first experience of a coup, Major Carrera had the idea of appealing directly to Santiago's many soldiers, both militia and veteran regulars, and on September 4, 1811, with Lucho and Juan José at the head of sixty infantrymen, José Miguel bravely presented himself at the regulars' barracks to explain the need for a new government. The Larrains' coup was successful. Carrera, the new favorite of the troops, then addressed the captive congress in a speech that was surprising in its revolutionary sweep. He blamed the corruption of King Fernando for the ruin of Spain, praised the French Revolution for its political ideas, and called for total independence for Chile as a true republic like the United States of America. By means of boldness, courage, and oratory, he launched his political career and solidified his brothers' ascendance as heads of the artillery and the cavalry. Happy to have a populist leader whom they could control, the Larrains proceeded to use José Miguel to deliver their message in the streets and at the barracks.

The Larrains consolidated their hold on government through patronage and nepotism, which did not include the Carreras. They installed Juan Martinez Rozas as head of a three-man junto: he represented the south of the country, Juan Mackenna the center (he was married to a Larrain), and Gaspar Marin the north. The Rozas-Mackenna-Marin junto worked with a new congress to create a supreme court, raise an army, and authorize the drafting of a constitution based on "enlightened liberty."

But an autocracy with Larrains in place of Spaniards did not appeal to José Miguel Carrera, who concluded that the Larrains' only interest in Chile was to make it "the patrimony of that family." If one family could claim all of Chile for itself, who was to stop the next one? To Major Carrera, power had to be earned; it was not a birthright or the result of intrigues. He expected Chile to become fully independent, with its own laws and government structures, and he expected to have to fight the king's forces to establish that independence. Only after a final victory could the new state be secure, and only then could the people be invested with rights and liberties. The Larrains had certainly achieved ascendancy, but had they earned it? Were they willing to fight for it?

Carrera's ambition—his obvious sense of himself as a man of destiny, intended for some glorious role in the birth of his nation—was not taken seriously except by Juan Mackenna, who assessed the Carreras as bully-boys at the head of a rabble-in-arms, with José Miguel, in his Spanish cavalry uniform, capable of crossing over from military commander to political demagogue. Mackenna warned his colleagues, but they gave no credence to his conspiracy theories about the Carreras, whom they regarded as mere tools.

On November 15, 1811, shortly before Poinsett's arrival, José Miguel Carrera led a military coup against the Larrains, and the streets remained calm under the bayonets of the Carreras' army. Thus, just nine weeks after helping to bring Rozas and Mackenna to power, Carrera ascended to the presidency of Chile himself. Two weeks later, he dismissed the congress and declared himself the guarantor of a new nation and a powerful patriot army that he would lead into war against Spain and its South American governor, Viceroy Abascal. Rozas, in the south, naturally disagreed.

José Miguel Carrera (1785–1821) trained as a cavalry officer in the Spanish army and returned to Chile just as the tide of revolution crested. The idol of the militia and the leader of the people's faction, he wrested control of the government from the moderates, freed the slaves, extended civil rights and public education to the working classes, and conducted a war of independence against the Spanish viceroy in Lima. Carrera chose U.S. Consul Poinsett as his closest advisor and military strategist. *(National Library of Chile)*

The more they talked, the more Poinsett admired Carrera as a political leader and as a soldier willing to take the fight into the field—a Chilean George Washington. With an American-style political base made up of working men and soldiers, Carrera had grown too big to be dislodged by the many rival aristocratic factions. Certain of the appeal of his populism, the tall, handsome Carrera projected a winning persona, suave, jovial, gallant, and romantic in his beautiful Spanish cavalry uniform. While he sought "the esteem of thinking men," he presented an "unaffected bearing, carefully displayed scorn for the privileged classes, and a generosity bordering on extravagance, [which] made him the idol of the troops and the common people." His vision of Chile was all-encompassing: the entire populace needed to be led out of the darkness so long imposed by the autocrats, toward their own sovereignty.

Poinsett knew that Americans enjoyed the good will of many Chilean Creoles, both historically and in the recent past. Where the British agents had overpromised munitions and support for the revolution, Americans had delivered. The expatriate American merchant Matthew Hoevel of Santiago had recently imported a ship's cargo of rifles, powder, and shot that was snapped up by Carrera's government.

Americans were no strangers in the ports of Chile; in fact, they had been regular visitors for many years. Since 1793, with Britain, France, and Spain embroiled in war, the Pacific had been left open to hard-driving Yankee captains flying a neutral nation's flag and scoffing at Spanish claims as they opened a smuggling trade on the west coast of South America. The Chileans, otherwise restricted to buying Spanish goods at Spanish prices, had quickly developed a taste for American offerings and had been happy to pay in gold and silver for the cargoes that Americans kept unloading. It was no coincidence that Chileans, upon deposing their Spanish overlord in 1810, had instituted free trade as one of their first acts of independence.

Consonant with this history, Poinsett worked with Carrera to introduce an innovation to Chile: its first newspaper, produced by three American printers on a printing press they sold to Carrera's government. The first issue of *Aurora de Chile* came out in February 1812 with a front-page article entitled "Basic Ideas About the Rights of The People." The newspaper's impact was sensational: "Men ran through the streets with an *Aurora* in their hand, detaining as many as they met, and read and re-read its contents, expressing congratulations for such happiness, and prophesying that, by this means, the ignorance and blindness in which they had lived until then would be banished." The four-pager, edited by liberal priest Camilo Henriquez, was packed with pro-American content, starting with a flattering piece about Poinsett's own reception and continuing in praise of America and its freedoms and the basics of democracy. Soon everyone was reading the *Aurora* or having it read to them. There was nothing of Britain or Spain in its pages—only America, and translations of speeches by Jefferson and Madison, and messages from Carrera about the wonders of the Chile that would become the United States of South America.

But Poinsett was not blinded by his own propaganda. Chile was a great geopolitical prize, with a million people, vast quantities of copper and wheat, many gold and silver mines, fertile plains and valleys, several seaports, some good roads, and 2,650 miles of Pacific coastline. Success in Chile might win great advantages for his country and glory for him—the sort that could open doors to a splendid career—but Chile had a history, the special nature of which he grasped early on. It posed challenges quite different from those of Buenos Aires: "the comparatively concentrated population, and its military organization, which has grown out of a system nearly resembling the feudal," meant that there were explosive "consequences of that system, when great and powerful families divide the state into violent and irreconcilable factions." He was not wrong about the vengeful rivalries.

Revolutionary Chile remained hostage to its internecine divisions, north versus south, youth versus age, Carrera (twenty-six) versus Rozas (fifty-two). The tragedy of civil war seemed inevitable. Carrera, though intent on serving as commander in chief in the field, remained in the capital as long as possible to organize his forces and guard against insurrections. In March 1812, he sent his father, Ignacio, south to Talca with a few companies, after which his brother Juan José joined Ignacio with a division near the River Maule, the northern border of southern Chile. Rozas' opposing army arrived near the river by early April, commanded by his protégé, also from the south: Bernardo O'Higgins, son of the former viceroy of Peru, an Irishman who had risen to the top of the Spanish structure in the Pacific.

It was a great irony that Bernardo, sent from Chile to be educated in England in the 1790s, had come under the influence of Francisco Miranda and other radical Spanish Americans exiled in Britain, and had returned to Chile with a love of English freedoms and a set of political beliefs completely opposed to those of his father. Viceroy O'Higgins had died before the uprising of 1810, and Bernardo's colleague Juan Mackenna, an Irish engineer who had served in the royal Spanish forces, had finally evolved into a Moderado, far to the right of Bernardo but deeply loyal to him as the chosen one—the future leader of an independent Chile. Although he had no military experience, O'Higgins had to be respected. He had his own adherents and his own sense of Chile's destiny, and there was no doubt that he, unlike Rozas, would fight. Fortunately, he was known to be reasonable and even tractable.

General Carrera himself traveled south when he learned that Rozas had been persuaded to accompany O'Higgins. In a meeting by the riverside, Rozas told Carrera that he wanted to have the congress reconvene; Carrera asked Rozas to give up his southern junto and come to Santiago. While they negotiated, the rainy season began, and in late April they agreed to send home their armies. Neither leader was rewarded for this outcome. Carrera, welcomed with jubilation at the capital, was challenged by his jealous brother Juan. Cannily, he did not resist but resigned his junto post to their father. Rozas, denounced for refusing to fight, lost his following. O'Higgins retreated to his estate at Las Canteras and considered moving with his mother to Argentina, where the rebels were united in a real revolution against the royalists.

In Santiago, it did not take long for Carrera and his brother to reconcile. Restored to power, José Miguel decreed the banishment of Rozas over the Andes to Mendoza. The order was carried out, and Rozas, the troubled godfather of Chile's independence movement, died in exile within a year.

Carrera resumed his meetings with El Consul Poinsett, who warned him that he looked like a dictator and needed to create republican institutions and to tolerate dissent. Carrera defended his methods and his junto as the only effective means of building an army and preventing his enemies from hijacking the movement, but he agreed to call a new congress and draft a constitution. Without the pressures of agitation in the south or the crisis of impending civil war, he focused on the work of creating a republic and making Santiago into the military, political, and intellectual center of a new nation.

While outwardly traditional, Santiago had been transformed by populist revolutionary spirit. Congress already had effected great reforms. Certain financial powers of the church had been revoked. Spurred by Carrera, the lawmakers had taken on the issue of slavery: children of enslaved people were declared free, people who had been imported as slaves were to be liberated within a few years, and, after the deaths of the oldest enslaved people, slavery would no longer exist in Chile. Virtually everyone felt the excitement of change and possibility and the hope that independence from Spain might be achieved peacefully.

Joel Roberts Poinsett (1779–1851), polymath and linguist, traveled the world in his twenties. The elegant Charlestonian returned to the United States in 1809 hoping for a career as an army general but instead was sent to Buenos Aires as a State Department spy, a position that he soon parlayed into U.S. consul general for southern South America. In revolutionary Chile beginning in 1811, he became a nation-builder, drafting the new republic's constitution, advising its president, and leading its armies into battle. (*from* Portfolio of Living American Statesmen, 1837–47, *by Charles Fenderich*)

Carrera opened up society to debate and discussion, promoted education and the importation of books and scientific instruments, and founded a national library and a university for science and foreign languages. His programs produced results that "were almost inconceivable. Suddenly people had fallen in love with literature and studying, and the products of the press had given the masses a knowledge of various forms of government best suited to advance their rights."

For the first time, schools opened in every district of Valparaiso and the other cities, mandatory and free to the children of the illiterate poor. Each school day began with a republican catechism:

"What nationality are you?"

"I am American."

"What are your duties?"

"To love God and country, devote my life to their service, obey government orders, and fight to defend republican principles."

"What are the republican maxims?"

"They are designed for human happiness. All are born equal and by natural law have certain inalienable rights."

The teacher would proceed to list the rights and privileges of the citizens of a republic, contrasted with the restrictions of the colonial system. The students held a weekly debate in which one would take the side of a Spanish European, advocating for the divine right of kings and the power of conquest against an ever-victorious champion of human rights and republican values.

Behind the scenes, Consul Poinsett became deeply involved in the new government as its chief philosopher and statesman—a role well beyond the ordinary reach of an American consul, but, in this case, a great and perhaps unique opportunity to build a new nation in the image of the United States. Although an admirer of O'Higgins, the young revolutionary leader from the south, Poinsett learned that O'Higgins was an Anglophile who wished to transform Chile into "the England of South America." Carrera, on the other hand, represented a complete break with the past and offered a future that no one had thought about. He wanted a true revolution, over-turning the forms of colonialism to create a new basis for society at all levels.

Poinsett formed the belief that Carrera, as the commander in chief, had done what was necessary to protect and foster independence in a way that could be made to benefit the United States, still the world's only example of a national republic formed after having undergone the passions and hatreds of a war of independence. Was the same thing possible in Chile? Poinsett was not sure. The Larrains remained in the wings, darkly plotting, holding on to great amounts of wealth and potential power. Carrera had won the love of the people and the loyalty of the army, all subject to another coup, a loss in battle, or a decision by Buenos Aires to intervene. Chile's revolution was based on the ascendancy of one man, and one man might easily fail—a possibility that no one felt with greater urgency than Joel Roberts Poinsett.

In his reports to Washington, the consul general did not mention that he and six others, at his house, over the course of weeks, had been drafting a Chilean constitution. It specified liberal civil rights for all men, freedom of the press, separation of church and state, and a governing struc-ture consisting of three branches: the courts, the congress, and the execu-tive, with the latter made up of a three-man junto chosen by the senate and responsible for the military and for foreign policy.

On July 4, 1812, the anniversary of the first meeting of the Chilean congress, Santiago held a gala public event to announce the independence of Chile and to unveil its new constitution. Representatives arrived from the south, where O'Higgins and his adherents had agreed to recognize Carrera as the leader of an inclusive government. Carrera and Poinsett raised the new Chilean flag—blue, white, and yellow—alongside the flag of the United States, and they jointly led an audience of thousands of soldiers and citizens in the singing of a new national anthem and several other patriotic songs.*

José Miguel Carrera, resplendent in uniform, received the adulation of his people, but Chile was a long way from being a republic. Poinsett

---

* That night, at the dance hosted by Poinsett, the three American printers got so drunk that Poinsett ordered that they be taken to their lodgings. On the way, they traded insults with the police, who opened fire and shot eight people, one of whom, printer William H. Burbidge, died four days later. The incident did not diminish Poinsett's stature or the importance of the products of the press.

saw the difficulty of turning ideas into realities in a society that had no experience of democracy: nothing had yet been done to create a process for electing representatives throughout the country; regional leaders in the south were still raising their own troops; church authorities resisted all reforms; the congress was slow to gather; and consideration of the constitution was delayed. The general populace of Chile, wrote the printer Samuel B. Johnston, knew nothing about political systems, having just "emerged from a state of the most abject slavery, which they and their forefathers had endured for centuries" of "ignorance, superstition, and the most blinded bigotry." Like Poinsett, Johnston admired Carrera for taking on the "arduous task" of creating a government for a people who had been "suddenly elevated to the rank of freemen, before the dawning of their political reason had learned to distinguish between liberty and licentiousness."

Overcoming bitter rivals, abysmal ignorance, and his own despotic tendencies, Carrera had developed a "system of national independence," wrote Consul Poinsett, who, with editor Henriquez, had continued to use the *Aurora* "to arm Carrera with the language of liberty and virtue." Carrera needed real arms, too, preferably from Poinsett's United States, including two frigates to support the taking of Lima. Poinsett kept sending out encrypted communications by mule train, hoping they would reach Washington, hoping that Washington would recognize the new republic and send it the assistance it deserved.

In September 1812, Poinsett received the electrifying news that in June the United States had declared war on England. He had been in Santiago for nine months by then, trying to make his own judgments about America's best interests, even while becoming a leading figure in the new nation of Chile. He and Carrera kept working to build republican structures into the government and to increase the size of the army and improve its capabilities. Carrera had sent 500 of his own men to Buenos Aires to fight against the royalists there, and he provided them with news and intelligence, as they did him. The Argentinians deserved support, having led the way toward independence in southern South America; and their junto had offered to send troops to Chile in time of need. Carrera knew that he would have little support from the outside world once the fighting started.

Rumors flew in the first months of 1813 from the sea and from over the mountains. Viceroy Abascal had reached the end of his patience, it was said. Naval vessels had gathered at Callao, and troops were drilling at Lima. Fernando VII had been restored to the Spanish throne and was seeking vengeance against those in the empire who had betrayed the fatherland. Perhaps some of it was true.

Poinsett continued to hope that the revolution in Chile might make it the fulcrum for a continent-wide movement for independence. This possibility gave profound meaning to all his years of wandering, observing, posing, and studying in preparation for some unknown opportunity, some grand purpose. And for more than a year, he had retained the confidence of the patriots while carefully finessing the issue of American involvement. Support was coming, he assured them, but logistics were difficult. It was important to his standing, and his country's, that he be seen as capable of getting his government to deliver.

He was both popular and credible, but an English merchant had matched Hoevel's achievement by importing a shipment of weapons for sale to the rebels, leaving Poinsett unable to counter. The silence of Washington and the rumblings from London as the British Empire's rulers slowly, tentatively, turned their attention to matters in Chile kept him awake nights. Still, he relied on the promises of President Madison, and he conducted himself as if it were only a matter of time before his government, now at war, took decisive and dramatic action. With the arrival of a decree of formal recognition for the new republic, or multiple shipments of arms, or a frigate-class American battleship, Chile would know who its true friend was.

Poinsett heard that two American whalers had been captured by a privateer and a British armed whaleship, and that the American sealing ship *Hope*, far to the south at San Carlos, had been taken and her men sent to prison in Callao. As consul general, part of his mission was to protect American seamen and American property. He protested to Viceroy Abascal but received no response. It was extremely frustrating: after more than a year of trying to bring about conditions for a Chilean war that would convulse the continent and change the course of history, Poinsett had to accept the silence of the enemy and of his own government.

And so, on the afternoon that he received word in Santiago that the U.S. frigate *Essex* had arrived in Valparaiso, Consul General Poinsett assumed that his many entreaties had been heard and acted upon. Captain David Porter must be the hero he had been awaiting—Madison's emissary, the herald of his nation's commitment to the brave patriots of Spanish America.

Chapter Six

A New America

In the harbor at Valparaiso on March 14, 1813, as Captain David Porter watched the barge of the seaport governor returning to the *Essex* with Lieutenant Downes on board, he prepared for the worst—a disaster at home, or a Spanish declaration of war on the United States.

In fact, the port captain joyfully called up to them, Valparaiso is free! Chile is independent! Vivan los Estados Unidos! The Chileans, he said, "had shaken off their allegiance" to Spain and now had an army, a constitution, and a new nation. America, he assured them, was their model. They "looked up to the United States of America for example and protection," and they welcomed Porter as a liberator.

Amused, Porter gave independent Chile a twenty-one-gun salute that was "punctually returned" by the fort. He went ashore and met with a surprised Governor Francisco de la Lastra. Lastra said that recently he had heard from Buenos Aires that the *Essex* was in the Atlantic, cruising with a squadron off Brazil, and that Porter's commander, William Bainbridge of the *Constitution*, had won a brilliant victory, as had James Lawrence and the *Hornet*. Porter was thrilled and jealous at this news and eager to hear more. Through an interpreter he spoke at length with the congenial Lastra, who had been an officer in the Spanish Royal Navy and had fought Napoleon's forces in Spain. Porter explained that this was his second cruise; on the first, in the Atlantic, he had captured several of the enemy's merchant vessels and had been the first to defeat a vessel of the Royal Navy, an inferior ship that he had sent in to New York. His triumph, he noted ruefully, had soon been eclipsed by the resounding victory of Captain Isaac Hull and the *Constitution*. Still, said Lastra, to El Capitan Porter belonged a great honor.

Lastra confessed that he had reservations about recent events in his homeland. He worried about "staunch republicans, men filled with revolutionary principles, and apparently desirous of establishing a government founded on liberty." Chile did not seem ready for liberty: it was suddenly a republic, although it had no experience of self-government; its slogan was democracy, but most of the people were ignorant and illiterate. There was a sense of unreality to it all, a feeling of improvisation and impermanence. Nonetheless, Lastra conceded, the revolution was probably necessary to introduce a better system of government. Spain was fading as an imperial power, and its colonies had an opportunity to be free. Lastra and other ruling-class Creoles felt that they could run Chile better than their Spanish overlords, but they did not believe in democracy or in republican government. In Lastra's opinion, the rebellion was moving too fast and making too many changes.

Chile had always been an autocracy, with the richest and best-educated running things. For centuries, the poor had been kept in their place, living out their lives in a state of ignorance and complacency that would help them to accept their lowly but useful roles in society. Some of this, said Lastra, was as it should be—there was a natural order involved. The idealists in the independence movement did not appreciate how deeply rooted were the old ways in this kingdom and how bitterly opposed to innovation were those who held privileged positions. Conservative royalists were numerous, and many of the wisest and most powerful moderates favored only limited reforms. They remained respectful of Viceroy Abascal, enthroned at Lima, technically the ruler of Chile in the name of Fernando VII; they did not want to suffer the devastation of war, and they did not want their sons fighting for a makeshift, radical government. They were grateful to Abascal for his forbearance in not sending troops into Chile.

Lastra thought he could see things clearly. Certainly he had a good vantage point, for his sister-in-law's brothers were the three Carreras, who first had taken over the army and then the congress. Now José Miguel Carrera was the leader of the new republic, and it was he who had made Lastra the chief of the Chilean navy, which, as Porter could see, had no ships.

Governor Lastra, obviously fascinated by the *Essex*, came on board with his retinue and seemed to Porter to be "much pleased and astonished that Anglo-Americans, as they styled us, could build, equip, and manage ships of so large a size." The governor ended his visit by inviting Porter and his officers to a party to be held in their honor.

Valparaiso Bay, Chile, looking south from the battery at Castello el Baron. At center is the harbor anchorage; to the right is the Point of Angels.

Valparaiso Harbor in the early nineteenth century. Toward the end of the British-French world war (1793–1815), several of Spain's South American colonies asserted their independence. Chileans, whose main port was Valparaiso, had long carried on a smuggling trade with visiting American whalers and merchant vessels. Revolutionaries opened the port to free trade in 1810.

At dawn the next day, Porter received an envelope from Santiago, the capital, fifty-seven miles away. He read the letter with concern; there was an American consul in Chile, one Joel Roberts Poinsett, who congratulated him on his timely arrival. War matters had reached a serious pass, Poinsett wrote, and U.S. intervention would make all the difference in Chile. Poinsett reported that news of the arrival of the *Essex* had set off joyous demonstrations in Santiago. Crowds had gathered in jubilation, "bells had been rung the whole day, and illuminations had taken place" all night. Horses and carriages were being sent to Valparaiso to carry Porter and his officers to the outskirts of the capital, to be met by President Carrera and his own cavalry unit, which would escort the captain in a triumphal parade through the city.

This was bad news for Porter, who, for the first time, understood that the war he carried with him might not be his own. He wrote with annoyance in his journal that Poinsett "believed that I had brought from my country nothing less than proposals for a friendly alliance with Chile and assurances of assistance in their struggle for independence." This Consul Poinsett seemed to think that the situation in Chile was highly important to the future of the United States in the Pacific. However that might be, Porter was quite sure that an official of the Department of State had no authority over a navy captain. He sent a message to Poinsett regretting that he and his officers would not be going to the capital or marching in any parades.

On the following day, as the men of the *Essex* loaded provisions and Porter played tourist, Consul Poinsett arrived from Santiago. He was dashing, handsome, and full of enthusiasm for Chilean independence. He remonstrated with Porter, hoping that there had been some mistake. In fact, there were many, and they all added up to a refusal. Porter had not been sent to Chile to support the revolution; he had known nothing about it when he had sailed from the Delaware River in October. Porter was on a mission to hunt down British whaleships in the Pacific and could not lose a day—if the Spanish sent word out to sea, the whalers might escape or seek protection in ports. The *Essex* had no orders to stay in Chile or to become involved in the wars of other nations. It was just a coincidence that Porter had come to Valparaiso to get supplies—he had meant to put into the Bay of Concepcion. Obviously, he could not allow the Chileans to lionize him under false pretenses.

Poinsett was shaken, dismayed, incredulous. His entire mission was being placed in jeopardy thanks to this American captain, his own countryman. Naturally, everyone in Santiago had given Poinsett credit for the arrival of the much-hoped-for battleship symbolizing America's commitment to their revolutionary state and its war of independence. The *Essex* had such strength and such firepower, at thirty-two guns, that she could dominate the Pacific coastline. Amid the cheering and fireworks in Santiago, Poinsett had done nothing to curb their jubilation at this example of the magnificent generosity of the United States. In fact, he had long expected Madison to live up to their private agreement to provide assistance to the patriots and to recognize the existence of their new republic.

Within twenty-four hours of the coming of the *Essex*, Poinsett went from elation to despair, and much of Chile with him. No doubt he pressed Porter hard to undo the damage, to no avail. Poinsett regarded Porter's refusal to stay on as a great error. War was imminent between rebel Chile and royalist Peru, and Abascal was behaving like an enemy, preying on American vessels, capturing three of them and imprisoning their crews, and ignoring Poinsett's demands. The *Essex* was uniquely able to prevent further depredations and, in case of war, to cut off a naval attack from Lima and limit the transport of troops by sea. But Porter insisted that his mission was to damage the enemy by capturing English whalers. Not to protect American whalers and trading vessels? Well, yes, that too.*

Consul General Poinsett was committed to the fight for Chilean independence. He was already advising President Carrera and planned to join him on the battlefield if necessary. Porter, however, could not be drawn in; he was not game for Poinsett's war or wars along the shores of Spanish America, and he wondered at the man's devotion to the cause, which made him seem more like a Roman consul, intent on a triumph against enemy armies, than a modern consular bureaucrat. It was not, however, the place of David Porter to question the deportment of a duly authorized consul general. If Poinsett was a partisan, perhaps that was what Washington wanted.

After a few days, Porter was willing to concede Poinsett's acumen, for it was apparent that "the whole power and force of the kingdom of Chile" was in the hands of Poinsett's friends the Carrera brothers. President José Miguel Carrera led the cavalry of this "kingdom," while the infantry was commanded by Juan José Carrera, the giant, and the artillery by Luis Carrera, the gentleman. Consul Poinsett had a high opinion of General Carrera and a firm

---

* Long after he had come on the Chilean coast, Porter, in his journal, wrote that he had realized that he might be useful in protecting American whalers—an afterthought.

belief in the importance of Chile's revolution. But Porter supposed that the Carreras were no more devoted to the ideals of a republic than to their own self-interest, nor were any of their rivals and subordinates, who waited for the Carreras to weaken and be devoured by their own monster.

Busy loading his provisions and resisting Poinsett and his suggestions, Porter took a summary view of the situation and missed, or avoided, the complexities. In his view the "patriots" were Creoles, "young dashing native Chileans," opposed by "invariably crusty, old, formal Castilians" sent out from Madrid to manage the colonies. Although the rebels were in charge, a large group of royalists called "Saracens" was said to be "a strong and secret party" out to assassinate certain Creoles.

Porter's arrival had been a coincidence, nothing more, although the Chileans still wanted him to be their hero. He resented their assumptions without bothering to refute them. In a few days he would be over the horizon, hunting for British whalers, far from these importunate strangers at whom he smiled and nodded, cynically encouraging "a belief that suited my views and accorded with their wishes." In truth, he was more interested in their women than in their revolution.

No one in Valparaiso—certainly not Poinsett—knew what had really brought David Porter to the Pacific and how much he had risked by rounding the Horn. For months it had been the little captain's own secret, one that tore at him, a compulsion and an irresistible temptation that overwhelmed his better judgment.

Governor Lastra, overseer of the seaport and its forts, hosted a farewell ball in honor of El Capitan Porter and the officers of the *Essex*. Porter, eager for female company after months at sea, was surprised and pleased to encounter "a much larger and more brilliant assemblage of ladies than we could have expected." The night's dancing began with elegant minuets, followed by folk dances and then an American cotillion, which "the ladies," all made up with rouge and powder, "had the complaisance and patience to attempt."

Porter and his happy officers "could almost fancy we had gotten amongst our own fair country-women" until the next dance began—"and in one moment the illusion vanished." To the music of the *balas de tierra*, a sort of polka, the pale, graceful ladies suddenly began making "the most indelicate and lascivious motions, gradually increasing in energy and violence"—most keenly observed—"until the fair one, apparently overcome with passion," was "compelled to retire to her seat." There a transformation occurred: "her rosy cheeks and fair complexion disappeared in the large drops of sweat which ran trickling down her neck and breast," revealing "the sallow tinge which nature had bountifully bestowed."

Despite his private crudity and reflexive American racism, Porter was not so uncouth as to express his thoughts except to the future readers of the journal he was writing. But he loathed some of the behaviors of his hosts and decided that "the customs of the inhabitants of Valparaiso differ so materially from our own (and perhaps from those of every other people) that I cannot help noticing a few particulars." His hosts had not explained to him how extensive were their multicourse meals, nor how to eat certain dishes. They had not mentioned that elegant ladies might prance around like pagans but would never show the slightest sign of public affection. These were the matters that "struck [Porter] as the most singular" about a society in the midst of revolution and a courageous people who, on the verge of fighting for their freedom, had graciously paused to pay tribute to a man who had bitterly disappointed them, their xenophobic guest of honor, a pure product of the closed society of the U.S. Navy and a betrayer of the cause.

At Valparaiso after the ball, Porter turned down many other invitations while the vessel loading proceeded. On Saturday he was interrupted by the arrival from Santiago of Don Luis Carrera, one of the military leaders of the rebellion, along with a new English commercial consul and two Americans.* On Sunday, Porter rested from his labors and invited ladies and gentlemen to spend the afternoon on board ship prior to attending an evening ball. After a pleasant visit in which "we had all laid aside our national and religious prejudices," Porter and his guests had just gone ashore when a cry went up, followed by a shot of warning from the outermost fort. A large vessel was making her way in—a warship, without doubt. The *Essex* was an easy target at anchor in the outer harbor, so Porter and his fellow officers, along with Poinsett and Carrera and his retinue, ran to the dock, jumped into the captain's gig, and flew back to their ship. Porter ordered the anchor cables cut and got her under way to meet the advancing enemy. A British frigate or ship of the line would have a great advantage over the *Essex*, still in the harbor with little room to maneuver.

The frigate kept coming, and the *Essex* sallied forth to offer combat.

---

* Perhaps the Americans were Captain Massena Monson and first mate Edward Barnewall of the merchant vessel *Colt*, moored in the harbor, to whom Porter evidently detached a couple of his sailors toward a navy for Lastra and Carrera.

On the yellow hillsides of Valparaiso, crowds gathered—men, women, and children—to view the battle to be fought by the gallant Anglo-Americans. On board, Luis Carrera, twenty-two, head of the rebel army's artillery, was excited; he kept urging Porter to take the enemy by storm and allow him to lead a boarding party. The *Essex* was in fighting trim by the time she caught up to the stranger, which proved to be the Portuguese merchantman *San José de la Fama* arriving from Rio for a cargo of flour. When the two vessels passed in silence, the cheated crowds grumbled and returned to the city. On board the *Essex* the intrepid Don Luis, deprived of this chance at glory, soon experienced the humiliation of seasickness. "However warlike he might have felt on first coming aboard," smirked Porter, "he was now as weak as an infant."

Other than this mistaken chance for one-on-one naval combat, Porter was vastly indifferent to events along the coast of Chile. Much had happened, and was happening, in the Pacific that required the attention of an American commander. He might have convoyed the American whalers home from Talcahuano, and he might have stayed on to work with Poinsett in the impending conflict with the Spanish royalists, whose vessels had been preying on American shipping. Clearly the consul believed that, in the war between England and America, the triumph of an independent Chile would be a strategic victory of the greatest importance to the United States. Poinsett's career would have been made, and Porter would have taken his place in the history books as a liberator and a hero of the Pacific far greater than Anson. But Porter had entered the ocean on his own, concerned with personal goals and fantasies that did not include freedom-fighting or nation-building.

Next morning, Porter finished loading and noticed that Governor Lastra, with flags and banners flying at the fort, had made a "great preparation" to honor the Americans. Once again, Porter went ashore. The extravaganza, in an enormous tent, was sponsored by the national leaders, who had come from Santiago: Consul-General Poinsett, members of the junto, heads of departments, President Carrera and his brothers, and various other military leaders, gallant young men like cavalry captains Diego Benavente and Manuel Rodriguez and their lieutenants. In the tent were the flags of all nations, a carpeted floor, handsome banquet tables with glinting silver services at every one, and a twenty-course dinner to be served to all, including Porter and his men and some Britons as well. The wine flowed freely, and the young Chileans became so impassioned in their toasts and speeches in praise of independence and American liberty that they had to withdraw before insulting the British further. After the feast, Porter was given a tour of the fort and then escorted to another ball, in which the ladies achieved a kind of "splendor." Amid "much hilarity" the dance broke up at one in the morning, and Poinsett and Carrera, amigos, headed off to Santiago.

At nine o'clock in the morning the *Essex* herself was invaded, as the dancing ladies came on board to enjoy themselves until noon, at which time they departed to an eleven-gun salute, which was returned by Don Francisco de la Lastra, governor of Valparaiso, head of the Chilean navy, from his fortress on the harbor. Porter finished his busy week at Valparaiso by sending a letter to Poinsett to be forwarded to Bainbridge—his last effort to communicate with his former commander. Porter and the *Essex* then stood to sea on a fresh southerly breeze. Even if news had reached Lima of the presence of an American frigate on the coast, it was now too late for British officials there to alert the English vessels on the whaling grounds. Recognizing that, Porter set free all but one of his British prisoners, collected from Atlantic encounters.

So ended that brief but intense love affair, entirely one-sided. The rebels of Chile bade farewell to the man who had arrived by coincidence and not out of a sense of destiny, and the tawny ladies of Valparaiso waved their hankies to see the odd little captain sail away, perhaps forever.

On March 31, 1813, with the *Essex* only days over the horizon, the leaders of Chile learned that Viceroy Abascal had begun an invasion by sea at the south, taking advantage of the rebels' complete lack of a navy.

Santiago went mad with patriotic fervor. Johnston, the printer, was on the scene, writing, "[I]t is impossible for me to give you an idea of the enthusiasm which prevails among the people. The palace is surrounded from morning till night by persons who offer not only their personal services to the government but bring with them their treasures also," including money, material, and squads of soldiers fully equipped and supported by rich individuals. "The rage for military fame is likewise indescribable," wrote Johnston. "Volunteer companies are formed and the first the government know of their organizations is when they see them armed and accoutered at their own private expense, offering their services and ready to march at a moment's warning . . . to join the legions of the country."

José Miguel Carrera, commander in chief, placed his political power in the hands of a junto of three prominent Santiago politicians. He trusted only one other man to join him as general of the armies: his *asesor*, El Consul, Roberts Poinsett, the confidential advisor needed if he were to survive the impossible mission that he had set for himself. Poinsett, still sending messages to Washington but never hearing back, questioned himself severely about this new role. Once before he had grappled with a similar question when Czar Alexander had asked him to consider fighting for Russia against the invader Napoleon. Then, Poinsett had reluctantly declined, fearing that there was no American purpose served by such service, however personally desirable. And he had been sure of his identity as an American, with no wish to become Russian. Now he knew that there were American prisoners, hundreds of them, held at Talcahuano, and that they could only be rescued by force. He knew, too, that Peruvian privateers had attacked the New York merchantman *Colt* and three whaleships off the upper coast. To his protests, Abascal had responded by upbraiding the Santiago junto for "harboring a French spy under the specious title of Consul-General of the United States."

When the news arrived that the ten American whalers were among the spoils of the viceroy's troops at the Bay of Concepcion, Poinsett decided that he "could not sit tamely, and see our flag insulted, our ships seized, and our citizens loaded (in) irons. My influence in Chile," he wrote Secretary Monroe, "enabled me to act as I thought my duty imperiously called upon me to do, for I could no longer consider these as the acts of a neutral, but as the wanton aggressions of a man who, in the arbitrary exercise of uncontrolled power, knows no right, and who, as an ally of Great Britain, looks forward to a war with the United States as a necessary consequence of that alliance and as a justification of his violent proceedings."

Throughout his adult life, Poinsett had wandered the world, learning from many experiences but always convinced of the superiority of the United States and equally convinced that it was his destiny to lead an army in defense of his country and its ideals. If that army was made up of Chilean rebels, and the enemy was Chilean royalists, perhaps his silent superiors in Washington would understand. "Induced by my devotion to liberty," he wrote to Secretary Monroe, and by a desire to avenge Viceroy Abascal's brutal treatment of Americans, "I joined the army of Chile, and directed its movements."

General Poinsett, the chief strategist, along with General Carrera and cavalry Captain Diego Benavente, headed south to establish an army base at Talca on the Maule River, the boundary between the provinces of Santiago and Concepcion. The two general officers had no experience in commanding an army, and their army had never fought a battle. To put an army in the field was not just to resort to overwhelming violence in service to policy, but to take responsibility for feeding, clothing, arming, and sheltering the men, far from familiar surroundings and predictable resources. Without infrastructure or supply networks, Carrera would depend on local people to contribute to the upkeep of soldiers occupying their territory—always a strain, and potentially disastrous to the civilians and to the morale of the army. A short war would be best for all.

Poinsett and Carrera assumed that the enemy force was larger and better organized, with Spanish officers and mainly Peruvian Creole soldiers, but their own Creoles, they believed, would fight harder for Chile than those fighting for Spain and its phantom king. They worried that the southern Chileans might rally to the royalist cause, for lower Concepcion province had long been guarded by the Spanish king's troops as a bulwark against the fierce Arauco tribe of Native Americans, potentially allies in war.

And there was the problem of the rebels who had sided with Rozas, Carrera's former rival. They would not necessarily welcome the patriots coming from Santiago, even if O'Higgins did. Carrera and Poinsett could only hope that the militia of the towns of Chillan, Valdivia, and Concepcion would join them. With civil war only recently averted, no one wanted to imagine a new one pitting northern Creoles against their southern cousins.

Poinsett knew that the concept of war—of large groups of men and boys serving as soldiers, commanded by officers and moving *en masse* across great distances to fight in formation—was entirely foreign to Chileans. The independence movement, to date, had been political, not military; no one other than a few leaders had been asked to give up his safety and his place in society and risk his life for something larger. War was an event that took place in Europe, with real battlefields, famous generals and strategists, and vast numbers of regular troops led by trained officers. Nothing like that existed here.

Poinsett was, however, thrilled to get his chance. He had steered the Chilean rebellion in the direction of a republic and toward outright alliance with the United States. His own nation was at war with the British, who were backing the royalists in Spain. Carrera's defeat of the Spanish invader would ensure that the revolution continued, and a decisive defeat might inspire the United States to recognize Chilean nationhood and to support "the one great movement" that Poinsett had envisioned for an independent South America. It could start right now, with him as catalyst.

Chapter Seven

Americans at War

Soon after leaving the Bay of Valparaiso to hunt for British whalers, Porter experienced a moment of excitement when he spotted a whaleship, but she proved to be American, the *George* of Nantucket. Her captain, Benjamin Worth, was the sort of man Porter had been seeking since entering the Pacific—a man with answers. Worth, forty-five, was an old salt; he had been at sea for thirty years, eighteen of them as a shipmaster. He had ranged the Peruvian whaling grounds for more than a decade and had been the first American to ascend the coast and hunt sperm whales in the Pacific Northwest. Now, coming aboard the *Essex*, the efficient Captain Worth lamented the time and money he had lost in Lima, having been captured by the Spanish and then forced to go through a lawsuit to regain the freedom of the seas. Porter questioned him about English whalers, and Worth mentioned that a few days earlier, while cruising with three other American vessels, he had encountered two English armed whalers whose captains had politely reported that their two governments were at war—the first the Americans had known of it. Worth claimed that the English "had no orders to capture American vessels" but "were in daily expectation of authority to that effect."

Worth had further heard that one American ship had already been captured by a British privateer, the recently arrived *Seringapatam*, but that Lima authorities—hoping to preserve the neutrality of their port and avoid antagonizing Americans—had refused to accept her as a prize. The *Seringapatam* was large, well built, heavily armed, and said to be commanded by "a bold and unprincipled adventurer" whose main interest was prizes, not whales. The captured American ship, Worth understood, was being sailed by an English crew to Cape Horn and on to St. Helena, off Africa, to join a convoy bound for England.* If Porter thought of giving chase, he thought again when, he claimed, Worth urged him to head for the Galápagos Islands, where many American whalers were unaware of the new war and were "entirely exposed to attack and capture by the armed English [whale] ships in those seas, carrying from 14 to 20 guns."

This was exactly what Porter wanted to hear. On he sailed to hunt the hunters, headed, at last, for a rendezvous. Next morning, March 25, at daybreak, the lookout spotted a sail to the northeast, and before long they came up with the Nantucket whaleship *Charles*, out thirteen months under Grafton Gardner, who told a harrowing tale. Four months earlier, whaling off the coast of Peru, he and his men had been attacked by a Spanish colonial privateer and sent as prisoners into Callao, the port of Lima. As with Captain Worth more recently, Gardner had sued for his freedom and won it. Back at sea, the *Charles* had fallen in with two other Nantucket whalers and together they had cruised until just two days before. Approaching the port of Coquimbo in northern Chile, they had been intercepted by two armed vessels, one English, the other Spanish. The whalers had crowded on sail as the fast-moving strangers had begun firing their guns. Gardner and the *Charles*, farthest off, had kept pulling away, but the New Bedford whalers *Walker*, under Paul West, and *Barclay*, under Gideon Randall, had surrendered.

Next day off Coquimbo, Porter spied a sail, and by noon the *Essex* had drawn close enough to see that she carried American whaleboats and an array of heavy cannon. When she hoisted Spanish colors, Porter responded with the flag of Britain, and the two vessels closed within a mile. Porter decided that she was "one of the picaroons that had been for a long time harassing our commerce"—but his English disguise would guarantee the stranger's good behavior. Suddenly, the Spanish privateer fired a shot across his bow, which so infuriated Porter that he almost forgot that "the insult was not intended for the American flag." He lobbed a few high shots to show the power that he was holding back.

• The Nantucket whaler *Edward*, with its captain, Seth Folger, fell captive to the British fourteen-gun ship *Seringapatam* and its captain, William Stavers, dispatched from the Orient to harass American shipping in the Pacific and to do some whaling as well. *Seringapatam* was not a letter-of-marque; she had no official government commission to prey on enemy shipping.

A boat was lowered from the other vessel, but the armed occupants were ordered to return with their papers and an apology. This they did, and her second lieutenant informed the "English" commander that she was the *Nereyda*, fifteen guns, sailing for the Viceroy of Lima and as a friend of the British, but under a commission that had expired three months before. To Porter, this made them pirates. Proudly the young officer related that the *Nereyda* had recently captured two American whalers, the *Barclay* and the *Walker*, and that when he had arrived at Coquimbo with the two prizes, Captain Perry of the British brig *Nimrod*, eighteen guns, had muscled his way over to the *Walker*, dismissed her Peruvian crew, and sailed away with the American vessel. The sick captain of the *Nereyda* had gamely begun pursuit to reclaim his stolen goods, and had mistaken the *Essex* and the *Charles* for the *Nimrod* and the *Walker*—thus the firing of a bow shot.

Porter summoned the first lieutenant on board and toyed with his young visitor. The lieutenant, who had not noticed the trappings and uniforms of the U.S. Navy all around him, explained that Peruvians were great admirers of the British despite the piratical actions of Perry—and that "his sole object was the capture of American vessels." In fact, he was holding more than twenty Americans—the *Barclay*'s crew and the captain and part of the crew of the *Walker*—imprisoned belowdecks. Porter played out his hand, demanding a visit from the American captain of the *Walker* and a crewman of the *Barclay*. Upon their arrival, he took them aside and said that they were on board an American frigate. Amazed and overjoyed, Captain West reported that the *Nereyda* "was a pirate, that she took everything she came across," that he and the other twenty-three Americans had been "plundered" by their captors solely because they were Americans. Whalers, with holds full of oil, they had done no smuggling.

Returning to the deck, Porter ordered the dousing of British colors and the raising of the big American flag, accompanied by two cannonballs fired into the *Nereyda*, whose captain promptly surrendered. Next day Porter had Downes heave overboard her guns, ammunition, arms, light sails, and topmasts. To the Yankees' surprise, all of her cannon but one were made of iron, and their shot was copper—the reverse of other nations', which were cast in bronze, firing iron shot. Porter then brought the liberated American whalemen on board the *Essex*.

Porter's handling of this situation was disingenuous at best, for he had heard repeatedly from American whaling captains that Callao's Spanish privateers, and not English whaleships, were the problem in the Pacific. Although Porter had treated her as a nuisance freelancing against American shipping, the *Nereyda* actually sailed under Abascal's patent as an instrument of anti-American policy, and her preying on Americans was cause for formal protest if not outright reprisal. In fact, Abascal had launched a full-scale war against Chile, which included an order to impound all American vessels found in Chilean waters.

The Spanish authorities at Callao must have been horrified to see an American battleship enter their port, evidently part of an invasion by Chilean and American forces. Callao, as it happened, had never been more vulnerable, since Viceroy Abascal had just dispatched a five-vessel fleet for Chile and so relied for protection on the *Nereyda*, which Porter, almost by accident and certainly without due understanding of its significance, had just captured and neutered. Unlike Poinsett, who was opposed to Abascal's Spanish royalists in the name of the republic, Porter did not wish to antagonize the Spanish viceroy if it would interfere with his pursuit of British whaleships. He sent in the *Nereyda* and her crew with a letter for Abascal, deploring their capture of two American whalers and their crews and noting that her officers had admitted to "cruising as the allies of Great Britain," although Porter was sure that "they had not your Excellency's authority for such proceedings." His certainty was, of course, totally misplaced. His obsession with British whalers had left him unaware, or unwilling to accept, that Abascal had declared war on the rebel state of Chile and had adopted a policy of aggression against Americans as part of that war.

Porter offered the shipless Yankee mariners the choice of joining the crew of the *Essex* or going ashore. Nine went with Porter. In his continuing state of ignorance, he urged Captains Gardner and West to take their vessels into Peruvian ports—a sure way to lose them again—and he thought about hunting down the *Nimrod*, which was likely chasing the *Barclay* and her captors. Since he could not launch his campaign against British whalers until he was sure that the Royal Navy battleship *Standard* had gone beyond the Galápagos, he decided to pursue the *Nimrod* provided it did not "interfere too much with my other views"—the vision of a conquered fleet of twenty well-filled whaleships worth millions.

And there was another consideration, one that had been a long time coming: Porter, for the first time, realized that his intended capture of the British whaling fleet would also protect unarmed American whaleships, whose masters may not have known about the Anglo-American war or about the presence of Peruvian and English sea wolves. Porter told himself that "if I should only succeed in driving the British from that ocean, and leaving it free for our own vessels, I conceive that I shall have rendered an essential service to my country"—at the same time reaping untold wealth and giving him cover with his navy superiors. As he contemplated his pursuit of the *Nimrod* and perhaps the *Seringapatam*, he reminded himself, in his journal, to re-frame his renegade adventure as a rescue of the Pacific fleet of American whalers. That noble aim "would be considered a justification for departing from the letter of my instructions" and might earn him forgiveness for having gone rogue.

On March 28, Porter had his crew swarming to disguise the *Essex* with a false deck and a new paint job that concealed most of her guns. A few days later, this ersatz Spanish merchantman began chasing three vessels standing in for Callao. The lead ship, the American-flagged *Barclay*, soon struck, but suddenly all were becalmed, so Porter sent out his boats to tow the prize against the incoming tide. In full view of the shipping and defenders of the harbor, Porter himself ran up the English flag on the *Essex*. At Callao, the colors of every vessel were hastily raised too, in honor of the unexpected English battleship: all were Spanish except for one Briton, not the *Nimrod*. From the deck of the *Essex*, the master of the recaptured *Barclay*, Gideon Randall, a recent prisoner on the *Nereyda*, looked on, hoping to resume his command; however, his men preferred the *Essex* and would not return to the whaler. Randall therefore sailed with only three Americans, all of them sick with scurvy contracted after seven months at sea. Randall could not risk putting into a Peruvian port since Porter had trashed the *Barclay*'s captor, the *Nereyda*, and he could not pursue sperm whales without a crew. Porter solved the problem by offering "to put on board hands enough to work his vessel," and Randall promised to guide him to the Galápagos haunts of the British whalers. Midshipman John S. Cowan and eight men now joined the skeleton crew under Captain Randall. Together, the *Essex* and the *Barclay* stood off to the north to touch at Paita, thence to the killing grounds.

Porter now had some idea what he was looking for. Before leaving him, Captains Worth and West had supplied a list of all whaleships in the Pacific, with details about the twenty English-flagged vessels, each about 400 tons burthen. There were twenty-three American vessels, two from New

Bedford and the rest from Nantucket. They reported that a large part of the American whaling fleet had already sailed south, seeking safety in the Creole ports of lower Chile. Typical was the *President* of Nantucket, commanded by Solomon Folger. Gamming with the Nantucket whaler *Atlas*, he had learned about the start of the Anglo-American war from Captain Obed Joy, who had it from the courteous Captain Obed Wyer of Nantucket, commanding the British-flagged armed whaler *Atlantic*. Thanks to the timely alert from Wyer, Joy and Folger had decided to head south to get a convoy to the United States. Putting in at Talcahuano, they came upon ten American whalers and crews also waiting for an escort. David Porter, unaware, had sailed right past them in early March; now, courtesy of Worth and West, Porter was fully aware of their desperate situation, and it was not too late for the *Essex* to help them.

Porter and the *Essex* approached Paita trailed by the *Barclay*. On the way, in the thick of an immense flock of birds, Porter noticed "small red specks" like blood clotting the sea, which he supposed to have come from "some hog killed on board"; looking closer, he saw that the specks had a "quick motion," so he lowered a bucket and found them to be "young craw-fish," swimming randomly. "[T]hey did not appear to be governed by any general laws, each one pursuing his own course and shifting for himself." Perhaps Porter recognized something familiar in their behavior.

The *Essex* was never free of problems, with more than 300 men on board. Not long before, the frigate's supply of fresh water had turned brackish. Some were suffering from its effects, but none suffered more than James Spafford, the gunner's mate, writhing in slow-dying agony. The poor man had been accidentally shot by near-sighted Lieutenant Stephen McKnight while they had foraged on Mocha Island three weeks before. Finally, on April 4, Spafford expired, and his body "was committed to the deep, according to the funeral ceremonies of the church." With his passing, his friends were left to reflect on the unpredictability of life and death at sea, where a murderous storm might spare them all, but a man's own officer might accidentally shoot him down—a bad omen indeed for the superstitious sailors of the *Essex*.

Porter sailed on through waters alive with seals and the turbulence of fish-chasing whales. And they were not alone: two small sailing vessels off Paita proved to be "rafts or catamarans, steering by the wind, each having six men to work them," each consisting of eight long logs lashed together and carrying deck cargoes of cocoa, bound from Guayaquil to Guacho, a voyage of 600 miles and two months. The decks were strewn with fish bones and garbage, and Porter reflected that the ocean was indeed pacific if these "barbarous vessels" could make such a long trip in safety. The crude rafts offended him as a mariner, but fascinated him too; their shabbiness was a "convincing instance of the unenlightened state of the people of this part of the world." The whole coasting trade of Peru, he decided, was clear evidence of a people so "behind-hand in civilization and intelligence with the rest of the world that the appearance of all the vessels built on the Spanish coast of the Pacific (except the few built at Guayaquil) bespeaks the extreme ignorance of the constructor as well as the navigator."

Porter's own ignorance was far more impressive. He had not cared much about the Chilenos and their revolution. He had not felt the tremors of a coast that was quaking with war; he had not seen that Americans were targets and that the few brave Americans fighting for an independent Chile might soon be held in a prison under a death sentence brought on by Porter's own actions. Given the choice between chasing whaleships and fostering national independence under a leader who idolized the United States, he had chosen plunder. From the railing of his battleship, Porter called down questions to the lowly raftmen, who answered that no foreign vessels were to be found in the harbor of Paita. The great captain waved his thanks, and the frigate altered course, steering west-northwest away from South America. The rafts sailed on toward the undefended port of Valparaiso.

José Miguel Carrera and Joel Roberts Poinsett, generals of the army, appeared at Talca on April 5, 1813, with a small force but with the countryside mobilizing and some of the 9,000 provincial militiamen and their officers starting to arrive in camp. Within a few hours, Bernardo O'Higgins rode in from his adventures in the south. His news was not good. Viceroy Abascal's commander, Pareja, had landed at the island of Chiloe with five vessels filled with arms, uniforms, and supplies, together with fifty Spanish officers who had taken command of the 1,500 Chilean militiamen at Chiloe and Valdivia.

O'Higgins had marched from his plantation toward Concepcion at the head of 100 soldiers whom he had personally trained and equipped. On the way, having learned of the fall of Concepcion, he had disbanded his men to avoid capture and had ridden on with a couple of friends to offer his services to Carrera. O'Higgins reported that Pareja's army had doubled in size along the way as putative rebels had gone over to the royalists. It was the worst scenario for the prospects of a united Chilean state: the men of the south were evidently willing to serve in the armed forces of the royalists, and indeed to make up the bulk of their army. At Talcahuano they created a blockade against any rebel reinforcements or provisions that might arrive by sea. Lastra, at Valparaiso, was responsible for the Chilean nationalist navy, which had never been organized and which, in the absence of Porter and the *Essex*, had no battleship available to break through the royalist barriers.

South of the Maule River, 200 rebel militiamen were pinned down by the vanguard of Pareja's army, which was camped at Linares. One night O'Higgins and a strike force galloped off into the darkness and went charging into the plaza at Linares, making prisoners of many of the surprised enemy cavalrymen. Sent over the Maule, the captives defected, and the militiamen marched north to join them in the rebel army. O'Higgins' boldness and courage were inspiring to all. By April 18, the Chilean forces had large numbers, including Luis Carrera's 200 artillerists with 400 mules and 16 small field pieces as well as 600 infantry, 1,500 cavalrymen, 200 national guardsmen, and assorted militia.

Carrera, advised by Poinsett, decided to create a salient south of the river, with earthworks and trenches blocking the enemy's path to the Maule. Just then Juan Mackenna, who had been briefly detained by Carreristas at Santiago, came into camp to serve as quartermaster and to apply his considerable experience as a field engineer. Carrera had deployed his army in three blocs between Talca and the Maule, under him and his brothers, with Bernardo O'Higgins holding the salient to the south that Poinsett had chosen. When O'Higgins fell severely ill, his 600 men came under the command of militia colonel Juan Puga, a brave soldier assisted by Lieutenant Henry Ross, a military engineer from Baltimore.

Mackenna persuaded Carrera to abandon the forward salient, but before this order reached Puga and Ross, they led their men on a midnight raid against the enemy vanguard and encountered them at the village of Yerbas Buenas. Incredibly, they smashed into the headquarters camp of General Pareja himself, who awoke to blood-curdling cries of *Muerto al Rey!* Death to the King! *Viva La Patria!* Long live our country! Pareja fled naked on horseback, and some of his best officers were cut down with swords as they tried to escape. In the confusion, the royalist troops opened fire on each other as well as the rebels. The battle continued until daylight, when Puga retreated in good order with prisoners and spoils.

On his way back to the main corps, Puga's command was cut off by a stray company of royalist cavalry. Pareja's troops then overran Puga's men and inflicted severe losses. Henry Ross was shot eight times in the thick of the fighting but still was able to escape. Puga's retreat set off panic in the rebel army. When Carrera withdrew from the Maule to form a new line at Talca, Pareja ordered his army to attack, but his southern troops would not cross the Maule into the province of Santiago. Many of them realized that they had no interest in dying for the king.

Discovering that Pareja's army was crumbling, Carrera and Poinsett sent their three divisions after the royalists, who retreated south toward Concepcion. April was the beginning of the rainy season, and Carrera lacked supplies and equipment. His men had fought well but could not be expected to pass the winter in the open. At a meeting of his top advisors, Mackenna favored an assault on Chillan, while Poinsett counseled bypassing Chillan and attacking the royalist garrisons at the key seaports of Concepcion and Talcahuano, where, he knew, the ten American whaleships had been captured by the royalists.

Carrera agreed with Poinsett. By taking the seaports, they would isolate Chillan in an otherwise all-rebel southern Concepcion province, and such a strategy was consistent with their plan of naval attack from the Pacific, which Carrera had arranged by authorizing the acquisition of two vessels at Valparaiso: the Colt, a mid-sized brig from New York, and the Pearl, a large former Boston ship used as a packet. Once properly armed and manned, they were to proceed to the Bay of Concepcion and blockade the royalists.

The vessels had been renamed La Perla and El Potrillo. The latter's former first mate, Edward Barnewall, now served Chile in command of both vessels, and Samuel B. Johnston, printer of the Aurora, had accepted a first lieutenant's commission as he "metamorphosed into a son of Neptune, going 'to seek reputation, e'en in the cannon's mouth.'" Barnewall and Johnston had taken on a nineteen-year-old Bostonian, Samuel Dusenbury, to help them hire a crew. They had enlisted only twenty-three Americans and so had hired another sixty-seven from a mix of Chileno and Spanish sailors and men from the visiting Portuguese Fama. Francisco Lastra, head of the Chilean navy and governor of Valparaiso, outfitted the vessels with munitions and cannon. The smaller Potrillo, under Captain Barnewall, mounted two swivel guns and twenty cannon, while La Perla had twenty-four guns and 150 men and sailed under a Chilean, José Vicente Barba, with a Yankee purser and pilot, John King, and the rest of the unruly crew drawn from *Fama* and the waterfront taverns.

Barnewall and Johnston were the toast of Valparaiso and frequent guests in the homes of the rich and beautiful. With the shocking departure of the *Essex* and Porter, these two and Barba comprised the entire officer corps of Chile's navy. By April 26, *Potrillo* was ready to head south to Talcahuano to support the forces of Carrera and O'Higgins. It was taking longer for Captain Barba to outfit *La Perla*.

At Talcahuano, Solomon Folger of the *President* and his fellow American whaling captains—masters of ten unarmed, slow-moving vessels full of whale oil—had been waiting for assistance for two months. They had learned that an American battleship had arrived in the Pacific, presumably to give them a convoy into the Atlantic and a safe return home. But instead of Porter and the *Essex*, in late March two Peruvian warships arrived, and their 1,500 royalist troops took the port from the rebels after a brief battle. The royalists boarded the *President* and found a bag of gold in Captain Folger's cabin, which gave them an excuse to arrest him for smuggling and to imprison him and all his men, to be carried off to Lima. The other American captains could not let that happen; one night they held a council of war and hatched a plan that would create such mayhem that they—or those who survived—might escape into the Pacific.

The desperate whaling captains knew nothing at all about the expedition of *La Perla* and *Potrillo*, due to sail from Valparaiso on Monday, May 3.

As Johnston described it, Captain Barnewall was hosting a dinner for "the American gentlemen then in Valparaiso" and some Chilean friends and the officers of *La Perla* when suddenly the cliffs of the port echoed with cannon fire, and the men rose from the table. The royalist warship *Warren*, "a privateer from Lima which for some time past had been cruising off the port, stood in and fired a gun as a challenge to us." Barnewall received Governor Lastra's permission to answer the challenge, and crowds of people came boiling up out of the city and onto the hills of the bay to see the naval action between the royalists and the patriots.

"The *Pearl* cut her cables and stood out," wrote Lieutenant Johnston. "We weighed our anchor by hand, and, in about ten minutes after, stood out likewise. We made directly for the privateer, but were much alarmed on seeing that the *Pearl* stood from us with a crowd of sail," almost as if she were trying to escape. "Not able to account for this strange maneuver (which was at first attributed to a wish of the Captain to get his men well to their stations, and at the same time amuse the enemy), we made all sail for him to speak him and know his intentions. As we passed the privateer [Warren] she commenced firing her bow guns at us, and continued it for upwards of an hour, to the number of 87 shot, without killing or wounding a man, and doing but very little damage to our sails or rigging." It was all very odd.

Still, Barnewall kept coming, determined to get signals straight with Captain Barba and La Perla. As El Potrillo approached, La Perla fired at her with stern chasers. Barnewall thought this was part of a decoy, and he held course, gaining on his partner until "within hail, and, on inquiring the cause of such strange proceedings," he was answered by three broadsides of grapeshot accompanied by cheers for the king of Spain and the viceroy of Lima, "which were immediately answered by the Spanish and Portuguese part of our crew, in the same words."

"Petrified with horror at these villainous proceedings on the part of the Pearl," wrote Johnston, "and finding ourselves in a small brig with a large ship on each side of us, and our own crew in a state of mutiny, we determined to make sail, and endeavor to regain the port." But that would not happen. For weeks Valparaiso had seethed with secret plots, and now, with the main topsail halyards cut, Barnewall and the other Yankees were overpowered until Johnston found himself alone on deck, calling for help and trying to steer the Potrillo toward the wharves. The crew yelled "To Lima! To Lima!" and he was surrounded by "soldiers [who] pointed their loaded muskets at my breast, and bid me surrender, if I wished to save my life." He did so, and went below, leaving both vessels in control of the royalists, who sailed off to the northward, out to sea. The people on shore had no idea what they had just witnessed, but pilot John King, having jumped into the harbor from La Perla, swam to shore and finally gained the strength to tell the story of the betrayal and loss of Lastra's Chilean navy.

The captive patriots were transported to Lima to be locked in a dungeon pending execution. The British members of the imprisoned crew were relieved of their fetters and confined in better quarters, while the Yanks were left to rot in the dark in reprisal for David Porter's attack on Abascal's Nereyda, flying the flag of Spain, a nation not at war with his own. It was only through the courageous and persistent intervention of an American merchant in Peru, Samuel Curson, in close contact with Poinsett, that his incarcerated countrymen would be spared the execution of their death sentences.

Abascal had landed 1,500 troops under Juan Francisco Sanchez at Talcahuano in April, to combine with Pareja's army, making a force of perhaps 3,000 infantrymen and 5,000 horsemen. Poinsett would contend that Abascal had no right to invade the province of Concepcion, which was under "a government acknowledged by the regency of Spain." On May 15, Carrera's army encountered the Sanchez-Pareja forces marching toward Chillan, near the town of San Carlos. A major battle commenced "at 11 o'clock in the forenoon and was fought with great obstinacy on both sides," recalled Poinsett. Sanchez, with twenty cannon, drew up the royalists in a strong position on a hillside, with cavalry at the flanks. Carrera, with 1,200 infantry troops and 6,000 cavalry, consulted with Poinsett about forcing a decisive all-out battle.

The attack began as planned, but Juan José Carrera did not coordinate the movements of the second division with the rest of the troops. In a bayonet charge toward the center, his men were decimated by the royalist artillery, while the patriot artillery fell silent as the guns went crashing off their worn-out carriages. Under Mackenna and Luis Carrera, the infantry regrouped and engaged the enemy for more than three hours of hard fighting and heavy losses. Carrera and Poinsett continued to confer. If this were to be the major battle of the campaign—perhaps of the war—Poinsett decided that, after all his strategizing and advising, he must take the chance for glory. Saddling up and presenting himself to a large detachment of cavalrymen, he led a charge into the smoke and chaos at the center of the fighting, then swerved and began a hard gallop to the enemy's right, outflanking the royalists' own cavalry and finally wheeling about and striking their infantry from the rear. The result was mayhem in the ranks until the artillery blew holes in Poinsett's hussars, but nightfall brought a cessation.

The Pareja-Sanchez army marched on in the darkness, crossing the Rio Nuble and taking up quarters at the well-protected city of Chillan. Carrera, with his men badly bloodied, decided not to pursue. For a month, the patriot army camped in the vicinity of Chillan, probing its defenses. The strategy debate continued in Carrera's camp, with Poinsett arguing for taking the seaports and ignoring Chillan—let the royalists remain holed up where they could do no damage and claim no advantage in the rest of the province.

Having proven himself in battle, Poinsett had the trust of the Chilean soldiers. In mid-June, with a detachment of 400 men, he marched off toward the coast. Carrera soon followed.

Just before dawn on June 29, the imprisoned American whaling captains at Talcahuano were about to try to make their escape when the town was rocked by the thunder of artillery. People poured into the streets, screaming and crying. On the heights overlooking the harbor, they could see a gun emplacement manned by a large company, with three cannons firing down on the harbor. The target was not the town or its vessels; it was the small fort that guarded the harbor's entrance and the nearby barracks of the royalist soldiers.

A small army of attackers came shouting and marching down the hillsides, carrying the tri-color flag of Chile. After "a smart action," the field "was carried by storm." The patriot commander sent a rider under a flag of truce to demand the unconditional surrender of the port. The royalist officers, unable to organize a defense, set fire to their artillery and ran up the white flag at their fort. Talcahuano had been liberated by El Consul, Roberts Poinsett.

General Poinsett was greeted with jubilation in the streets. His first act was to free the American whalemen, and, in their place, to imprison the royalist soldiers. He sent a gunboat out into the bay to intercept the royalists' main warship, now laden with refugee treasure, but she was too strong to stop. Then came word that Carrera had taken the port of Concepcion. Poinsett's strategy had paid off; the patriot army now held all of Concepcion province outside Chillan. Poinsett set his men to repairing the damaged cannons that the royalists had torched, and began improving the defenses by land and sea. He decided to fly the Spanish flag in case a royalist vessel should come calling. Sure enough, a British privateering whaler sailed into port, and Poinsett stripped it of armament. A few days later a large ship arrived from Callao with several Spanish officers on board. Poinsett made them his prisoners, and they told him that his ridiculous navy at Valparaiso had been captured before it had left the bay and that his ships and his foolish American sailors had been delivered to Viceroy Abascal.

Colonel Bernardo O'Higgins soon appeared at Talcahuano with fresh troops from the area of his home plantation, Las Canteras, which had been destroyed by royalists. His troop was augmented by many soldiers who had defected to him on his northward march. Carrera massed the combined patriot army on the outskirts of Chillan, and there began a siege. They had hoped it would not come to this. Although Pareja soon died there, his place was taken by Sanchez. Chillan was well fortified and well provisioned, and the royalist troops had comfortable quarters. The winter rains came down, and the rebel soldiers suffered from poor shelter and scanty meals. Finally, they were forced to pillage the surrounding countryside for their subsistence. The locals turned against them, and the rebel army slowly dissolved in the incessant downpour and cold mud.

Desperate to break the impasse, Juan Mackenna lured a large royalist force outside the city defenses, and on August 2, Mackenna and Luis Carrera attacked with 800 men, infantry and cavalry, supported by artillery. Their assault succeeded, and the enemy forces retreated into the city, hotly pursued. Inside, the commanders lost control of their men. The hungry rebels broke into stores and houses, at first for food and drink and then for looting and rape. Lucho's officers finally exerted their authority, and the rebels withdrew. Next day, the attack was renewed, and the patriots penetrated into the city in the face of great resistance. Hundreds were killed on both sides, and the householders formed a third army, organized as guerillas and firing at both rebels and royalists. Gaining the central plaza of Chillan, the patriot vanguard was torn apart by concentrated artillery fire, and again the assault devolved into mayhem.

Poinsett, opposed by Mackenna in strategic counsels, decided to return to Santiago late in July. "Having obtained the end I harbored in taking up arms, I left the army and returned to Santiago." He was ready to go home to the United States, tormented that he "remained banished at a moment when my country was engaged in a glorious struggle against her natural enemy, a moment which I had always looked forward to with hope and anxiety," as he wrote to his cousin on September 2, 1813. "I returned last night from the army of Chile, whose movements I had directed in a short and brilliant campaign, during which the province of Concepcion has been reconquered." Poinsett worried about the correctness of his fighting for Chile. "I may be blamed by government and by my fellow citizens, but I have acted right." He was certain of it, since he had used the opportunity to liberate ten American vessels and more than 200 American sailors, and he was confident in his own judgment, having been "so long a solitary wanderer that I am accustomed to content myself with my own approbation."

To Secretary Monroe, he was more particular in defense of his actions, citing many evidences of American vessels that had been captured or harassed by the Spanish privateers: "I shall take an early opportunity of enclosing such documents as will convince you that, although my conduct does not appear to have been that of a neutral agent, it is justified by my obligation to protect the flag of my country from insult, and the property of her citizens from lawless and piratical depredations." He noted his own success in helping to direct the patriot army, and he reported on the success of Porter and the frigate *Essex* "in her cruise in these seas," sending in two British whalers as prizes, and, at Callao, defeating the Lima privateer that had captured two American whaleships.

Despite these successes, Poinsett did not wish to remain in Chile. He had made a huge contribution to the creation of the new republic. He had done everything possible to influence Carrera in a direction favorable to the United States, and he had guided the patriot armies to victory in their battles against the royalists. But he had become controversial, not just as a partisan of the patriots but as an adherent of Carrera. He could not justify continuing as a leader in a foreign country unless he had orders to do so, and he had heard nothing at all from Madison or Monroe for more than a year, which left him "shut out from the world." He had learned that the war against the British was not going well at home, and he felt that his patriotic duty—as well as his personal ambition—was to lead troops into battle in the uniform of the U.S. Army. He noted that the *Essex* afforded a possible means of escape; "should she touch here on her way home, the temptation will be too great to resist." On the back of the letter, he wrote, "to be quoted: anxiety to return to serve in the war at home."

Chapter Eight

A-whaling

B y mid-April 1813, David Porter had been at sea for nearly six months on his self-assigned mission and had yet to sight his first British whaler. He wrote in his journal that in the fabled Galápagos archipelago, 600 miles off the coast of South America, he was sure to find these vessels that were "the constant subject of our conversation and solicitude; and we did not calculate on a number less than ten or twelve; indeed we calculated on making more prizes there than we could man, and hoped to be thus indemnified for all loss of time, fatigues, and anxieties." His search did not include the American whaling fleet, formerly represented as being in great peril at the Galápagos: his sole interest was in capturing British ships.

Heading west from the continent, Porter wondered about himself, that he would come so far, at such peril, without permission and without any guarantee of redemption. He could not discuss his fears and doubts with his officers or allow his misgivings to affect his public role as the decisive leader of this cruise. At night in his cabin, he tried to repress his fears of disgrace for running off into the wrong sea, mad for glory. The cure for his dread was to hunt for the British even as they hunted the whale. He knew that he would have a huge advantage in firepower, experience, and attitude if he could find them. Where had they gone? Had they anticipated his arrival? Had the armed British whalers captured the unarmed American whalers and sailed off toward the Orient?

He entered the volcanic archipelago on April 17, 1813. Charles Island proved a distraction; he explored it thoroughly to see if it might yield food and water enough that American vessels, in future, would not be required to put in at the off-limits Spanish ports to the east. Whaling captains had been coming to these islands for thirty years, but Porter's ego would not permit him to learn from them, and he was enough of a scientist, historian, and navigator to welcome all this newness and try to make himself a public authority on the Pacific. Like Captain Cook, he was attentive to the public-relations opportunity; he indulged in fiction in his journal—flattering himself and puffing his cruise into an epic—while accurately describing the features of this exotic part of the world.

Porter's next stop was forty-five miles west at the island of Albemarle and the whalers' "general rendezvous" of Banks' Bay. In the manner of a conqueror, if not a discoverer, he bestowed names on the already named geography that he encountered, although he did not bother to take soundings or chart the coast. Behind "Point Essex" they found a small hidden bay—no whalers in sight—and a very good landing. Porter and company started off into the bushes but then stopped short in sheer terror; they stood amid acres of large iguanas, four-foot-long mini-dragons, thousands of them, all glaring at the intruders, who "supposed them prepared to attack us." The men made a feint at their enemy and "discovered them to be the most timid of animals, and in a few moments [we] knocked down hundreds of them with our clubs." Most of the dead iguanas were left for carrion, but those that were carried off "proved to be excellent eating."

The royalty of the Galápagos bestiary were the giant tortoises, numerous on almost every island and big enough for a man to ride. Porter discerned slight differences among the tortoises from island to island: on one the carapace might be thicker; on another, the feet might be larger. Tortoises, they found, were even more delicious than iguanas, and they could be stored alive in the hold of a vessel for months at a time, surviving without food or water.

Twenty-two years before Charles Darwin would visit the Galápagos aboard HMS *Beagle*, Porter closely observed the island wildlife and thought about what he saw. He had no explanation for how the Galápagos came to be populated with "their supply of tortoises and guanas, and other animals of the reptile kind," but it did seem "that those islands have every appearance of being newly created, and that those perhaps are the only part of the animal creation that could subsist on them."

Although Porter kept imagining that the British fleet lay just ahead, around the next point, unaware of his approach, the reality was otherwise.

No matter what one tried to do in the Galápagos, the islands had a different plan; all the rules were skewed there, and nothing was quite as it seemed. Compass headings and course plots were subject to powerful unseen forces, strong currents overruled the tides and winds, and a good sailing breeze might suddenly drop to a dead calm for five days.

Perversely reading these phenomena as portents, Porter predicted to his men that they had reached the moment of triumph. Full of manic inspiration, he broke his own rule against sailing among the islands by night and headed for Narborough "in order that we might have the whole of the next day for securing our prizes in Banks' Bay." His prediction of epic prize-taking on the morrow represented a big risk, and he slept little that night.

In the morning he was proved a false prophet. The men, he knew, were buzzing; his officers were wary. Some now wondered about his mental balance, and the impetuous Porter had his own doubts. He experienced "great uneasiness" and "could not resist those anxious feelings, which cannot be repelled at such moments." For no particular reason, he had set himself up for failure, and failure had obliged. Porter and the whole company of the *Essex* had crossed into a zone of delusion in which the captain misjudged almost everything he encountered.

He placed his crew on high alert and repeatedly sent them to battle stations, but the enemy remained a phantom, and the *Essex* sailed on. For two days they fought only the currents, and the men seethed toward a state of psychosis. They could stand it no more, and began climbing the rigging until the *Essex* was top-heavy with "seamen and officers whose anxiety had taken them aloft" to scan the great waters. Finally, the tension was broken with a cry of Sail ho!, and then another, which "seemed to electrify every man on board." From the manic heights, however, they descended in "sudden dejection," as the sails "proved to be only white appearances on the shore," ghostly images that left them fooled and profoundly shaken.

The crew could not trust their captain. Even with his spyglass, he was literally seeing things. Three hundred Americans now felt kidnapped, imprisoned in the Galápagos with no prey to be found and perhaps no way out. If Porter was wrong about the British whalers, what else was he wrong about? James Rynard and others began questioning their captain's fitness and grousing about this cruise that seemed more like one man's delusion than an operation of the U.S. Navy. The islands had come to seem haunted, with Porter himself a specter among the shape-shifting Encantadas, not so much enchanted as accursed.

After six days among the islands, hearing his men, Porter decided to break the spell and clear out for South America. The *Essex*, however, could not buck the current; for another six days she was borne away against the captain's will. On April 28, Porter passed "a sleepless and anxious night" and had just nodded off when, at dawn, a dozen voices cried out "Sail ho!"

All doubts suddenly fled, and Porter was restored to credibility; he had found his white whale. The sail belonged to a large ship bearing west. Jubilantly, they chased her and then discovered two more. Porter ordered the raising of British colors and their large pennant reading "Free Trade and Sailors' Rights" flown from the main topmast.

The mighty *Essex* came alongside the much-smaller British whale-ship *Montezuma* under Captain Baxter of Nantucket, with a largely American crew and 1,400 barrels of sperm oil. Affecting an English accent, Porter lured Baxter on board and sprang the trap. Poor Baxter, now a prisoner, was glad to see the wind drop with eight miles of ocean between the *Essex* and her other prey, hull down on the horizon, but Porter had his men pursue with three cutters, a gig, a pinnace, a whaleboat, and a jolly boat. In the fierce heat and dead calm, men and boys strained at the oars and closed the gap, converging on the 280-ton *Georgiana*, under Captain Pitts, with a crew of Yankee whalemen. Midshipman Feltus wrote that his cutter boldly pulled up under her stern: "She had two guns pointed at us; we immediately hoisted the American ensign, [whereupon] the ship gave us three cheers, which we did not return [but] boarded her. She immediately struck to us. We manned her and went to the next. She had one gun run out abaft and one in each gangway and ready to fire. We ran alongside and boarded" the 275-ton *Policy*, whose Captain Bowman prudently struck her colors.

The frigate sailed on, going nowhere, with the poky *Montezuma* in tow and the *Barclay* to starboard and the *Policy* to port. Late on the afternoon of May 28, the lookouts spotted what proved to be the British whaler *Atlantic*, mounting six eighteen-pounders and commanded by Obed Wyer of Nantucket, just up from the Bay of Concepcion. The ruse of a fake flag and an English accent sufficed to prompt a visit from Wyer, from whom Porter learned much about naval matters in the South Atlantic, including the fact that HMS *Java*, searching for the *Essex*, instead had encountered Bainbridge and the *Constitution*, which, incredibly, had sent the great battleship to the bottom.

With ghoulish pleasure, Porter kept Wyer talking. He toyed with the earnest Nantucket captain who had been so helpful to the Americans holed up at Talcahuano. Little did Wyer know that he was now cast in an elaborate piece of theater, produced, directed, and acted by David Porter, who was playing God. Porter kept it up long enough to confirm that the "polished gentleman" Wyer "evidently possessed a corrupt heart, and, like all other renegadoes, was desirous of doing his native country all the injury in his power." Suddenly the interview was over, and Wyer was confronted with the truth. Chagrined, he tried "to apologize away the impression his conduct had made, improvising artfully" as he pleaded his cause. Porter, having already scored a "triumph over the wretch," was "willing to make some allowances for his conduct"—one renegado to another.

At that moment a cry went up as another sail was sighted. Drawing alongside in the night, Porter ordered the captain to surrender but was loudly refused. In response, Porter fired a cannonball between her masts and threatened a broadside, which proved persuasive to John Shuttleworth of the ten-gun whale ship *Greenwich*. He clambered aboard the *Essex* drunk and full of fight, but Porter merely laughed and locked him in a cabin with Wyer. Later, Porter paid a visit to "this haughty Englishman" and "this renegade" and worked himself into such a fury that he had them groveling. "They would have licked the dust from my feet," he wrote, "had it been required of them to do so."

David Porter now moved out at the head of a fleet of six vessels. He had found 800 tortoises and 100 tons of water on his prizes, which solved his provisioning needs. Lieutenant McKnight was given command of the *Atlantic*, while the *Greenwich* was put under Lieutenant John Gamble of the marines, a non-sailor whose nautical ignorance was balanced by advice from his mates, both expert seamen.

On the night of June 6, 1813, as they ghosted along, a volcano erupted nearby, which "illuminated the whole atmosphere"—a seaman's good omen, for next day the winds freshened from the southeast and finally, after six weeks of trying, they sailed out of the clutches of the Encantadas and into the wide blue waters of the Pacific.

Porter headed for the Peruvian coast looking for food, water, and buyers for some of his ships. So recently despairing of finding any prey, Porter now could not find a way to dispose of his surfeit of prizes. They constituted the fortune that he had intended to make and the evidence that his renegade action was more than a manic episode, but they also made him vulnerable to attack by Peruvian privateers or by a Royal Navy squadron, and Viceroy Abascal certainly would not permit him to sell British vessels at Callao.

Porter put in at the port of Tumbez. Although it had no market for ships or oil, the mayor agreed to find buyers at nearby Guayaquil on commission. Meanwhile, Porter and a few others played tourist in the "wretched" bayou town, whose friendly inhabitants "invited me into their huts." As usual, the locals did not measure up: "The men of this place seem to be of the lowest class of those who call themselves civilized; and the women, although of fine forms, animated, cheerful, and handsome countenances, are destitute of all that delicacy the possession of which only can render the female lovely in our eyes."

Porter's Guayaquil connection did not pay off, and this rejection was accompanied by the news that three well-armed British whalers were headed for the Galápagos to hunt him down. Returning in a foul mood to the *Essex*, he found his deck officer, Lieutenant James P. Wilmer, stinking drunk and passed out in his cabin. Wilmer, an alcoholic, had stayed dry for months, but his relapse was total. Roughly awakened, he quietly stated that he intended to kill himself as soon as possible.

With Wilmer sidelined and the officer corps spread throughout his growing fleet, Porter decided to make changes. Downes, off on a side trip, remained first officer. McKnight was moved up to second officer and rejoined the *Essex* from the *Atlantic*, which was put under David Adams—the only navy chaplain ever to command an armed vessel. In another surprise move, Porter played favorites and awarded McKnight's vacated third lieutenancy to the doughty sailing master, John Glover Cowell, twenty-eight. Midshipman John S. Cowan, twenty-one, was promoted to fourth lieutenant, and Midshipman William H. Odenheimer got Cowell's former job. Porter thrilled the younger midshipmen by making them prize masters of the captured vessels "with careful seamen," he wrote, "in whom I could confide, to take care of them." With a new team in place, Porter prepared to head back to the Galápagos, but first he had to recover his purser, Shaw, who had not returned from haggling for provisions in Tumbez.

On the morning of June 24, three ships approached the harbor of Tumbez. Porter prepared for an attack, but it proved to be John Downes in the *Georgiana* followed by two new prizes, the 270-ton whaleships *Hector* and *Catherine*. Cheered on board the *Essex*, Downes reported that, off James Island, he had easily taken the ships *Catherine* and *Rose* but had been resisted by the *Hector*. Downes had fired a damaging shot into her stern and repeated his demand for surrender. Crying "No, no!" her captain had ordered his men to make sail and defend themselves. Downes had let loose with five unanswered broadsides that killed two sailors and wounded six more. Starting for Tumbez with his prizes, Downes had found the *Rose* too slow, and so he had dumped her guns and oil, put seventy-five prisoners aboard, and sent her for St. Helena in the South Atlantic.

Porter rewarded Downes with command of the superior *Atlantic*, refitted with twenty guns and renamed (by Porter) *Essex Junior*. After converting *Greenwich* into an armed store ship, with food and water enough for the fleet for seven months—but still without rum—Porter prepared for sea. Once more he put midshipmen in charge of prizes: William Feltus, fourteen, proudly commanded the *Montezuma*. Porter's last act was to free his prisoners; the boats took them into Tumbez, and he said goodbye to Shuttleworth and Wyer. On July 1, Porter and company cleared the Gulf of Guayaquil, nine handsome vessels stretching "away to the westward, to fall in with the easterly trade winds."

Next day, Porter wrote to his old adversary Navy Secretary Paul Hamilton for the first time since leaving the Delaware, not knowing that Hamilton had been replaced by William Jones, a man with a very different outlook on naval operations. Porter recounted his Pacific triumphs, from the taking of the *Nereyda* to the capture of eight British whalers mounting a total of sixty-three guns, and the recapture of the American whaler *Barclay*. "The Governors in Peru," he wrote proudly, were "excessively alarmed at my appearance on the coast, as my fleet now amounts to nine sail of vessels, all formidable." The viceroy's minions "would, if they dare, treat us with a hostility little short of declared enemies." He boasted of prizes "which would be worth in England two millions of dollars." Referring indirectly to Poinsett, he wrote, "the State Department will no doubt inform you of the effect our presence has produced in a political view [so] on that head I will be silent"—a silence that concealed his blunders regarding Abascal and Carrera, driving one toward the British and leaving the other without a naval force as he tried to create a new nation. Warning that "it is not probable that you will hear of me for several months to come unless some disaster happens," he closed, "I expect to be pursued, but shall be prepared."

On the other side of the continent, British captain James Hillyar was arriving at Rio after a short voyage from London, where he had been selected to carry out a secret mission. Temperate, deliberate, and deeply devout, Hillyar had earned the confidence of the Admiralty for steadiness in combat and a profound sense of duty to the king and his navy. He was no aristocrat and had none of the arrogance typical of his rank. At forty-three, he was still strapping, with a sturdy physique, fair, wavy hair, and a boyishly ruddy complexion.

Before departing Britain, he had been briefed on imperial policy toward Spain and Spanish America. There was little doubt that Britain's coalition forces would prevail in Europe in the next year or so. Napoleon's invasion of Russia had failed disastrously; the Prussians were about to reenter the war; and General Wellesley, Marquess (later Duke) of Wellington—who, in two years, would defeat Napoleon for good at Waterloo—had scored great victories over the French with his English-Spanish-Portuguese army in Spain. London intended to restore Fernando to the Spanish throne, subject to the Spanish Constitution of 1812, combining a weak monarchy with a republican parliament like Britain's own. The future of Spanish America was unclear; the colonial system was disintegrating, and patriot juntos controlled many areas, as in Chile, where the rebels had a government and an army but had yet to win a war of independence.

Hillyar's secret assignment from the Admiralty in London was to go to the Pacific and destroy the American trading post on the Northwest coast.* It was no longer just a matter of fur-trading rivalries, but of war, in which London intended to annex the entire area to Canada and to achieve total domination of the upper Pacific coast. An English merchant brig had already been sent ahead to inform the "Spanish ports" in Chile, Peru, and Mexico that "the object of the expedition" would not bring harm to them.

At Rio, Hillyar met with Admiral Sir Manley Dixon, chief of station at the center of British power in the South Atlantic, who had a very different mission for the new arrival and his squadron. To fail at it would cost Hillyar his career and perhaps his life. Dixon, who had arrived at Rio just as the U.S. Congress had declared war on Britain, knew everything worth knowing about conditions in South America; through dozens of agents and informers, he tracked the progress of the continent's independence movements, and he was well aware of Poinsett's anti-British successes at Buenos Aires and his partisan role in Chile. In many regions, Spain's colonial viceroys contended

---

* Hillyar was "to destroy and, if possible, totally annihilate any settlements which the Americans may have formed either on the Columbia River or on the neighboring coasts." His orders from London did not include pursuit of Porter or negotiation with Abascal or the Chileans. The purpose was to preserve British dominance in the area by dispossessing the Americans of their newly built fort, Astoria, from which they conducted a fur trade sponsored by John Jacob Astor of Manhattan. The Americans there realized what was afoot and cannily sold Astoria to their British colleagues.

James Hillyar (1769–1843), a devout Christian and distinguished captain in the Royal Navy, befriended the young Commander David Porter, USN, in 1804 while the two men were on joint maneuvers in the Mediterranean. Ten years later, Hillyar was given the assignment of hunting down Porter and eliminating the American presence in the Pacific in order to ensure British postwar dominance there. *(National Maritime Museum, London)*

with Bolivar, San Martin, Carrera, and other revolutionists. Spanish armies near Buenos Aires had been defeated by the forces of the United Provinces. Of England's possible imperial rivals in South America, Portugal could do no more than hold onto Brazil, and the United States, with a tiny navy, was obviously incapable of extending protection and support to potential client states. This made the success achieved by Poinsett—"the arch-enemy of British interests in the region"—all the more unacceptable.

Dixon had deftly managed the South American enterprise. Establishing Britain as the naval giant of the continent, he had driven the Yankees out of the South Atlantic and had befriended all players in their struggles to get power or hold onto it. On the Pacific side, the great prizes were the resource-rich markets of Chile and Peru, opened up after 300 years of Spanish monopoly. London was aware of American influence in Chile, and one faction of rebel leaders was known to admire the United States. Consul Poinsett was agitating at Santiago, and Captain Porter, Dixon understood, was protecting American shipping. But the status of the Chilean rebellion was doubtful, and the Americans had yet to send munitions or even to recognize Chile as a nation. This he heard from British merchants in Valparaiso, good friends of the port's governor, Lastra, and good at smuggling weapons and powder to his colleagues, especially O'Higgins.

Dixon had assessed Viceroy Abascal as capable of maintaining authority in Peru and perhaps regaining control of Chile. Certainly, he should be well disposed to Britain, the champion of the anti-Napoleonic forces in Spain and fully capable, through sea power, of dominating the Pacific coast. Under Abascal or as a semi-autonomous state, Chile might well be reconciled to Spain, especially if Fernando were restored to the throne. However these matters played out, London expected to establish British commerce as preeminent on the postwar seas of the South Atlantic and Pacific.

The one wild card was Porter and the *Essex*. Dixon, unaware of the renegade nature of Porter's cruise, admired the U.S. Navy planners for their presumed acuity in sending him into the Pacific to tear up the British whaling fleet and to work with Poinsett to support Carrera's revolution in Chile. Like the Admiralty in London, Dixon had been concerned about the Pacific; he had just ordered a foray by the sloops of war *Cherub*, twenty-six guns, and *Racoon*, eighteen guns, to hunt down the *Essex*.* Now Hillyar came to him bound for the Pacific as well. Reviewing the two missions—his own decision to stop Porter and the Admiralty's wish to capture the trading post—Admiral Dixon decided to combine them under Hillyar, whose record was well known. In December 1810, Hillyar had defeated a French flotilla off Madagascar, creating an impressive advantage for his squadron before engaging in battle. Since then, he had been stationed in the Orient without opportunity for further honors. The Pacific venture would give him that chance.

If Hillyar did his job, British trade at Concepcion and Valparaiso could continue prosperously and usefully, and Porter's British prizes could easily be retaken by the Royal Navy. Hillyar was to find Porter and stop his rampage; after that, he would be expected to play the diplomat with the viceroy and to act as the Pacific emissary of Great Britain, forging positive, permanent relations on the west coast of the Americas while eliminating any and all United States presence from Nootka Sound to the Bay of Concepcion.

Hillyar was given a four-vessel battle group and broad authority for the results. In issuing his orders, Dixon regretted that spies in Rio and Buenos Aires would inform Poinsett about Hillyar's destinations "long before you arrive there." Some of his British opponents had a healthy respect for Poinsett; one British captain noted that Poinsett had damaged Britain badly at Buenos Aires, "and now again [in Chile] Mr. Poinsett is busy in contaminating the whole population on that side of the continent."

British merchant vessels, Dixon had learned, had been detained by Abascal for reasons unknown, and something had to be done about that without inflaming the royalists or encouraging the rebels. Hillyar had thorough guidance from Dixon: "On your arrival at the Spanish ports, you are to use every endeavor to cultivate the most friendly understanding between the two nations, and if you should find any reprisals to have been made of British vessels or their cargoes by Spanish privateers or Garda Costas, or by

---

* A sloop of war was not a sloop as the term is understood today—i.e., a single-masted sailing vessel; rather, it was a large, ship-rigged vessel with three masts, built stoutly for warfare and carrying many large guns and up to 200 men.

the authorities of their ports (relative to which the accompanying intelligence speaks positively), you are to inquire the cause thereof and to do your utmost by conciliation to leave them restored, according to the laws subsisting between the two nations." Should he be refused, he was "to have the case drawn up" for the information of the Admiralty, making certain not to become embroiled in any "cause of politics between Spain and her colonies, but to act with the most perfect neutrality towards them both."

The pressure of this mission on Hillyar was compounded by the shock of learning that his prey was David Porter—his dear companion from the days of their service in the Mediterranean, when the young American had been an intimate of the Hillyar family. It was a strange fortune of war to be tracking him down, perhaps to kill him, but Hillyar recognized it as part of his duty,* and on July 9, 1813, he departed from Rio for Cape Horn in command of the *Phoebe*, the *Cherub*, the *Racoon*, and the armed store ship *Isaac Todd*.

After six weeks of hard sailing, the warships made it through to the Pacific and proceeded up the coast of Chile separately from the store ship. At the island of Juan Fernandez, Hillyar was informed that not one but two American frigates were cruising nearby and had recently taken an armed British vessel, perhaps the *Todd*. These rumors changed things. Hillyar weighed his options and decided to stay on to make connections and to find the British whalers. He could not know that all of them had already sailed for home or been captured by Porter, nor could he know that the *Isaac Todd* was bowling along northward to California. He sent the *Racoon* to the Northwest coast to "annihilate" the American trading post while he and Captain Tucker of the *Cherub* looked for the frigates, the whalers, and the missing store ship.

As Hillyar was making his way from Rio to Cape Horn, Porter, his prey, tried once more to sell some of his prizes. Lieutenant John Downes and the *Essex Junior* were sent to Valparaiso with the *Barclay* and four other vessels, three of which were to be sold there while the oil-laden *Policy* was to sail for the United States. Downes was to get provisions and plenty of rum and reunite with the *Essex* at the Galápagos.

Downes' squadron had a smooth voyage south, though one that was not without its moments of excitement. The whaling captain Gideon Randall, on board his former command the *Barclay*, blew up at her captain, twelve-year-old Midshipman Glasgow "Gatty" Farragut. Swearing that

---

* Perhaps Hillyar did not tell Dixon about his old acquaintance with Porter.

he would not work for a "damned nutshell" and would shoot anyone who touched a rope without his orders, Randall slatted off to get his pistols below. Gatty coolly ordered a sailor to inform the old whaleman that he ought to take a long nap in his cabin if he did not wish to be thrown overboard.

Downes could not know it, but Porter had turned his full attention to the pursuit of his own long-held fantasy of life and lust in paradise. Porter had given him sealed orders, to be opened only after Downes had departed Valparaiso, telling him to proceed to the Galápagos and check for messages in bottles buried at certain beaches, but not to expect a rendezvous, for Porter would be long-gone to "the island of Chitahoo, or Santa Christiana, one of the Marquesas, where you will find me at anchor, or hear from me, at Resolution Bay, in the latter part of September, and first of October. I intend there to refit my ship."

The Marquesas were three thousand miles to the west, and October was a long way off.

Porter arrived in the Galápagos once more on July 12 and hove to off Charles Island. Two days later, in the morning, while cruising toward Banks' Bay, he spotted three sails "standing on a wind, some distance from each other"—the same vessels that had left Tumbez to capture the *Essex*. In short order, Porter and Adams captured the ten-gun *Charlton* and the *New Zealander* without a fight. Volcanoes were erupting on nearby islands as the third ship, heavily armed, tried to escape. From the deck of the *Essex*, Porter and his men followed the maneuvers of Marine Lieutenant Gamble in the *Greenwich*, with eighteen men and ten guns, as they approached *Seringapatam* with thirty-one men and fourteen guns. As the *Greenwich* came within distant pistol shot of her opponent, the silence was shattered by thunderous broadsides. Each vessel passed unscathed out of the smoke. Over time, four more broadsides were exchanged, with neither crew able to top the other. Cool and patient, Gamble eventually outmaneuvered his opponent, gave them a devastating broadside, and watched as her flag came down.

The 357-ton *Seringapatam* was the finest British ship in the Pacific, and Porter took great pleasure in possessing her, for her Captain Stavers had captured the American whaleship *Edward* of Nantucket and still held American prisoners, who now joyously signed on with their liberator. In Porter's opinion, Stavers "might have done great injury to the American commerce in those seas"—had there been any such commerce. Porter well knew that the Americans had all cleared out for home and that no other British vessel had captured even one other American; instead, they had been busy catching whales. Stavers had an expired commission as a privateer, which technically made him a pirate. Porter clapped him in irons but spared his officers, of whom the former prisoners gave a good report, unlike Stavers himself.

Once again in the grip of powerful ocean currents, Porter shed some of his fleet. The old *Charlton* he gave to her captain to take to Rio de Janeiro with forty-eight prisoners who, as Porter well knew, were mostly Americans from Nantucket with no interest in warfare or navies. They begged to be set adrift in whaleboats rather than be doomed to impressment into the Royal Navy, but Porter remained firm, and the whalemen accepted their fate with such good grace that they departed giving "three hearty cheers" to Porter's fleet. Porter had no love for Nantucketers under any flag. Still blind to the viceroy's anti-American policy and declaration of war on the Chilean rebels, he wrote an angry letter to the *Edward*'s owner alleging that Folger, putting greed ahead of honor, had cooperated with Stavers rather than proceed to recover his vessel in Lima "on a simple representation of the case to the Viceroy."

Porter sent *Georgiana*, loaded with sperm oil, for the Atlantic; he calculated that the voyage would take five months. She stood a better chance of making an American port in wintertime, and Porter could shed the worst and sickest of his sailors whose enlistments had expired. Further, he could dispose of William Stavers, who was good at outguessing him. On July 25, Lieutenant James Wilson ordered the joyful men of the *Georgiana* to set the topsails and begin their voyage home.

Having captured almost every one of the British-flagged whalers in the Pacific, Porter needed an exit strategy. The Royal Navy would send out a squadron to hunt him down with his vulnerable fleet of whalers. In the absence of legal commerce and motivated buyers, none could be sold in the Pacific; all would have to get to American ports. To fail in this with even one prize was to forfeit great riches; to fail largely would be a disaster, not just in value unrealized but in existential terms: Why had he gone rogue and run such high risks if he were so likely to lose it all?

Porter, however, had unfinished business in the Galápagos. As far as he could tell, British-flagged whalers still roamed there, and he wanted all of them. Sure enough, while becalmed off Albemarle he "discovered a strange sail" which "appeared to be close on a wind under her topsails, with fresh breezes" as if sailing in a different sea. Porter caught a zephyr and started the chase, but the wind dropped and the current carried the *Essex* toward the seas heaving against the Rodondo shore with ship-crushing violence. All seemed lost as the frigate drifted closer to the killer coast, and only the sudden arrival of a "smart breeze" saved the *Essex* and her men. Porter, of course, continued to push his luck, doubtless to the dismay of his crew, who knew an ill omen when they saw one.

Unable to take this last prize, Porter focused on loading tortoises and, in his journal, excoriating Colnett, his British predecessor in these islands, whose charts Porter found so defective that he filled several pages with outraged contempt. As he did so, a tragedy unfolded. The rivalry between his new fourth lieutenant, John Cowan, and his chief of marines, John Gamble, was intense, and Porter, as their chief, failed to manage the problem. It culminated in a duel on shore at dawn, with seconds and perhaps others attending. After the countdown, each fired his pistol. Fortunately, both missed; unfortunately, they wished to continue. No one thought to notify their commander, and no one intervened. Instead, the young officers paced off and took another shot at each other; and again the bullets missed. On the third exchange, Cowan fell dead.

The Marquesas were calling, and the *Essex* was infested with rats. Porter hunted down and captured one more hapless British-flagged whaler, *Sir Andrew Hammond*, and celebrated by hosting a feast for his crew, washed down with two captured puncheons "of choice Jamaica spirits." The navy men, without their dram since clearing Tumbez, were soon inebriated, and "many were taken to their hammocks perfectly drunk." And the rum started them grumbling. It was a critical moment in the history of this strange cruise, for the crew had good reasons to kick against Porter. There were, evidently, no more whaleships to capture, and their enlistments had expired. When were they going home? Porter heard them in their cups and was inclined to lenity, except toward James Rynard, a quartermaster who, in the past, had advocated for the crew and played peacemaker with the officers. Porter could not tolerate any degree of divided allegiance; he still had big plans that must be kept secret, and he needed to know if his men were still with him. Had the foxy Rynard kindled serious discontent?

Seeing his chance, Porter put on a show, accosting the half-drunk Rynard and ordering him to go aboard one of the prizes and get to work. Predictably, Rynard objected, at which Porter called him out for drunkenness and ordered him aft until he was sober. Instead, Rynard defiantly rushed forward past Porter, for which he was made to sit under guard. His messmates brought him supper, but he threw it overboard and left the deck. Porter had him put in irons; Rynard groused that his enlistment was up, and Porter put him on board the *Seringapatam* to be deposited ashore.

Rynard showed no fear or remorse; he was glad to go. In their set piece he had pushed back at every insult, and Porter had affirmed his authority at the very edge of sadism. For Rynard, banishment from the *Essex* community was not some unthinkable punishment; it was liberation, even if it left him stranded on a desert island.

Porter rightly wondered about the effect on the crew. Not one of them, presumably, would have signed up for a cruise that was in its tenth month with no end in sight. But the showdown had "rendered every man in the ship sober, attentive, and active in the discharge of his duty, and assiduous to please." Porter still owned them, and he was not yet ready to depart.

New Zealander was caulked and *Sir Andrew Hammond* was painted. Each of the five vessels was stocked with tortoise and made ready for an extended cruise, and on August 28, 1813, just as these preparations were completed, Lieutenant John Downes showed up. Received with three cheers, he brought much news from Valparaiso. Peru and Chile were fighting an all-out war. Madison had been reelected president, and the navy had triumphed "in every instance where our ships had encountered an enemy of equal force."

Downes reported that he had left the prizes *Montezuma*, *Catherine*, and *Hector* at Valparaiso, which was still in the hands of Carrera's rebels, and he had learned that several British merchant ships were expected with valuable cargoes, while another, the *Mary Ann*, was already there, "richly laden, and on the point of sailing for India." He had escorted four American whalers from Valparaiso partway to Concepcion, along with the *Policy*, which he had ordered into the Atlantic in the track of the *Georgiana*. The last free British whaleship in the Pacific, the *Comet*, a twenty-gun letter of marque (privateer), now lay at Talcahuano, shorn of her guns by the Chilean rebels.

Finally, Downes handed Porter a packet from Poinsett, just received from a spy in Buenos Aires, who wrote: "on the 5th July the British frigate *Phoebe*, of 36 guns, and the *Raccoon* and *Cherub* sloops of war, of 24 guns each, accompanied by a store-ship of 20 guns, had sailed from Rio de Janeiro for the Pacific Ocean, in pursuit of the *Essex*." Porter was not surprised; it was news that he had long expected, and he welcomed it. But it came with a truly disturbing twist at the end: his British nemesis, the head of the wolf pack sent to hunt him down, was a man who knew him very well. It was none other than Porter's only friend in the Royal Navy, his dear companion from happy days at Gibraltar, the admirable Captain James Hillyar.

At Chillan, Carrera kept up the siege while his army devoured the crops and cattle of the unwilling people of the province. Far to the south, the royalists retook the large port of Valdivia and built up their base at the island of Chiloe. They formed an alliance with the Arauco chiefs and made good use of the many shipments of munitions and provisions that arrived regularly on vessels sent from the viceroy's warehouses at Callao, free of any concerns about a patriot naval force.

The Chilean army, or what was left of it, remained loyal to José Miguel Carrera and the dream of an independent Chile. Poinsett remained at Santiago, out of the fight; Carrera, without his advisor, relied on O'Higgins to stir up battles. At El Roble the fight went against them, and Carrera, targeted by the enemy, fled on horseback toward the camp of his brother Juan; O'Higgins, though wounded, directed a successful counterattack. As usual, the battle meant nothing strategically, but it did raise O'Higgins in the esteem of the men.

Six months had passed since Carrera had made himself commander in chief and gone to the front, leaving a hastily appointed Santiago junto to run the government. He had given his all to the war, and had not returned to Santiago or taken a break, but had relied on the people and officials of the capital to support him and his army in the field. His faith was badly misplaced.

In Santiago, the Larrains, far removed from battle and bloodshed, had never once conceded the control of Chile to Carrera and his adherents. Throughout the military campaign, they had undermined his leadership and criticized his motives and abilities. Remaining in the field to lead the army and to continue the siege that Mackenna had advised, Carrera, by his absence, gave his rivals an opportunity to betray him in the capital.

On October 8, the Larrain faction took control of the government and installed José Ignacio Cienfuegos, a Dominican friar and bitter enemy of Carrera, as head of the new junto. Leaving Father Joaquin Larrain in charge at Santiago with his own fighting force, the junto moved 160 miles south to Talca, where they arranged for the arrival of a battalion of 300 Buenos Airean soldiers from Mendoza. The foreigners were commanded by Colonel Marcos Balcarce, who had been the governor of Cuyo, western Argentina, until succeeded the year before by General José Francisco de San Martin, just arrived from years of fighting in Spain.

Without informing Carrera of their presence, Cienfuegos and the junto contacted Sanchez, the royalist commander at Chillan, demanding his surrender. When he scornfully refused, they sent a messenger to General José Miguel Carrera ordering him to resign. Carrera reacted violently, accusing them of treason and defying their authority in the strongest possible terms. O'Higgins agreed, and wrote to the junto to support Carrera and his brothers, brave soldiers who had devoted everything to winning the war. "Once the independence of the country has been achieved," wrote O'Higgins, "they will make any sacrifice to secure its civil liberty."

The junto was not much interested in civil liberty. In fact, they had decided to replace Carrera with their own Argentinian mercenary, Balcarce. Unknown to O'Higgins, Mackenna had gone to Talca to meet with his relatives in the junto and to plot against his hated rivals, the Carreras. When Mackenna suggested to the junto that Balcarce could not lead the Chilean army, and that their only choice was his friend O'Higgins, the junto decreed the appointment of Bernardo O'Higgins as commander in chief. Carrera, receiving the message at Concepcion, tore it up and threw the messenger in prison. His entire officer corps reacted with disgust and outrage and refused to accept the decree.

Split between the army in the south and the politicians in the north, between Larrains and Carreras, between appeasement and independence, the republic of Chile was coming apart.

Chapter Nine

Opotee in Nooaheevah

T he Porter fleet started out across the Pacific with the *Essex* as flagship, followed by the well-armed *Seringapatam*, the *Greenwich*, the *New Zealander*, the *Sir Andrew Hammond*, and the *Essex Junior* under John Downes. Having formerly deserted the Atlantic and the wartime constraints of duty, authority, and responsibility, Porter now was leaving behind the last coast of the modern world and crossing a 3,000-mile stretch of ocean into the islands of a Stone Age people. He went with no regrets about his apostasy or his ignorance of the fate of his beleaguered country or old friends and famous ships on which he had served.

American armies had not done well. Their invasion of Canada had been turned back, and the Canadians and British had destroyed the town of Buffalo and crossed the Great Lakes frontier. The British, with their naval power, seemed capable of landing an army at any point along the coast; they had captured towns in Maine and burned plantations in the south. General Jackson, in the south and west, was engaging and occasionally slaughtering Indian tribes, but most people in the United States realized that they were losing the war and might even forfeit their independence.

Only the U.S. Navy had given them some hope for military success. Having appointed William Jones as navy secretary in January 1813, President Madison had reinstated naval planning as a priority in the overall war effort. By virtue of victories in ship-to-ship duels, the navy had won over the American public and the U.S. Congress, which had allotted funds for the construction of six forty-four-gun heavy frigates and four seventy-four-gun ships of the line, the largest vessels ever built in America. Conceding the immense strength of the British blockade along the American seacoast, Jones made two key recommendations: build some smaller vessels, and defend the lakes along the Canadian border, where a strong American naval presence might block supply lines essential to any major British invasion.

Congress authorized Jones to produce freshwater warships, including two corvettes for Lake Erie, and to begin construction of six seagoing battleships of a new class. Smaller than frigates and produced faster and cheaper, these so-called sloops of war would be superior commerce raiders and perhaps cause the British to divert some blockading vessels. A good example was the *Wasp*, to be built at Newburyport, up the coast from the Salem shipyard that had produced the *Essex*. With about half the crew of a frigate, she would match up if necessary against Royal Navy sloops and brigs of war. The *Wasp* would displace 509 tons, carry twenty-two cannon and 173 men, and would measure 117 feet in length and 31.5 feet in beam, with a draft of 14.5 feet. The *Essex*, displacing 864 tons, measured 141 feet long and 37 feet in beam, with a deeper draft.

The navy's most ambitious commanders, formerly colleagues of David Porter, lined up to get a crack at these new vessels or to build their own. On Lake Erie, Captain Oliver Hazard Perry rapidly assembled a squadron of nine warships, including the new corvettes *Lawrence* and *Niagara*. On September 10, 1813, Perry sailed against the British lake fleet. In the first large-scale battle of the inland naval war, he brought up his vessels in a battle line, got a favorable wind shift, and won the fight. As the victor at the Battle of Lake Erie, Perry blocked the British effort in the west and became the idol of his nation.

In the larger war overseas, the tide had finally turned against Napoleon. In Spain, Wellington's combined army—British, Spanish, and Portuguese—had been winning battles throughout the spring of 1813, and in June, at the Battle of Vitoria, Wellington defeated the vastly outnumbered Napoleonic forces. By the end of the year, all Spanish territory was held by the British alliance, which made possible the restoration of the Bourbon king, Fernando VII.

The war went no better for Napoleon on the eastern front. His invasion of Russia, while penetrating all the way to Moscow, had resulted in disaster as his huge Grand Armée was decimated by disease and the ravages of a Russian winter. Defeated in Spain, Russia, and then Germany, Napoleon retreated into France with his remaining forces and would abdicate his throne in April 1814.

These events left London in an even stronger position to block-ade the coasts of North and South America and to defeat the American armies. Soon large numbers of troops would be transported to Canada, and a Royal Navy fleet would be cruising in the Chesapeake Bay while another squelched maritime commerce from New York to Maine. Despite the daunt-ing strength of Britain in Atlantic waters, however, personal glory might still be won in naval battles between smaller cruisers. Assigned to supervise construction of the *Wasp*, Commander Johnston Blakeley turned over the brig of war *Enterprize*—once commanded by David Porter in the Mediter-ranean—to Lieutenant William Burrows, who, on September 5, 1813, off the coast of Maine, defeated the Royal Navy's *Boxer*. With more such fast, elusive warships, Americans could take the war across the Atlantic to Africa, Europe, and even to Britain's home waters, preying on shipping there and adding measurably to the enormous toll, in the hundreds of vessels and the millions of pounds sterling in property, that was already being taken by American privateers.

As the names of Burrows, Lawrence, Hull, Bainbridge, and Decatur passed gloriously into history, the name of David Porter faded away, vanished from the theater of war and the pantheon of heroes, evidently lost at sea.

Porter's fleet made an impressive parade of vessels crossing the broad ocean. In battle formation, with no enemy in sight, they surged through the gor-geous days under a dome "of the most delicate blue, except along the skirts of the horizon, where you might see a thin drapery of pale clouds which never varied their form or color. The long, measured, dirge-like swell of the Pacific came rolling along, with its surface broken by little tiny waves, sparkling in the sunshine. Every now and then a shoal of flying fish, scared from the water under the bows, would leap into the air and fall the next mo-ment like a shower of silver into the sea." Tuna, whales, and sharks would appear, and "at times, some shapeless monster of the deep, floating on the surface, would, as we approached, sink slowly into the blue waters and fade away from sight. But the most impressive feature of the scene was the almost unbroken silence that reigned over sky and water."

For the men, with enlistments expired and enduring the longest cruise in American naval history, the beauty of the Pacific was the backdrop to daily military drills at the great guns, at small arms, and at the game of single stick—swordplay done with wood, not steel, to hone their skills in boarding. As usual, they did not know their exact destination, although their captain had told them why they were disappearing into Polynesia: "Firstly, that we may put the ship in a suitable condition to enable us to take advantage of the most favorable season for our return home; Secondly, I am desirous that you should have some relaxation and amusement after being so long at sea, as from your late good conduct you deserve it."

He warned them about the dangerous, faithless beings they would soon encounter, whose smiles and friendliness masked a ruthless bloodlust but whose women were fair game. His men perked up instantly at this message; all of them, from fuzzy midshipmen to grizzled tars, had heard tales—or were they legends?—about the naked ladies of the tropical islands, so free with their favors. Now, as they closed in on the summer isles, their endless cruise was charged with excitement. The party had almost started; the girls were nearly real. "Everyone imagined them Venuses and amply indulged themselves in fancied bliss, impatient of our arrival at that Cytherean Paradise where all their wishes were to be gratified." Presumably Porter did not interview them about their imaginings; he was projecting his own.

In his journal, Porter indulged in other, more extensive fantasies. He was careful to shape his saga as an epic triumph, full of great victories over man and nature—and over the ghost of Lord George Anson. He was the first U.S. Navy captain to enter the Pacific, the eclipser of Anson in the annals of oceanic glory, and the rival of Captain Cook himself. He was a conqueror and the object of the enemy's obsessions, with a British squadron on its way. In the unwinding narrative of the cruise that he was creating, he, the author, suspected that the best part—the moment of truth, the chance for abounding glory—was yet to come, however it would happen, however it might end.

In the catalog of his achievements, foremost was the break-up of the British whale fishery, by which he claimed to have "deprived the enemy of property in the amount of two and a half millions of dollars, and of the services of 360 seamen" who were "not to serve against the United States until regularly exchanged." He had also protected American whalers. The *Essex Junior* had convoyed four of them, along with "my prize the *Policy*," from Valparaiso out to sea "a sufficient distance beyond the usual cruising grounds of British armed ships" so as to "take advantage of the winter season for getting into a port of the United States." Charleston, South Carolina, the nearest such port, was eight thousand miles away and heavily blockaded.

He had hurt the enemy in several ways, including the expense and diversion of the squadron that had been sent after him, if they were still afloat. "Whether the said ships will succeed in doubling Cape Horn, or meet the fate of Lord Anson's squadron, time alone will show," wrote Porter, as if rounding the Horn were not a regular event for hundreds of smaller vessels in recent years. He went so far as to deny that these reportedly "dull sailers" from the Royal Navy could ever pose a threat to the *Essex*, "even if they should all keep together and fall in with her; and if they should cruise separately they will have more to fear from our enterprise than we have to apprehend from theirs."

In toting up the value of his Pacific cruise, Porter dealt in sensational figures: $2.5 million in prizes and cargoes taken; $2.5 million in American vessels "which would in all probability have been captured had we not arrived"; and $250,000 in British squadron costs for "equipping and employing in one year one frigate, two sloops of war, and a store-ship"—all told, $5.17 million, having deducted the one-year expenses of the *Essex* at $80,000, or about the cost of outfitting the voyage of a whaleship. Porter's exaggerated numbers were also completely hypothetical;* not one penny had yet been realized in exchange for the prizes and their cargoes.

During this peaceful Pacific crossing, he wrote about himself as a patriot, motivated by damaging the enemy, but he could not restrain his Anson-mania and his money-lust, in which he asserted the rights of the predator, himself, versus the interests of his country.† It was too tantalizing, too close to being real, not to think obsessively about the value of the British whalers and their oil, of which his share as captain was 8.5 percent, or a cool $227,500, at a time that a first-rate full-rigged ship sold for $20,000. The problem—the great problem—was the lack of useful markets in the Pacific; but such markets might be found in Asia and perhaps Europe, and surely in the United States.

On a sunny day in late October 1813, the *Essex* made landfall in the outermost islands of the Washington Group of the Marquesas. The

---

* Most commentators consider Porter's numbers to have been inflated by a factor of two or three.

† Porter expressed greed as a first principle in his journal: "The object of the government is to injure the enemy; it derives no advantage from captures, however valuable they may prove; by our captures we have effected the object of government, and whether we sell or destroy them is of importance only to ourselves." In fact, the government had a large financial stake in all of this, for it claimed half the value of any captured vessel and cargo at the time of sale.

Marquesas were not an accidental destination: a Polynesian orgy was a major goal of this cruise, as had been made explicit in the Atlantic.* Porter's men had not clamored for such an opportunity; rather, Porter had offered it out of the pent-up desires inspired by accounts of European visitors to Oceania. He was determined to live out the fantasy, however awkward the circumstances. Also it galled him terribly that the French and English had ignored the primacy of the American "discovery" of these singular Pacific islands. It was true that the southern part of the Marquesas had first been visited by Spaniards in the 1500s and then again by Captain Cook in the 1760s, but the northern group of islands was first reached by outsiders in May 1791 with the arrival of Captain Joseph Ingraham and the crew of the *Hope*, of Boston. A year later, Captain Josiah Roberts, also of Boston, looking to trade for sandalwood, had sailed into the same group, which he had explored, described, named, and dubbed collectively the Washington Islands. With no one to dissuade him, Porter could imagine that the Marquesas were a strategic asset for whichever great power wanted an expansive presence in the Pacific. He told himself that Congress would wish for him to "do justice to the discovery of Mr. Ingraham" so that "posterity will know them only as Washington's Group." Natives, even those with two thousand years of occupancy, had no standing in this; it was a Western competition, and Porter knew that winning the war of words was a key to successful imperialism, ratified by treaties and books yet only secured by conquest.

Porter assumed that the British squadron sailing in pursuit of him had arrived at Valparaiso in late July, and that he was safe hiding out in paradise, trying to decide if he wanted to flee west into the Orient. But now that he had arrived, the Marquesas gambit was complicated by the Marquesans themselves, who were not fantasies. Though lusting for orgies, Porter feared these people; his habitual low-grade paranoia struggled with his swollen libido. With "savages" abounding, a Marquesan island was not a good site for refitting vessels; it introduced a specter of bloodshed that did not exist on uninhabited islands such as the Galápagos, where, since he had cleaned out the whaling fleet, he would have been free, months before, to smoke out rats and make repairs. But the Galápagos had iguanas, and Porter wanted girls.

Next day, Porter dropped down to steep-sided Ua Huka ("Ruahuga, called by us Adams' Island," he wrote), which was a summit, like all the Mar-

---

* In Porter's journal, the Marquesas are first mentioned during his Galápagos sojourn as the getaway place of his quasi alter ego, the infamous island hermit Red Patrick, sailing off in the imaginary *Black Prince*.

quesas, of an immense volcanic mountain range at the northeastern edge of Polynesia. Only Easter Island, with its staring stone heads, stands farther to the east. It seemed "barren and desolate" at first, but then the mariners were thrilled at the sight of "fertile valleys, whose beauties were heightened by the pleasant streams and clusters of houses, and intervened by groups of natives on the hills inviting us to land." As the *Essex* rounded a point, a canoe came off toward them "with eight of the natives, one of whom was seated in the bow with his head ornamented with some yellow leaves." A Tahitian on board the *Essex*, Tamaha, spoke a tongue similar to theirs, and eventually he communicated Porter's invitation to trade. Positioning the canoe under the frigate's high stern, they received a bucket full of metal items and sent up a few fish and "a belt made of the fibers of the cocoanut, garnished with the small teeth of a hog." They smiled and kept urging, *Taya, taya*, friends, friends, and invited the strangers to the shore, "where," Porter was quick to notice, "they assured us, by the most expressive gesticulations, that the *vahienas*, or women, were entirely at our service."

Porter had brought along a box of sperm-whale teeth that, he understood, were irresistible to these men, who "were entirely naked, and their chief ornament consisted in the dark and fanciful lines formed by tattooing, which covered them." Looking much closer, Porter saw that "the foreskin of their privates was drawn so close over and tied with a strip of bark as to force that member entirely into their bodies, and gave them a strange and unnatural appearance." When he flashed a couple of whale's teeth, the boaters "promised to return to the shore and bring us in exchange for them fruit and *vahienas*; not, however, before I had assured them that, as an additional compensation, I would cause their heads and privates to be shaved," for this, Porter had somehow discerned, "was what they seemed most to desire."

He finished at Ua Huka with a visit to another cove and a beachfront gathering of three women and about fifty tattooed men. From the shallows, standing in his longboat, Porter could observe these tall, handsome, smiling people, who "made altogether no inelegant appearance." Some were "highly ornamented" with plumes of black feathers, large gorgets, white fans, and a kind of cloak formed of white paper-like cloth. Tattooing, he would find, was pervasive, inscribed by sharks-teeth needles. Women were lightly marked, with some dots or fine lines and a tree-form or plant on a hip; men, starting with a few swirls and ovals in boyhood, were adorned until they wore an entire suit of beautiful skin designs. Geometric and also representational, these traditional symbolic patterns and colors varied with each individual, and the skin of an older man might be entirely blackened from the density of his tattoos.

Porter cheerfully "gave to each a small present; but they had no article to offer in return but their women: and as two of them were not more than sixteen years of age, and both handsome, they no doubt considered them the most acceptable present they could offer us." The girls, thought Porter, "showed no disinclination to grant every favor we might be disposed to ask; and to render themselves the more attractive, they retired and soon appeared clad in clean and, no doubt, their best attire, which consisted of a white and thin paper cloth, which enveloped their whole persons, with the exception of one arm and breast: and this simple drapery, when contrasted with the nakedness of the men, gave them an appearance of grace and modesty that we had little expected to find among savages."* After a lifetime of fantasies, Porter now came face-to-face with the reality: two sweet sixteen-year-old "savages" offered up as objects for his sexual gratification. For once, however, something like conscience overtook him, and he decided that he did not need to degrade himself and his men, that maybe he had misjudged these friendly people and that there was more to them than he had understood.

The girls warily entered the strangers' boat, but soon relaxed. The men were greatly amused by their innocent cavorting, and returned them to the beach to their own people. Porter grasped that "their modesty was more evident than that of the women of any place we have visited since leaving our own country; and if they suffered themselves (although with apparent timidity and reluctance) to be presented naked to strangers, may it not be in compliance with a custom which teached them to sacrifice to hospitality all that is most estimable?"

A night of heavy squalls ensued, and then Porter departed for Madison's Island, the largest in the group—Nukuhiva, or Nooaheevah, as it was pronounced—a gray-green mass rising from the sea not far to the west.† Twelve miles wide at most points, Nukuhiva presented a spectacular appearance, all steep mountains and valleys, with seaside cliffs. On first encounter, "the land heaved up in peaks and rising vales; it fell in cliffs and buttresses; its colour ran through fifty modulations in the scale of pearl and rose and olive; and it was crowned above by opalescent clouds. The suffusion of vague

---

* Porter was so taken with this first view of a beautiful island girl that he drew a picture, which appeared as an engraving in the first edition of his published journal.

† Today the island's name is spelled Nukuhiva or Nuku Hiva, but the internal "k" sound was evolving in the dialect, and in 1813 was usually pronounced with a vestigial "ng" sound, as in Nu'ahiva or Nooaheevah, as Porter and other English speakers invariably spelled it. The author uses the standard spelling except when referring to the American sailors.

hues deceived the eye; the shadows of the clouds were confounded with the articulations of the mountain; and the isle and its insubstantial canopy rose and shimmered before us like a single mass." Approaching on the south side, Porter looked in at Comptroller's Bay—large but open to the sea—and decided to enter the next one, about nine miles in circumference, approached "by a narrow entrance flanked on either side by two small twin islets"—the Sentinels—"which soar conically to the height of some five hundred feet." The view from the inside was spectacular: "a vast natural ampitheatre in decay, and overgrown with vines, [with] deep glens that furrowed its sides appearing like enormous fissures caused by the ravages of time."

Shortly after anchoring near the entrance, Porter was amazed to see three white men in a whaleboat, one of them "perfectly naked" except for a loincloth, and "his body was all over tattooed." Deciding that they were reprobate "seamen who had deserted from some vessels here," he ignored their shouts of joy, which, after a while, trailed off in abject despair. At last, the three pulled away toward the beach in doomed silence, followed by several native canoes. Porter sent some marines in boats to save them, just in time; and all were astonished when one of the bushy-bearded brown beachcombers spoke up and identified himself as John M. Maury, a midshipman of the U.S. Navy. The near-fatal incident was an indication that the islands were a different world, to be understood in their own terms and not judged by assumptions. Maury explained that he had been marooned for nearly two years after a botched sandalwood voyage. He introduced the others as an American seaman, Baker, and a veteran islander named Wilson, an Englishman who had gone native.

Porter took an immediate shine to Wilson, whom he thought "an inoffensive, honest, good-hearted fellow." On the spot, Porter made this rum-soaked Briton his translator and advisor for dealing with the islanders.* Translation, in all its meanings, was essential to the cooperation of the two peoples, but Porter came to Nukuhiva as a western conquistador among savages, while to the Enana, as they called themselves, he was an unwelcome stranger, the leader of a tribe of wandering white men with unknown intentions, whom they believed had come from the moon. Porter, typically, had misjudged Wilson, who would prove to be his equal in talent for misrepresentation.

Wanting to socialize, Porter walked up to a group of natives, and "all their apprehensions seemed to cease: the women, who had retired at a

---

* Enana was the name for "the people" in the northern Marquesas; in the southern islands they were Enata.

distance, came down to join the male natives; and even the landing of the marines, as well as the rest of the party, did not seem to occasion any uneasiness among them." These people were of the Teii tribe, and this was their valley and their bay, which was rapidly filling up with ships from Porter's fleet. Noticing that the steep hills were "covered with numerous groups of natives," Porter learned from Wilson that they were the "warlike" Hapa'a, "residing beyond the mountains, [who] had been for several weeks at war with the natives of the valley."

Porter decided that he, the new lord of the isles, was the protector of the Teii and the enemy of the Hapa'a. War being his business, he sent an incendiary message to the cliffs: "I have come with a force sufficiently strong to drive you from the island: and if you presume to enter the valley while I remain there, I shall send a body of men to chastise you; you must cease all hostilities so long as I remain among you; and, if you have hogs or fruit to dispose of, you might come and trade freely with us, as I shall not permit the natives of the valley to injure or molest you."

Porter, through Wilson, and backed by his phalanx of marines, turned to address his naked Teii allies, urging them to "look on us as brethren: and I shall protect you against the Happahs should they again venture to descend from the mountains." Leave your spears, slings, and clubs at home, he told them, "so that we might know [you] from the Happahs." With a little more oratorical persuasion, they dropped their weapons. Porter was ecstatic at their compliance; he had achieved a coup without one shot fired in anger, and he now thought it possible to create a permanent American outpost in the Pacific.

Porter found that his speechmaking had proved a lot more interesting to his new friends than to his marines, who had "formed with the female part of the community an intimacy" in the houses and the bushes. Although Porter's horny stalwarts had defied his orders, he did not blame them, for "if an allowance can be made for a departure from prudential measures," he wrote, "it is when a handsome and sprightly girl of sixteen, whose almost every charm [is] exposed to view, invites to follow her."

Captain Porter fixed on "a handsome young woman of about eighteen years of age, her complexion fairer than common, her carriage majestic, and her dress better and somewhat different from the other females." Piteenee was the grandchild of "the chief, or greatest man in the valley," named Gattanewa. "Neat, sleek, and comely," she proved irresistible to Porter, who meant to make her his teen queen. The captain's advances, however, were very much unwanted; she met them "with a coldness and hauteur which

Taiohae Bay, Nukuhiva, Marquesas Islands, which David Porter renamed "Massachusetts Bay" upon arriving there with the men of the *Essex*, many prisoners, and several captured vessels. Inflating a minor tribal skirmish into deadly warfare of a sort previously unknown there, he built Fort Madison (atop the hill) and the village of Madisonville and took formal possession of Nukuhiva for the United States of America, which, as it turned out, had no interest in Porter's imperialism. *(from Journal of a Cruise made to the Pacific Ocean, David Porter, 1815)*

would have suited a princess, and repelled everything like familiarity with a sternness that astonished me."

Porter gazed at his enemies on the mountains. He was angry at having been rejected, and his mind filled with violent fantasies and cannibal lore. He had no knowledge of their history and traditions and no thought that they might be enacting a ritual designed to end things short of warfare.

Gattanewa was visiting a mountain fort when he got word to come meet Porter. He was not a chief, for, in spite of Porter's assumptions, the Enana had no chiefs—and no kings or queens, no castles or estates. Most clans recognized a tribal patriarch, but some were totally democratic. The patriarch was a wise man, but no autocrat; he inherited a good deal of property, but he shared it with everyone else. He married off most of his children to the children of leaders in other tribal valleys, which kept the whole island connected by kinship. He shared public honors with the *tau'a* shaman-priests (often a younger brother) and with the leaders of the warriors, athletic skirmishers to whom the patriarch loaned out his many wives if they were willing. Sometimes he might have to act as a judge, but not often, as there was no crime, no theft, and very little violence. The Enana were all of one class, with few distinctions, personal or public. Most lived in groups of houses built on huge stone platforms near the island streams. They bathed frequently and dined on fish, pork, dog, and chicken, as well as abundant tropical wild fruits and vegetables. No agriculture was necessary, and wild island herbs provided topicals for injuries and medicines for sickness.

Back aboard the *Essex*, Porter decided on a close-in mooring and found his men inspired by glad tidings from grinning marines. The crew rowed strenuously for hours, towing their heavy frigate to an anchorage within easy view of the beach crowd, mainly female, "waving their white cloaks or *cahoes* for us to come on shore." The boats went in and ferried out women "of all ages and descriptions," reported Porter. Having visited ships before, many "had been taught by the men some few English words of the most indecent kind, which they pronounced too plain to be misunderstood. Indeed, the ship was a perfect bedlam from the time of their arrival until their departure, which was not until morning, when they were put on shore, not only with whatever was given them by all such as had shared their favors but with whatever they could lay their hands on." Presumably some laid their hands on Captain Porter to assuage his failure with Piteenee, who, it turned out, was quite partial to one of his officers.

The midshipmen were segregated under the Reverend David P. Adams. "During our stay at this island," wrote Gatty Farragut, "the 'youngsters' were sent on board the vessel commanded by our chaplain, for the purpose of continuing our studies, away from temptation. We were allowed, when not occupied with our duties, to ramble about on the shore in company with the native boys. From them we learned to throw the spear and walk on stilts; but the most useful accomplishment we acquired was the art of swimming," at which the Enana children excelled, even as infants: "to my astonishment, the little creatures could swim like young ducks."

Chaplain Adams and his charges also came to appreciate what they could understand of a highly successful civilization. Over the course of two millennia, the Enana had regulated their society so as to avoid war and to limit the extent of male violence. In effect, they had created a paradise of sorts at Nukuhiva, where peace and harmony reigned and no one had to work or worry. About 50,000 people inhabited six major valleys, each with a tribe comprising several clans, all speaking the same language and worshipping the same gods.

The "warlike attitude of the Happahs" on the mountainsides was Porter's excuse for not initiating repairs to the *Essex*. Before he could take the next step, he was called upon to welcome Gattanewa, coming out in a boat. Porter had been much impressed with the big, strong, plumed, cloaked, tattooed, ornamented warriors at the beach; now he eagerly await-ed the arrival of the leader. Gattanewa was helped over the rail, and there he stood—a small, black, bent old man, leaning on a stick and wearing only "a clout about his loins and a piece of palm leaf tied about his head." He was also drunk, having been imbibing *kava*, a fermented nectar for priests and patriarchs. Porter was astonished; the great man's face and body were "entirely covered" with dense dark tattoos, "and his skin was rough and appeared to be peeling off in scales."

Porter assembled his crew at attention and fired a salute, but the old man only griped. After a short nap, he felt better and decided either that he liked Porter or that he had no choice but to like him, and he proposed, therefore, a name exchange, by which they would share everything, wives and ancestors included. Porter agreed and added a wish for peace, at which Gattanewa declared that the Hapa'a "had cursed the bones of his mother," recently dead, who was now Porter's deceased mother too.

Opotee—the islanders' word for Porter—sent him ashore, and next morning a sober Gattanewa looked out and saw five more of the moon men's ships. In hopes of forestalling an invasion, he sent out boats piled high with coconuts and plantains, enough to feed the crews of the just-ar-rived prize fleet. The *Essex Junior*, too, had showed up the day before, with the put-upon Lieutenant Downes reporting that he had found no trace of the *Mary Ann*, that India-bound British phantom. Porter gave Downes the newly rescued Midshipman John Maury as his chief officer and filled him in on his plans.

Big things started happening next day. The topmasts of the *Essex* were removed, her sails went ashore, and water casks were landed to form a perimeter of what was to become a large American camp situated between the two hostile tribes on a spot that had been placed under a *tapu*, pro-scribing its occupation on pain of divine retribution. Such matters meant nothing to Porter. He had a large tent put up, guarded by marines. In the afternoon, the officers went ashore to visit some villages, but Porter, on board the *Essex*, noticed the reappearance of Hapa'a warriors descending from the mountains into the valley. He fired his guns as a warning, and Teii men drove them upward in retreat. Only then did the interpreter Wilson reveal to Porter that the Hapa'a visitations were required by an island ritual, enjoined by a *tapu* "of the strictest nature," due to their having killed a Teii shaman in an ambush. Porter did not understand, or chose not to.

The Hapa'a messenger returned with a derisive response to the intruder's ultimatum: Opotee was a coward whose camp they would wreck and whose sails they would carry away. Porter posted a large guard every evening on shore, but he heedlessly allowed his men complete liberty "in procuring sweethearts; and it was astonishing to us to see with what indifference fathers, husbands, and brothers would see their daughters, wives, and sisters fly from the embraces of one lover to that of another." The Teii men seemed to view it only as an accommodation to strangers who had claims on their hospitality. Porter's anthropological observations—and his research was personal, especially with teenage girls—began to give him an appreciation of just how different this culture was. The women seemed wanton, yet they were not; they were simply friendly and physical and did not view sex as shameful or particularly important. It was fun to do, and it made the visitors happy, and if the moon men were happy they might not blow apart the Teii's valley or slaughter their families as they seemed capable of doing.

While Porter began to pick up these cues, he missed many more, including the most obvious; he had not happened to glide into Taihoe Bay on the eve of the very first war in Marquesan history. Captain Cook before him, whose books he had read, had realized that his sudden and outsized appearance in the islands was a catalyst for unexpected responses. Cook had come among these isolated peoples as a fearsome shiva upon whom they projected the powers of preserver and destroyer, granter of forbidden wishes, agent of ultimate *tapu*. Unlike Porter, Cook had been selected by his government to explore and to make contact as an enlightened, educated representative of a civilization that had scientific and commercial interests in these new lands and peoples. At first Cook had misinterpreted his encounters with natives, and some had ended in violence, but over time he had grasped the incredible power of ritual in the island cultures and had learned to adjust his behaviors and exercise understanding.

Landing at Tahiti, Cook had suavely refused the invitation of one tribe to fight another; the rivals, he said, had never offended him and he "was not thoroughly acquainted with the dispute." The lesson was clear. Cook understood that he stirred extreme feelings in the peoples on whom he intruded and that, representing his nation, he was obliged "to display its character as well as its authority." Although Cook had been killed at Hawaii when he mistook his own role in a native ritual, he showed the way for others who came after.

Porter, a renegade westerner appearing in the midst of a typical in-tertribal conflict, brought about a distortion in the traditional process due to his gigantic presence and partisan hostility. Gattanewa had explained that often they fought "for weeks, nay for months sometimes, without kill-ing any on either side," but that was in the absence of intruders employing military tactics and fatally efficient weaponry. Opotee, the leader of this tribe of whites, seemed intent on breaking the ultimate *tapu*. At any point he could have sailed away from the Bay of Taihoe and found another spot in which to repair his vessels in peace. But he was committed to a war, by which he would establish ascendancy over all the tribes of the island for as long as he bothered to stay.

Opotee sent ashore one of his long-range cannon and told Gattan-ewa to haul it to the top of a mountain, so it could be fired "and drive away the Happahs." It was an impossible assignment—to carry a cannon up a nearly vertical cliff—but it gave Opotee an excuse to land one on the beach and demonstrate its power. First he had a six-pound ball fired almost straight up, "and a general shout of admiration marked the time of its fall into the water." Then he had a ball shot so as to skip across the bay, which the islanders applauded; and next he fired a cannister of grape shot, guar-anteed to tear men apart, which they liked best of all. When the shooting was over, "they hugged and kissed the gun, lay down beside it and fondled it with the utmost delight." Then, to Porter's astonishment, they "slung it to two long poles" and cheerfully marched off with their long, heavy idol to begin the climb up the mountain. Their natural cooperation, positive out-look, and incomparable skill and strength showed what sort of people they were, and Porter was deeply impressed.

In the meantime, along came Mouina, the chief soldier of the Teii. Opotee instantly admired this "prepossessing," tall, "well-shaped man of about thirty-five years of age, remarkably active, of an intelligent and open countenance." Mouina wanted them to fire a musket, or *bouhi*. The Hapa'a believed that muskets had no power to harm them, and Mouina wanted to be sure they were wrong. It happened that several Hapa'a men "were at the moment about the camp"—so much for a serious war—and Opotee took pleasure in firing his musket repeatedly at a distant mark the size of a man. Then he had the marines fire volleys at a cask, which they blew apart. Mou-ina smiled to see the power of the *bouhi*. "*Mattee! Mattee!*" he exclaimed, *killed, killed*, looking at the Hapa'a, but they just shook their heads. Opotee was a fraud; the *bouhis* could not "do them the injury that we pretended."

Mouina, Enana warrior. When Porter and the *Essex* arrived at Nukuhiva in 1813, Mouina was a leader of the Teii tribe, with whom Porter made an alliance against the rest of the islanders. Handsomely adorned with full-body tattoos, Mouina impressed Porter with his size, bearing, and gravitas. *(from* Journal of a Cruise made to the Pacific Ocean, *David Porter, 1815)*

Per Enana rules of engagement, Opotee had to prove his potency in actual combat.*

    Next morning at daybreak, October 29, on the beach of the compound, Porter sent off a combined war party of Downes and Mouina. A few minutes later, Gattenewa arrived, urging Porter to recall his men; he had just heard from his son-in-law, a chief of the Hapa'a, "who had come as an envoy to beg that [Opotee] would grant them peace." Porter did not believe Gattenewa. Suddenly he thought that he had sent his troops into a trap; "from the old man's solicitude for peace, when contrasted with his former desire for war, I for a moment believed some treachery on foot." Porter's men were "in the hands" of the Teii who accompanied them, but Porter had Gattanewa and roughly took him hostage. The old man was sure that this was the end; repeatedly he asked if he would be killed, and Porter's "assurances to the contrary did not relieve his anxiety." Why should they? Gattanewa figured that in this war between invaders and natives, Opotee, if displeased, would not hesitate to take vengeance on the nearest target.

    At noontime, near the summit, Downes and his men, with Mouina

---

* This was the first time in his journal that Porter mentioned the name of the Tayee (Teii).

and his Teii, faced a barrage of well-aimed rocks as the Hapa'a moved from place to place, unscathed, trying to wear out their slower, weighed-down opponents. When the Hapa'a retreated to a fort, the Americans "gave three cheers and rushed on through a shower of spears and stones, which the natives threw from behind the strong barrier."

Fighting was fierce in the moment of collision, and five of the young Hapa'a warriors "were at this instant shot dead." They had not believed in the power of these guns, and one had "fought until the muzzle of the piece was presented to his forehead, when the top of his head was entirely blown off." That was enough. In traditional Enana skirmishing, five dead men was a total massacre, so the Hapa'a fled in horror down the hill, full of the terrible knowledge of guns and bullets. Mouina and some of his men pounced on the bodies, dipping their spears in the blood and calling their spears by the names of the slain. Others ran down into the Hapa'a Valley to take the spoils.

Opotee liberated his brother Gattanewa. The old man "dreaded an ally so powerful" and could not leave fast enough. Next day he had recovered sufficiently to attend the victory ceremony on the plaza, with ranks of tall warriors in their tattoos and regalia, and the four bodies—the fifth man killed had been a Teii living with the Hapa'a—and the shaman Tawattaa chanting and shaking his wand, a palm branch twined with strands of hair. On cue, the warriors gave three shouts with loud claps, followed by five minutes of drumming and loud, animated singing, repeating the sequence twice more, each time with greater intensity as they boasted of their conquest and thanked the gods for sending Porter to their aid. Toward the end, a Hapa'a emissary appeared and was led fearfully to Opotee, who responded ominously by taking up his musket and firing it at a distant tree, hitting it at man-height, then inviting the warriors to try their slings and spears at doing the same. All of them refused, and praised his weapon.

At the American camp there was much tribute in the form of food and goods. The Hapa'a were granted terms of peace, and their leaders suggested that all of the tribes build a suitable town for the great *hekai* (chief), Opotee. Within two days, Porter received envoys from all over the island. Except for the proud Taipi people and their allies in the distant valley of Hannahow, each tribe agreed to supply provisions and to build a house, and to each leader Opotee gave a much-prized harpoon. Porter hastened to lay down the plan of "the village about to be built." At the rear of the camp, a barrier of water casks traced the crescent line of the proposed buildings, which would be in the style and materials of the Enana, each fifty feet long and twelve feet apart, connected by a wall four feet high to be extended to enclose the entire settlement. On the morning of November 3, a huge crowd of tribesmen—perhaps 4,000—arrived with construction materials and began their labors.

Incredulous, Porter watched them by the hour. "Nothing," he wrote, "can exceed the regularity with which these people carried on their work, without any chief to guide them, without confusion, and without much noise; they performed their labor with expedition and neatness; every man appeared to be master of his business, and every tribe appeared to strive which should complete their house with most expedition and in the most perfect manner." At the end of this remarkable day, before sunset, they had completed a residence for Porter and another for the officers, a sail loft, a cooper's shop, an infirmary, a bake house, a guard house, a shed for the sentinel, and all of the connecting walls. Opotee distributed more harpoons and iron hoops and gave a little speech thanking his benefactors for "our delightful village, which had been built as if by enchantment."

Porter was humbled by this enormous gift from the tribes and by their spirit of friendship, and he marveled at their unity and harmony, so unlike westerners, and wondered about the sources of this remarkable variant on human nature. "They appear to act with one mind, to have the same thought, and to be operated on by the same impulse." Porter had begun the week concerned about cannibalism; now he was "inclined to believe that an honester and more friendly and better disposed people do not exist under the sun. They have been stigmatized by the name of savages; it is a term wrongly applied; they rank high in the scale of human beings, whether we consider them morally or physically. We find them brave, generous, honest, and benevolent, acute, ingenious, and intelligent, and their beauty and regular proportions of their bodies correspond with the perfections of their minds." He might almost have been quoting from another westerner at his first encounter with a traditional island culture: "They are the best people in the world and above all the gentlest—without knowledge of what is evil—nor do they murder or steal. . . they love their neighbors as themselves and they have the sweetest talk in the world. . . always laughing." Those natives, "exhibiting great love toward all others," would be enslaved, raped, killed, and ultimately exterminated by the admiring writer, Christopher Columbus, and his successors in the New World.

The U.S. Navy frigate *Essex*, anchored just off the beach of the village, had been sealed tight and thoroughly smoked with cauldrons of charcoal in every part of every deck and hold, resulting in great piles of dead rodents. With the rats gone, the men spent days caulking the seams and making various repairs such as scraping clean the bottom of her hull and refastening her copper sheathing to ensure maximum speed for any conditions in the Pacific. "Among other defects," reported Porter, "we found her main-top-mast in a very decayed state." This mast, fitted into the top of the mainmast, carried the uppermost sails and enabled her to reach full speed even in light winds. In storms and in battles, the loss of the main topmast was often a fatal blow, for it might crash through the rigging and bring down the mainsails and mainmast with it. The *Essex* carried a spare.

The refitting of the *Essex* went on "with order and regularity," wrote Porter. "Every person was employed to the best advantage, and yet all were allowed sufficient time for amusement and relaxation." The men engaged in sports like wrestling, spear throwing, long jumping, and quoit pitching. This they did in preference to certain other activities, of which they had had enough, according to their captain.

"The girls, who had formerly engrossed the whole of their leisure time, were now less attended to, and indeed were frequently reduced to the necessity of suing, in vain."

Chapter Ten

Taipi

C aptain David Porter, the godlike Opotee, had a brand-new village full of fruit and hogs sent to him by the interior tribes. Amid all the activity, however, he had not missed an insult. Temaa Tipee, chief of the Shoueme clan, could not get his caravan past blockades in the Taipi Valley. Having demanded fealty from all, Porter could not allow the Taipi to oppose him, since, he wrote, "their example might change the conduct of others." Porter commanded a force of 200 on an island of perhaps 20,000 native men. It would not take much, he thought, for them to turn against him. Mouina, thinking of plunder, urged immediate reprisals; Gattenewa, pensive, finally pronounced that the Taipi were not aware of the effects of Opotee's weapons "and must not suffer in consequence of their ignorance."

Porter allowed Gattanewa's son to warn the Taipi of their peril. Two days later he returned with the message that the Teii and the Hapa'a were cowards and that Opotee and his men were "white lizards, mere dirt," the butts and balls of the Teii, contemptible *othouah* boasting about "chastising" a people who, "as their gods informed them, were never to be beaten." The Taipi leaders dared Opotee to find out how much they feared his guns.

Gattanewa himself now called for war, and Mouina stomped into the American village "boiling with rage" and spoiling for action. Porter took his time, slowly marshaling his forces and commissioning a fleet of twenty war canoes and construction of a fort on the hill by his village. As the natives labored, he lectured them—through his English interpreter Wilson—about the evil empire of Great Britain, and why it was their enemy as well as his. Overseen by a few of Porter's officers, the native workers leveled the top of a hill and made a breastwork out of dirt-filled casks, leaving embrasures for sixteen guns. "All worked with zeal, and, as the friendly tribes were coming in with presents, all joined in the labor," while their "chiefs requested that they might be admitted on the same footing as the Tayees." Opotee responded with a civics lesson about "the nature of our government," after which Gattanewa "requested that they might not only be our friends and brothers, but our countrymen."

Porter had taken on and resolved many problems at Nukuhiva: the resistance of friendly tribes, an escape plot by his British prisoners, a budding mutiny, and neglect of duty by marine sentries, a problem he solved by shooting a sleeping man through the meat of his thigh. He had not, however, imagined how the weeks might change his understanding of the islanders. The Enana, he concluded, were entirely admirable; in many ways, they had an ideal society, and he was proud, on this American-discovered island, to be the first to see how they might fit into the larger scheme. American commerce would be expanding in the Pacific, with great possibilities for development, colonization, and exploitation. From the *Albatros*, for example, traders George Ross and William Brudenell had come ashore with their stock, prepared to spend years there as sandalwood agents for their Philadelphia merchant house. Many others, on many other islands, would follow. Someday the Pacific would become a major battleground, economic and perhaps military, in which the United States ought to prevail. With flags flying and guns bristling, Porter's new fortress bade defiance to all comers and dominated—and defended—the Teii in their seaside town. But Fort Madison was something bigger than that, he realized; it was an outpost of his nation, an American beacon in the Pacific.

Porter had come many thousands of miles to exploit the Enana women sexually, and now he was prepared to stay for a while, amusing himself by meddling in tribal matters and using force if he thought it necessary. Porter the sexual predator had become Porter the conqueror, the possessor. It was strange, this turn toward imperialism, but he had no conscience about such matters and no orders to guide him. He was the law wherever he went, thanks to his guns, and he saw no need to try to understand "the Indians," although he liked and admired them. He and his men, with their prejudices and diseases, were bringing civilization to these people so long cut off from the world. He could, he believed, offer them a great future.

On November 19, Porter staged an impressive piece of theater. At the new fort, drawn up in colorful uniforms, his sailors and marines—the naked revelers of the night before—stood under the tropical sun. The Teii and the Hapa'a audience gathered by the hundreds and then by the thousands. Opotee, in his captain's regalia, came forward to the flagpole and raised the Stars and Stripes over the earthworks of Fort Madison. As the flag caught the breeze, he gave the order for a salute of seventeen guns from the fort's artillery. Their mighty reports were answered by his ships in the harbor, and the thunder rolled around the bay and echoed off the high peaks, and the smoke drifted across the waters.

Porter waited for the excited crowd to grow quiet. Then he proceeded to read, in a language unintelligible to his audience, a formal declaration of annexation by which he claimed sovereignty over "Nooaheevah, generally known by the name of Sir Henry Martin's Island, but now called Madison's Island." He proclaimed that "our rights to this island, being founded on priority of discovery, conquest, and possession, cannot be disputed." Nor were these the only means by which Madison's Island had been annexed to the United States, for the people themselves, he affirmed, fervently desired "to be admitted into the great American family, whose pure republican policy approaches so near their own."

Reading on, Porter stated that the thirty-one clans of the six tribes—Teii, Hapa'a, Maamatwuah, Attatoka, Nieekee, and Taipi—had sworn hostility to Great Britain and loyalty to the United States, and that "all have been willing to purchase, on any terms, a friendship which promises to them so many advantages." He closed by stating that he had acted to secure "to my country a fruitful and populous island" and to bring "civilization to a race of men who enjoy every mental and bodily endowment which nature can bestow, and which requires only art to perfect." As governor and ruler, he signed the instrument of annexation with his amazing embellished signature, and then he bestowed new names on the features of his domain: Madison's Island, Fort Madison, and Madisonville, all overlooking the dancing blue waters of the ludicrously rechristened Massachusetts Bay.

Porter believed his own propaganda and assumed that his audience sincerely accepted his terms; his astounding narcissism and his late-blooming admiration of the Enana left him unable to appreciate the degree to which they were simply enjoying a day of pageantry. "The object of this ceremony," he proudly recounted, "had been previously and was again explained to the natives. They were all much pleased at being *Melleekees*, as they called themselves, and wanted to know if their new chief was as great a man as Gattanewa."

In their valley the proud Taipi seethed with battle fever, playing their drums, singing their songs, sounding the war conch. Still nothing happened; no great vessels arrived at their high coast, no army appeared on their mountains or in the shallows of their beach. The people of the twelve clans sharpened new spears and added to the piles of polished stones, and kept vigil from the ridges.

Porter thought he knew what he was doing. By delaying, he had allowed the Taipi to consider peace and made the others desperate enough to join him in battle, for his demands for tribute had seriously depleted their resources and all were eager for a share of Taipi plunder. Whipped up by Opotee, they stood on the brink of intervalley war.

On November 28, at three in the morning, Porter slipped out of the bay at the head of a flotilla of five of his own boats and ten war canoes, sounding their conch horns eerily in the thick darkness. He had not reconnoitered the terrain of the Taipi nor assessed their strength or positions, and he had no battle plan. Consciously or not, he expected them to fold before the armed might of the moon men and the power of Opotee.

At sunrise, Porter and his men landed on the quarter-mile black-sand beach of the Taipi valley. One of the boats had disappeared, and Downes in the *Essex Junior* had lost his way and was just arriving, but the canoes landed safely with several hundred natives. On this perfect Pacific morning, Porter was pleased to see the nearby hillsides covered with Teii and Hapa'a tribesmen, his allies, painted for a fight and armed with clubs and spears. A few descended to the beach to join those who had come by canoe—Hapa'a on the left, Teii on the right, and Porter in the center, heading up a total force of 5,000 men, at least as many as the Taipi, and unprecedented in the two-thousand-year history of Nukuhiva.

Beyond the beach was the first obstacle, an "almost impenetrable swampy thicket" extending across the three-mile floor of the valley. Downes came ashore with Gattenewa, two ambassadors, the interpreter Wilson, and fifteen sailors and marines. These, added to Porter's twenty, were, he imagined, "fully sufficient" to over-awe his new enemies and "to incline them to terms." Porter kept forgetting that the proud Taipi had showed no fear of whites and no interest in compromise. They had the faith and strength of an independent people, safe in their valley and assured by their gods that they would always remain so.

As Taipi warriors began popping up from the bushes and raining stones down on the beachhead, Porter sent one of the tabooed ambassadors into the brush with a white flag held high. Very soon the man returned, "the picture of terror"—the Taipi had beaten him and chased him back under threat of death; *tapu* meant nothing in the face of war. A shower of Taipi rocks came flying, and a volley of American musket fire ripped into the bushes. The battle had commenced. A Taipi man cried out as he took a bullet in the leg. With Downes in front and Mouina leading a few braves, Porter gave the order to march. "Assailed by spears and stones," they entered the morass and heard "the snapping of the slings, the whistling of the stones," and spears that "came quivering by." Glancing back, Porter saw that the great mass of his native army stood at the beach, immobile. He was not their leader; this little strike force, he realized, was all he had.

Several hours later, Porter emerged from the thicket onto the beach, exhausted and all but defeated. Downes had been carried out early with a broken leg, while others had been bruised and wounded by stones and spears. However, late in the fight, while blocked by a huge stonewall, Porter had flushed out two Taipi warriors and killed them, and he had their corpses in his possession. "We returned to the beach," he wrote, "much fatigued and harassed with marching and fighting, and with no contemptible opinion of the enemy." There he found the men of the missing boat. All of his company, therefore, had survived the invasion.

Assuming "the air and language of a conqueror," Porter put on a show for the hillside spectators. To one of Gattanewa's ambassadors he made a loud speech: Go to the Taipi, he declaimed, and tell them that a handful of men had driven them into their fortifications, "that we had killed two and wounded several of them, and had now a force sufficient to drive them out of the valley; that I did not wish to do them further injury and still offered the terms I had first proposed."

Porter had fought like a tiger, but his hubris had led him deep in the direction of disaster. He resented the inactivity of the painted onlookers. They were not his allies; they were opportunists and they were Enana, like the Taipi against whom he had brought this war. And after all, he thought, no true conquistador ever counted on the locals. The fight had been his to lose or win, and they had witnessed his victory, however narrow.

The Taipi messenger told Opotee that they had many men and could afford to lose a few, as he could not. They had killed (they thought) his best fighter, wounded several others, and compelled a retreat. They derided the power of his muskets and "dared us to renew the contest and assured us that they would not retreat beyond where we had left them." At the beach, Porter found that Lieutenant Downes would recover, but the wounded were in agony and the rest were "disheartened." It was time to go. As he boarded the boats for the *Essex Junior*, the hillside Hapa'a and Shoueme came down from the ridges. Opotee was anxious, as "we were still but a handful, and were surrounded by several thousand Indians, and although they professed friendship I did not feel safe."

Suddenly the bushes came alive above the beach and Taipi warriors rushed out. Many of the other tribesmen fled in their canoes, but Porter and his men returned intrepidly in their boats, guns blazing, and the Hapa'a and Teii rallied and drove back the Taipi in a hail of stones. They captured a Taipi man, clubbed him to death, and carried away his body—a crucial turn of events enabling the would-be allies to share in the victory.

At Fort Madison, Porter reviewed his mistakes and moved fast to save his mission. By neutralizing the Taipi, he had bought time in which he could have finished repairing the *Essex* and departed, but his blood was up, and he did not stop to consider a strategic retreat. Porter's entire Pacific adventure was now at stake. He might never cash in his whale-oil fortune, or defeat a British battleship, or receive the laurels of a grateful nation. Instead he might die in a war with Stone Age men who ate their opponents.

Next day he organized a strike force of 200 sailors and marines, minus Lieutenant John Downes, *hors de combat*, and without the "noise and confusion of either of the tribes of Indians, whom we had always found useless to us." Porter hoped—but had no actual plan—to "take several prisoners, the possession of which would probably bring them to terms and save the necessity of bloodshed." That night he mustered his troops and told them that this time it would be just them, Americans, marching by starlight, over ridges and down into the enemy stronghold.

Ten hours later, Porter's weary men reached the ridge overlooking the scattered fires of villages far below. The Taipi were singing and drumming ecstatically, "celebrating the victory," said Wilson, "and calling on their gods to give them rain" to soak the white men and their guns. Porter decided to bivouac for the night, which brought a cold wind and heavy rains. Unable to sleep, fearful of falling, the Americans huddled in misery, awaiting the dawn. When it came, they were "as perfectly wet as though we had been under water the whole time," and half the ammunition was useless. A large body of Teii and Hapa'a had joined them, but they could not make a descent in the rain, so Porter ordered his men to form on the ridge and prepare to salute the Taipi valley. When the volley was fired—Porter said "it went off better than I expected"—the Taipi looked to the mountaintop in shock. Recovering, "they shouted, beat their drums, and blew their war conchs from one end of the valley to the other," but Porter heard the terror of a people facing annihilation.

For no apparent reason, Porter had given away the huge tactical advantage of surprise. He wrote that he hoped to impress the watching Hapa'a and to enable the Taipi to sequester their women and children. More likely, he simply could not bear the tension. The Americans and Teii spent another day and night in a Hapa'a village, where friendship reigned, the downpour ended, and the warriors rose "fresh and vigorous" and returned to the ridge. "Never in my life," wrote Porter, "did I witness a more delightful scene." The Taipi valley was about nine miles long and three or four wide, walled in by "lofty mountains." At the upper part, a grand cataract fell from "a precipice of many hundred feet in height." Villages "were scattered here and there, the bread-fruit and cocoa-nut trees flourished luxuriantly and in abundance; plantations . . . were in a state of high cultivation, and everything bespoke industry, abundance, and happiness."

Porter intended to lay waste to this vision and to kill as many people as possible. His idea of taking a few prisoners gave way to feelings of genocidal vengeance: "I had borne with their reproaches, and my moderation was called cowardice. I offered them friendship, and my offers were rejected with insulting scorn." He could destroy the tribe that "believed they had obtained an advantage over us"—a belief that stoked Porter's fear that the other tribes would turn against him. By waging a war of devastation, he could "secure the future tranquility of the island"—at least for as long as he intended to occupy it.

Porter's men began the descent toward the river and the music of drums and conch horns, into the homeland of an ancient and undefeated people. At the bottom, they rested on the riverbank, then crossed the ford without loss, firing away at the underbrush. Suddenly the chief warrior emerged, leading a large band of his elite fighters. Before them he fell dead, and another fighter with him, and several more were wounded as they retreated to higher ground. As Porter's soldiers took the village, followed by groups of Hapa'a and Teii, three were hit by spears and stones, but the Americans coolly kept firing, killing several more natives and driving the rest into the woods. In another skirmish, more Taipi were killed, yet the stones and spears continued to fly from the bushes, and Porter was "satis-fied, from the opposition made, that we should have to fight our whole way through the valley."

Before starting, he sent a warning to the Taipi that he would "destroy their villages" if they did not surrender. Receiving no response, he had Moui-na lead the main force to the next settlement, which they set on fire, and then the next one, and the next, until most of the upper valley was ablaze. Fighting their way toward the waterfall, Porter's army reached the capital and drove out its defenders. The "beauty and regularity of this place," he wrote, "was such as to strike every spectator with astonishment; and their grand site, or public square, was far superior to any other we had met with." Nevertheless, it was all put to the torch, and the Teii and Hapa'a "loaded themselves with plunder, after destroying bread-fruit and other trees and all the young plants they could find." The Americans now stood at the foot of the great cataract, looking back on their creation, a "scene of ruin and desolation" with thick clouds of smoke rolling up into the blue Pacific sky.

Were the Taipi ready to quit? Had they been punished enough for mocking Opotee and the moon men? Porter marched his forces back down the valley, avoiding the flames. After a half-hour break, they got ready for the big push toward the beach. "We formed the line of march," recalled Porter, "and in our route destroyed several other villages, at all of which we had some skirmishing with the enemy." Eventually they came to the strong-hold with the high stone wall. Porter ordered his men to tear it down, but they could do nothing; it was too well built. "This fortification appeared of ancient date," he decided, "and time alone can destroy it."

At the shore, Opotee was met by the chiefs of the Hapa'a, smiling and waving, and by Tavee, the natty chief of the Shoueme, bearing a white flag. Opotee "requested him to return and allay the fears of the women, who . . . were in the utmost terror, apprehensive of an attack" by the lunar killers. The Hapa'a chiefs, wrote Porter, invited him to their valley, "assuring me that an abundance of everything was already provided for us." As Porter's men ascended the first mountain on their journey home, he encountered Gattenewa. The old chief did not speak, but genuflected, placing Porter's hands on his head and resting his brow against the other's knees. Then he rose and put his hands on the white man's chest, exclaiming "Gattenewa!" and clapped his own chest, saying "Opotee!"

Porter turned "to contemplate that valley which, in the morning, we had viewed in all its beauty, the scene of abundance and happiness. A long line of smoking ruins now marked our traces from one end to the other; the opposite hills were covered with the unhappy fugitives, and the whole presented a scene of desolation and horror." The "heroic" Taipi were, he wrote, "victims of [their] own courage and mistaken pride."

At Madisonville, Porter and his men rested. A worn-out marine died a day later. By that time, the Taipi had told Opotee that "there was nothing they desired more than peace, and they would be willing to purchase my friendship on any terms." He required 400 hogs. The Taipi agreed to live peacefully with all the other tribes, who now sent in great amounts of tribute. Madisonville was overrun by swine, which could not even be corralled, so Porter set up a slaughtering operation on the beach.

"Peace now being established throughout the island," he wrote, "and the utmost harmony reigning, not only between us and the Indians, but between the tribes, they mixed with one another about our village in the most friendly manner, and the different chiefs with the priests came daily to visit me." But as great and admired as Opotee was, he had to move on. "I informed them that I should shortly leave them, and should return again at the expiration of a year," hoping to find them at peace, but fully prepared, in case of its absence, to punish the tribes "most in fault."

Porter had little to do for the next few weeks at Nukuhiva. As the refitting of the *Essex* went forward, he worked on his journal and wrote a formal report to the Navy Department recounting the challenges he had overcome and the splendid victories he had won.*

Porter thought about his next move. He could take his prizes and sail west like Lord Anson, across the wastes of the Pacific to Asia, greatly minimizing the chance of encountering British warships and likely gaining entry at Macao, Portugal's neutral port of entry to China. There he could sell his vessels and perhaps his oil, placing some of the proceeds with dependable American agents. Unencumbered by the prizes, the *Essex*, with a full crew, could complete her cruise by crossing the Indian Ocean and lurking off the Cape of Good Hope to intercept an English merchantman making her way home. Perhaps in the North Atlantic, not far from New York City, he might surprise a Royal Navy frigate and end his odyssey with

---

* In the seaport of Salem, whose Federalists had built the *Essex* and given her to the nation, Porter's report would be received with disgust, sarcasm, and incredulity, as reflected in the Federalist newspaper, the *Gazette*.

a spectacular victory. It seemed the prudent course, but there were other options and a greater temptation.

For months, Porter knew, he had been hunted, and he had been too smart for the hunters, hiding out at Nukuhiva and practicing the arts of a conqueror. If he really was something of a war god, if he had succeeded magnificently in this first cruise to the South Seas, nothing would seal his fame like surprising and destroying a superior force of pursuers. It was more than ironic that James Hillyar came for him, but in wartime no Briton was a friend. The reversal was irresistible. It would be a grand coup, written about first in his own book and then in the history books, and celebrated forever. He was certain that the *Essex* could out-sail these Britons and that his crew could outfight anyone. It was only a matter of sailing east and making contact; the rest was preordained.

Porter ordered that the *New Zealander* be loaded with barrels of whale oil from the other vessels and then sail for America under master's mate John King. The other three vessels would stay at Nukuhiva under Gamble and a skeleton crew, with a few British prisoners, to man the fort and inhabit Madisonville. If Porter had not returned or sent word within six months, Gamble was to destroy one vessel and take the other two to Valparaiso.

For his part, Porter and the *Essex* were bound for glory. He wrote, "I had done all the injury that could be done to British commerce in the Pacific, and still hoped to signalize my cruise by something more splendid before leaving that sea."

During his last days on the island, Opotee toured the remoter parts of the Teii valley, usually in the company of tribal shamans. People ran up to give him coconuts and other gifts, to which he responded with seeds from the American cornucopia, from melons and pumpkins to wheat and Indian corn. He had Wilson explain carefully the crops' cultivation and the proper way of protecting them from hogs and harvesting them, and he promised to return with whale's-tooth prizes for the best fruits and vegetables. Although the islanders had their own sort of bread, Opotee showed them how to make wheat into flour for baking bread like that produced at Madisonville's ovens, of which the women had become "extravagantly fond."

When not playing seed king or spending quality time at home with his fifteen-year-old lover, Opotee visited the interior of Nooahevah. "In one of those excursions," he wrote, "I was led to the chief place of religious ceremony" up in the Havvou valley. In a "large and handsome grove" of trees at the foot of a steep mountain, he encountered a shrine and a deity statue "formed of hard stone, about the common height of a man but larger-proportioned every other way." Around it were others, made of wood, all "handsomely decorated with streamers of white cloth, which give an elegant and picturesque appearance." To the right and left stood obelisks about thirty-five feet high, made of bamboo and palm leaves, festooned with the heads of hogs and tortoises, "offerings to their gods."

Nearby, Porter noticed four splendid war canoes, "furnished with their outriggers and decorated with ornaments of human hair, coral shells, etc., with abundance of white streamers." They seemed ready for a voyage, and Porter took a harder look: the big canoes were headed away from the shrine toward the mountainside, and in the stern of each, steering with a paddle, was the figure of a man "in full dress," ornamented with plumes, earrings, and other fashionable items. Through Wilson, Opotee inquired "who the dignified personage might be" in the largest canoe. He was informed that it was a corpse, that of "the priest who had been killed, not long since, by the Happahs."

Porter was fascinated. The "stench here was intolerable" as he approached the dead man's canoe and "found the bodies of two of the Typees, whom we had killed"—his own victims—"in a bloated state, at the bottom . . . and many other human carcasses, with the flesh still on them, lying about the canoe." Pursuing his ghastly interest, Opotee learned that the other canoes belonged to "warriors who had been killed or died not long since." The Taipi had been put in the big canoe, said the shaman, because the priest, now a god, could only be paddled to paradise by enemy warriors killed in battle. "A full crew" of ten was needed—two more dead Taipi fighters—and then the priest-god would begin his journey, with a sea stock of red hogs, which snuffled in an enclosure nearby, and choice coconuts and breadfruit. Opotee asked if he had far to go. No, said the shamans, pointing to a modest square enclosure of stones: "that was their heaven, that he was to go there" by way of a river of smoke and an island in the sky.

Opotee strolled over to inspect the wooden statues, whose facial features were exaggerated in typical *tiki* style. The shamans went with him, eager to call attention to symbols of their supernatural power. They grasped the icons' large ears, but their visitor seemed indifferent; they ran their hands over the wide lips as if to make them talk, and they widened their own eyes as they traced the enormous goggling eyes of the statues. Unmoved, Opotee told them that they treated their gods disrespectfully. No, they said, not at all. These were but attendants like themselves, guardians of the grove and of the small house in which resided the greatest of the gods.

Opotee wanted a look, but the shamans hesitated. They consulted in whispers, then walked over and ducked through the doorway of the shrine. When they came out, solemnly proceeding, they held an effigy lashed to a spear, with a head made of strips of cloth, resembling "a child in swaddling clothes." At the sight of this most sacred relic of the island people—so reminiscent of the divine infant of his own forgotten religion—their conqueror guffawed.

The shamans went stiff and looked at each other, then at the scoffing alien. "I could not help laughing at the ridiculous appearance of the god they worshipped," he confessed. The holy men recovered quickly. They appeased Opotee with animated nods and smiles and "a great deal of good humor, some of them dandling and nursing the god, as a child would her doll."

Chapter Eleven

Rendezvous

I n the first light of February 8, 1814, two vessels approached the high bluffs
of the Point of Angels at the entrance to Valparaiso Harbor. As they did
so, Captain James Hillyar, in command of the *Phoebe* and the squadron, and
Captain Tucker of the *Cherub* spotted a sloop sailing toward them with men
waving and a voice calling in English of a naval sort; it was George O'Brien,
mate of a British merchantman. He came up with *Phoebe* and stood in the
sheets of his little boat alongside the great warship, hollering that he had
news of the highest importance. He was taken up, and he was not wrong.
The American frigate *Essex*, he said, was anchored in the outer harbor two
miles off; her commander, David Porter, had thrown a grand party on board
ship the night before, with wine flowing freely and all the fine ladies and
gentlemen of Valparaiso dancing into the small hours. The *Essex* remained
vulnerable, with tents and awnings on deck, officers surely passed out in
their cabins, and half the men ashore in the city. There was another American vessel, a corvette of twenty guns, but not a real warship and not a threat:
Captain Hillyar would know what to do.

The visitor claimed to have been a lieutenant in the Royal Navy,
cashiered for youthful indiscretions but forever loyal and more than willing
to put his men at the captain's disposal. Aware of Porter's love of tricks and
impersonation, Hillyar wondered about this bold man O'Brien but judged
him a sincere patriot and sent word to Captain Tucker that the six-month
hunt for the *Essex* might well come to an end that very morning. Hillyar's
chief officer, the excellent Lieutenant William Ingram, ordered the drum-

mers to beat to quarters, and the decks of the *Phoebe* seethed with sailors and marines throwing on their clothes and rushing to battle stations to make an entrance that old Valparaiso would never forget.

Hillyar rounded the point and had to tack his way forward across the moderate breeze coming off the land. To the right, under cloudy skies, was the conquistadors' fort, Castello Viejo, on the cliffside at Point Antonio, forming one pillar of the harbor; in the distance, two miles to the east across the calm waters, stood the walls of another fort, the Castello el Baron. Presumably there was nothing to worry about. As Hillyar knew from having visited in September, Valparaiso welcomed all flags.

Dead ahead, in the outer anchorage off the old fort, the *Essex* lay at her mooring, not exactly the picture of disarray. Quietly Hillyar gave orders, and Ingram sent his lieutenants and midshipmen throughout the vessel to see that all was in readiness for the terrible surprise. It was 7:30. In half an hour, with two or three more stretches across the wind, the men of the *Phoebe* would be throwing a party of their own.

Porter was wide awake. Lieutenant Wilmer had roused him at six o'clock to say that he had received a signal from the *Essex Junior* offshore that two vessels were approaching, perhaps frigates. Porter had given the order to fire a shot, and in a few minutes the liberty-men, one-third of the well-drilled crew, had swarmed down to the wharves and into the boats. Porter directed that the *Essex* be prepared for action, and then he joined Downes on board *Essex Junior* to get a good look at the vessels in the offing. It was true: both were English, one a frigate, obviously intending to enter an open port guarded by three forts against any hostile action. Porter was back on board the *Essex* well before eight o'clock, eager for the rendezvous, fully prepared for the worst. The *Essex Junior* took a position nearby so that the two vessels could defend each other.

Entering the harbor, *Phoebe* was alone, guns thrust from her ports, sails taut on a reach, while *Cherub* fell off below the *Essex Junior*, out of view of the *Essex*. In the semi-darkness belowdecks, the gun crews strained forward and the boys stood by with their big, lighted matches, awaiting a command. *Phoebe* came on fast at the *Essex*, headed straight for her starboard stern quarter. Captain Hillyar stood at the port gunwale of his quarterdeck in his peacoat, grim-faced, sword drawn, with the fate of ships and men in his hand. Ahead of him, down along the rail, disguised by the shadows and the tangle of lines, a hundred armed men crouched in readiness for boarding. At the last second, Hillyar murmured the command, and the bow of the *Phoebe* swung in a tight arc, reversing her course. As she started to come alongside the *Essex*, Hillyar clenched; with his first clear view, he realized that it was all wrong. The target's railing and rigging were thick with armed men ready to board, and her gunports showed the black mouths of carronades. Hillyar had not sprung a trap; he had entered one. Quickly stepping up on an after gun, he did the only thing that might possibly undo the impending disaster: he called out, loudly and pleasantly as if across a London street, "Captain Hillyar's compliments to Captain Porter! Hoping Captain Porter is well!"

The crews of both vessels stood in a frenzy of anxiety, watching, waiting, breathless. Time and the world had contracted to this climactic moment, and to Porter. He looked at his men, poised for slaughter; then he met the gaze of his sworn enemy and old friend, just a few yards away, and shouted, "Very well, I thank you!" in civil captain's diction, as *Phoebe* came closer, "but I hope you will not come too near!" His voice was rising. "Some accident might take place! Some confusion," he yelled, "that would be disagreeable to you!" Porter's absurd words did not stop the aggressor. Staring at Hillyar, he saw the pained white mask and felt the wave of shocked silence as the ship of war, moving on its own, loomed closer and closer, thrusting and sidling toward conjunction.

Before Porter spoke again, a Yankee powder boy, still drunk from his big night ashore, saw a face grinning at him from an opposite gunport and snapped. "Damn your eyes, I'll stop you laughing at me!" He went to touch his match to the cannon's powder hole. In another second, the two ships would erupt in volcanic blood and fire, but Lieutenant McKnight, too quick, knocked the boy sprawling, and the gun stayed mute. Instead Porter roared, "Prepare to repel boarders!" Instantly, the kedge anchors went flying out to the ends of the yards, poised to drop to the enemy's deck and fasten them in a fatal embrace.

Hillyar ordered Ingram to back all yards, to reverse his ship's progress and get clear if still possible. Furious now, Porter did not notice. He called out a final warning, "Sir, I am prepared to receive you! But know that I shall only act on the defensive!" Hillyar gathered himself, affecting nonchalance. Coolly, almost casually, he said, "Oh sir! I have no such intentions." At that the bow of the *Phoebe* began pulling back in massive intimacy, very slowly, nearly grazing the forequarter of *Essex* alongside, almost touching the American's yards overhead. Every eye watched the subtle movements, entranced. *Phoebe* was uncontrollable at this point, unresponsive to her helm, but

Porter felt her malevolence, unaccompanied by any human hostility. "No contact! Not a rope yarn! All hands, prepare to board," he cried hoarsely, and his men pressed harder against the rails, and the boys held their matches a little closer. Still they watched, calibrating, wincing, and Porter bellowed once more, "Board her, men—board her the instant the hulls touch!" Hillyar dropped his pose and pleaded, abjectly, trying to prevent the explosion: "I had no intention of getting on board of you! I had no intention of coming so near you! I am sorry I came so near you!"

Out of her full stall—the classic maneuver for boarding the enemy, executed perfectly here in the Bay of Valparaiso—the *Phoebe* slowly slid away, stern foremost, toward the expectant *Essex Junior*, and at right angles to the silence of the bristling broadside carronades of the *Essex*.

"Don't be alarmed," called out Hillyar's Lieutenant Ingram, "we shall not touch you." From the *Essex*, sword and pistol at the ready, Lieutenant McKnight responded, "We are not at all alarmed! And we wish you *would* touch us!"

Hillyar raised his hands in surrender and apology, extending the moment, desperately trying to make contact across the years. Porter knew that Hillyar had meant to attack—but James kept calling to David, cajoling, apologizing for an accident, saying nothing hostile had been meant by it; it was a freak mistake. Horrified and calm, Hillyar endured the aftermath as his vessel backed into a position of total vulnerability. Porter had an ideal chance to destroy the *Phoebe*. In an instant, her deck would be swept by the gigantic firepower of the thirty-two-pound smashers, and she would not be able to answer; the carnage would be awesome.

Glory came calling, but David Porter just stood there. "The *Phoebe* is at this moment completely at my mercy," he thought. With a few words, he could still trigger the cataclysm to make the pleading face disappear and the vessel with it, in a chaos of smoke and thunder. The encounter would end in triumph, and the Pacific would be his. Porter, for once, held back. "I was disarmed by these assurances of Captain Hillyar," he bravely confessed. The encounter had touched him at some deep level, at a core of gratitude, ten years dormant, toward a kind man who had welcomed him into his family. Despite a lifetime of navy training, Porter let the long moment pass; then he raised his speaking trumpet and called over to the *Essex Junior*: "Hold your fire, Lieutenant Downes! Hold your fire! It is my intention to allow Captain Hillyar to extricate himself from this situation!"

Serenely, the drifting *Phoebe* swung around on her keel as the light breeze filled her sails, and James Hillyar got her under way and sailed right past the *Essex Junior*, looking straight ahead at the little fort in the distance with its unfamiliar flag. He brought *Phoebe* to anchor well beyond the range of Porter's carronades and stood quietly on the quarterdeck for a while, by himself, thanking God Almighty and reflecting on his incredible error and the miracle of having his life and career handed back to him.

Next day David Porter met with James Hillyar at the Englishman's request. Porter, thirty-three, was dark, small, "ardent and impetuous," and full of notions of chivalry. Hillyar, forty-four, was burly, pink, "cool and calculating." They sat together affably, almost as if nothing had happened. After pleasantries—each sirred the other, like knights, in high genteel style—they discussed the terms of being together in the harbor of Valparaiso in time of war. Porter wanted it understood that only the concept of neutrality, so dear to Americans, had saved *Phoebe* from destruction: Do you intend, he asked, to respect the neutrality of this port? Hillyar gave him a look and replied, "Sir, you have paid such respect to the neutrality of this port that I feel myself bound in honour to do the same." If Porter had not paid that respect, there would have been no meeting that morning of two brave captains who had flinched in the face of catastrophe—a good thing for them and for their men, but not for their careers or reputations—so this post-facto discussion of neutrality gave them some cover. Their old friendship and the shock of this encounter had suddenly turned them into inverse mirror images: Hillyar had been reckless, Porter restrained. Had Hillyar acted as intended, scores of Englishmen would have died and he would have lost his ship; had Porter reacted predictably, he would have won imperishable fame.

Hillyar sized up his companion. At Gibraltar, in days of American-British peace, he had known Porter as a charming, restless, curious specimen of American self-creation, eager to learn and always good company. He had not considered him as an opponent, but as a brash, interesting young friend. What did he know about him now, except that, in yesterday's showdown, each had surprised the other? Obviously Porter had been having it all his own way in the South Sea, ultimately embarrassing the Admiralty with his unexpected pillaging, but a rampage through a dozen undefended whaleships manned largely by American Quakers could not be considered a feat of naval arms. Bainbridge, Hull, and Lawrence had made their names as American heroes of the Atlantic, capable of defeating the best of the

Royal Navy in a fair fight, but Porter of the Pacific remained a rogue, a ruffian robbing civilians, untested in the rigorous and unforgiving arena of heavyweight combat at sea. Hillyar had fought those battles for years; he had learned the craft of the victor, and he had presided at the funerals of those who had helped him win his laurels. It was a serious business. God was in it, and it required the highest talents of good decision-making and the combination of several rare qualities in one man, able to exercise his gifts under great pressure, in extremity.

Looking into Porter's lively brown eyes, Hillyar wondered about this man with a face so sunburned and scarred, and thought about the meaning of their encounter the day before and its portents for the next one. What was he doing here? If he had captured all of the English whalers and sent them on their way across the seas, as he obviously had, why was he still at Valparaiso? Hillyar could reach no logical conclusion. It was a mystery, and they were both stuck with it.

Hillyar also wondered about himself, and whether he would have fired his guns had he stood in Porter's boots. For his part, he had miscalculated his opponent's strength and balked at the last second. It was not a good moment for him, and it might still cost him his life, yet he could feel that he had done the right thing. Porter was in the more difficult position. At the critical instant, he had not exercised the right of self-defense, especially when he had the upper hand over a superior force. Was it a noble and chivalrous forbearance, or was it a weakness, a failure? Porter must have had deeply mixed emotions as he sat sipping with his fortunate former friend.

Porter had been at Valparaiso for only five days before *Phoebe's* arrival; earlier, he had been cruising nearby for two weeks, looking for Hillyar and British shipping. As Opotee, fresh from Nukuhiva, he had been re-acclimating to the reality that he was matched against ruthless uniformed men, his equals, warriors sent out on fatal missions. He had called on the city governor, Francisco de la Lastra, to discuss the status of his anchorage in the harbor and his hope that he would be protected as his vessels lay under the guns of the city's forts. Porter did not realize, nor did Lastra inform him, that Hillyar had already visited Valparaiso on his mission to eliminate Americans from the Pacific.

Hillyar had met Lastra in January upon arriving from the palace at Lima, quite pleased at his progress with Abascal. Unable to hold power without the support of the British, whose army was closing out the war against Napoleon in Spain and whose navy dominated the seas, the viceroy had agreed with Hillyar on the shape of things to come, expressed in a peace treaty that would re-establish Spanish royal control over Chile without reprisals against the rebels. To show good faith, Abascal had given him eleven Chilean prisoners, captured during the debacle of the *Perla* and the *Potrillo*, to be taken to Valparaiso and set free.

Hillyar had divulged to Lastra that Abascal had authorized him to offer terms of peace in Chile, perhaps implying that these were not negotiable. Lastra had no intention of rejecting a proposal delivered by Captain Hillyar offering a way to end a conflict that was verging on civil war, and to restore the connection of Chile to its true king, Fernando VII. These were not the special pleadings of an individual but the policies of the great nations from which all power in the world ultimately derived. Indeed, Hillyar "might have been said to govern the country from the moment he came to an anchor in Valparaiso." Abascal's terms had been presented as follows: Chile should dissolve the junto, resume the former arrangement with Lima, and recognize the sovereignty of King Fernando; Lima would evacuate its troops from the territory of Chile; and Chile would be allowed to open her ports to the commerce of England.

Hillyar had known that Lastra would impress upon the junto the wisdom of acceptance. To give them time, Hillyar had gathered up his vessels and men and cleared the Bay of Valparaiso to go looking for the *Essex*.

Moving on from the chilly Lastra, Porter met with Samuel Johnston and Edward Barnewall and heard the story of their betrayal as officers of Lastra's Chilean navy. After five months of imprisonment, illness, and brutal treatment in Lima, they had been sent to Valparaiso in November. Then Hillyar met with Consul Poinsett and learned what Lastra had withheld from him: the Carreras had been betrayed—José Miguel and Luis were in prison at Chillan, and Juan José had been banished to Mendoza—and Hillyar was negotiating with the viceroy and with O'Higgins and the junto for the surrender of Chile.

With an imperial policy in place and a long record of achievement, Britain—defender of Spain and sender of ships, men, munitions, and Hillyar's squadron—had gained the advantage. Poinsett, fighting in the field for the nationalists, had done his best, but the U.S. Congress and Porter had not delivered in the ways that London and Hillyar had.

When Captain Hillyar next met with the governor, he insisted that Lastra seize Porter and his vessels and prizes in the harbor. The American had obviously violated neutrality and had no right to hold British whale-ships in Chilean waters. Lastra responded that he did not have the authority, at which Hillyar threatened to delegate the authority to himself. Then he went straight to the junto to see if they could be bullied.

Hillyar figured that Porter would try to escape soon, for other Royal Navy vessels were on their way. Flight was far more likely than fight; the *Essex* was much faster than Hillyar's vessels and could not vanquish the team of the *Phoebe*, at fifty-three actual guns,* and *Cherub*, at twenty-eight—the converted whaler called the *Essex Junior* would be nearly useless in a naval battle. Hillyar meant to get food and water aboard his ships swiftly and then blockade the Americans until reinforcements arrived, but he was unprepared for what happened next. Porter's men started taunting the English boatmen as they sailed past on their provision runs, and they took to singing songs and cheering the frequent displays of their pennant with the motto "Free Trade & Sailors' Rights." At first it was just annoying, but soon it became galling. Hillyar worried about his crew; many had been forced into service, and some might be tempted to defect. He authorized retaliation, and one day the *Phoebe* displayed its own pennant, emblazoned "God & Country, British Sailors' Best Rights, Traitors Offend Both." It was not as snappy as the Americans' motto, but the British sailors soon established themselves as the better singers, largely thanks to their band, which would strike up *God Save the King* several times a day accompanied by a full-throated glee club rendition, then swing to another tune about a "sweet little cherub," with three rousing cheers preceding and following.

The Americans, led by Porter, repeatedly belted out the national song, *Yankee Doodle*, complete with new stanzas and choice lyrics for their audience, and they raised a second pennant, inscribed "God, Our Country, and Liberty—Tyrants Offend Them." Both sides exchanged snide poems and bawdy chants, of which the Englishmen's were better performed but the Americans' were funnier. The competition was intense, and many skirmishes erupted. Longboats rammed each other in the harbor, and brutal blue-eyed brawls broke out along the wharves and byways of old Valparaiso. Quite disturbed about the level of ferocity, Hillyar, in closing a report to his superiors, wrote: "I expect an awful combat if the two ships meet, but

---

* Whatever the rating of a vessel in terms of her standard armament, the captain was at liberty to add more weaponry as long as it did not affect seaworthiness. Long guns were much heavier than carronades, for example, so that fewer long guns could make way for many more carronades or other types of shorter-range guns.

humbly wish to repose my trust in God's goodness for a favorable result."
Porter had no such concerns and no such trust.

Although the crews had worked up an intense loathing, none of this
achieved Porter's intended effect, which was to goad Hillyar into a one-on-
one battle. Ever mindful of the Admiralty's admonitions, prohibitions, and
expectations, Hillyar celebrated in his cabin when his provisioned vessels
finally sailed out of the harbor to take up a blocking position just offshore.
For a day or two, Porter watched them with the restless intensity of a tiger, snorting at their inferior sailing qualities and wanting desperately to
do something terrible to provoke them. One evening he towed one of his
English prizes to a central spot in the harbor and set her on fire, purely as an
insult, and for several hours the *Hector* lit up all of Valparaiso and its neutral
waters with her magnificent burning. Next day the dead body of the hull was
dragged away, charred and wallowing. Later, Porter, the battle-happy Achil-
les, further insulted British pride by setting fire to his prize the *Catharine*,
but this too failed to rile Hillyar to action.

Of course Hillyar was angry, and his anger was shared by the small
but influential British merchant group at Valparaiso, who demanded that
Lastra afford better treatment of their own vessels, moored not far from Porter's shocking bonfires. Their outrage flared higher when it was learned that
Porter kept English prisoners in the hold of his frigate, which he admitted
was true. It was also true that the prisoners were held in chains as punishment for their perfidy on a faraway island, and so they would remain until
Porter saw fit to set them at liberty, perhaps when Lastra was removed and
Carrera restored to power. Some felt that Porter deserved a come-uppance,
an attempt at which was exactly what he wanted.

At times Porter and the *Essex* made a feint at escape, but the two
British captains sailed together with vigilant lookouts, and the moment never came. Once, when the *Cherub* got far to leeward, Porter came out toward
the *Phoebe*, which fired a shot and had a shot returned before she jibed away
toward the *Cherub*, chased by two cannonballs from Porter's long twelves as
he returned the *Essex* to her mooring. Cheated of his epochal battle, Porter
seethed and smarted and denounced Hillyar as a coward in remarks that
were repeated in the streets and taverns of Valparaiso and finally reported
to Hillyar and his officers. A boat with a flag of truce approached the *Essex*
from the sea; it was Lieutenant William Ingram, Hillyar's chief officer, a
handsome fellow and a notable hothead. Much like Porter himself, he was
earnest, romantic in his conception of war, and full of the cant of chivalry

and honor. Ingram, wishing to deliver a letter from Hillyar, was welcomed aboard and invited to the officers' quarters to parley.

"I understand," said Ingram, "that you have called Captain Hillyar a coward for running away from the *Essex*, and I beg to know if this is the case."

Porter looked Ingram in the eye and said that he considered Captain Hillyar to have issued a challenge by charging upwind and firing his cannon. With his own salute, he had accepted, but instead of a fight he had got a look at his opponent's receding stern. Given the conduct of the *Phoebe* in bearing up and running away, he affirmed that "anything he might have said about that occasion was justifiable."

"I assure you, sir, that no challenge was intended," responded Ingram. "The firing of our cannon was an unfortunate accident."

"Accident or not," said Porter, "I supposed it to be a challenge, and made it plain that I accepted it. And let me say that it cannot be expected that I would take upon myself the responsibility of challenging a 36-gun frigate with a frigate of 32 guns, as my country would censure me should I prove unsuccessful." To make his position unmistakable, he added, "The difference of force will not prevent my accepting a challenge given by Captain Hillyar."

Ingram thanked Porter for his generous candor and asked to be given leave to return to his pinnace. Instead, Porter invited him on a tour. Stem to stern, deck by deck, Porter proudly showed off his beloved frigate and introduced the Englishman to members of the crew wherever encountered. Ingram was well received. Porter's young aide, Midshipman Farragut, wrote that Ingram's "manly, frank, and chivalrous bearing quite won the hearts of all on board. Whilst admiring her, he said it would be the happiest moment of his life to take *Essex* to England if we could take her in a fair fight; to which Captain Porter replied that, if such an event had to occur, he knew of no British officer to whom he would more readily yield his honor—and in this sentiment all our officers and crew sincerely coincided." The impressive Lieutenant Ingram shook hands all around and was helped over the side to his little boat, with his new friends wishing him well as he pushed away from the side of the noble *Essex* and began the trip back to report to his stolid and vigilant commander.

After that, Porter set his British prisoners free in Valparaiso, but he remained obsessed with Hillyar and *Phoebe*. Somehow she had to be brought to combat before she was reinforced and he could neither fight nor escape.

His restless inventiveness and piratical imagination led to more strange proceedings. One night Porter gathered his crews and filled ten boats with armed men. Away they went over the moonless sea toward the sleeping *Phoebe*, to take her by boarding. The Americans made it to their target undetected, and Porter himself got under her bows, ready to spring; but in the blackness above he heard the English crewmen chatting, and discovered that Captain Hillyar had them drilling that night at battle quarters.

Events in Chile had continued to be unfavorable to Poinsett and the interests of the United States. After being informed by the new junto that he was to surrender the command of the armies to O'Higgins, José Miguel Carrera was visited by O'Higgins in Concepcion. They had spent a year together fighting, not always happily but with respect and the deep friendship of brothers in arms. They had battled ceaselessly for their country, and Chile meant more to both of them than any personal interest. O'Higgins had come away from this meeting still loyal to his chief and had gone on to meet with the junto at Talca. There he had declared his unwillingness to take on the generalship, while allowing that Carrera had said he would be willing to step aside in order to save the republic of Chile.

O'Higgins reminded the junto members that he had begun as "an ordinary guerilla" and "lacked the training for a senior officer commanding armies." They had conferred, and replied that Carrera was out and would never be reinstated and that all of the Carreras had been stripped of their commissions and banished from service. O'Higgins had submitted without protest. Agreeing to consult the junto in all important war-related matters, he had returned to Concepcion. On February 2, 1814, O'Higgins had become commander in chief of the patriot army, reduced to 1,800 soldiers, with hundreds leaving in anger because of the expulsion of their leader, José Miguel Carrera, and his gallant brothers, Colonel Luis and General Juan José.

At about that same time, Viceroy Abascal had sent out a new commander, Brigadier General Gabino Gainza, with 200 troops and large amounts of arms and provisions, to land in the south at Arauco and demand the capitulation of Concepcion and the surrender of the rebels. O'Higgins, in his first test, had been advised by the junto to clear out of the south and retreat to the Maule River, which was held by the newly promoted General Juan Mackenna and his army. O'Higgins hesitated. Should he not renew the attack on Chillan before the two royalist forces combined? He continued to consult Carrera, whose brother Juan José Carrera, furious, organized a troop and set off for Santiago, vowing in public to overthrow the junto that had betrayed his great-hearted brother.

The junto ordered José Miguel and Luis to leave the province of Concepcion. With thirty-one loyal officers—the flower of the patriot army—and seventy retainers, they started out for Santiago on March 2, 1814. At dawn two days later, while sleeping at a farmhouse, the party was attacked by a detachment of royalists. Several of the guards were killed before the Carreras and other officers could surrender. As they were brought into Chillan, the royalist troops chanted, "Long live the king! Death to the Carreras!" They were led into the presence of Gainza, who sat with a big sombrero pulled down over his eyes at a small table with a candle on a watermelon rind. His prisoner boldly proposed that Gainza join him in a war against the Larrains; José Miguel Carrera had no doubt that he could take over the government at Santiago and restore independence to Chile. Gainza laughed and told Carrera that he was crazy and that he and his brother would be kept under guard until they were arraigned on charges of treason against the king.

After Carrera's resignation, the rebel army at Concepcion dwindled, and news arrived that Britain had achieved victory in Spain and restored the rule of Fernando VII, who intended to reassemble Spain's shattered empire. Under General Gainza, Abascal's army at Chillan was reinforced from Lima and began its march northward. The junto fled toward Santiago. On March 8, when the capital learned of the fall of Talca, "terror, dismay, and confusion reigned among all classes of its citizens."

The junto faced a crisis. Gainza's royalist army having defeated Mackenna's forces, Santiago was exposed and O'Higgins had to withdraw from Concepcion province. Forfeiting all to the royalists, he slowly went north, with his men dragging the cannons for lack of mules. Gainza moved between the two rebel armies. O'Higgins, coming on, engaged and defeated a small force. Mackenna's troops did the same. On March 23 they finally combined and began the sprint for Santiago to try to block Gainza.

Both armies raced across the Rio Maule. Gainza, with the smaller force, saw that he could not sustain an attack on Santiago due to the oncoming winter and the need to increase the size and supply lines for his troops. He decided to withdraw to Talca or Chillan. The patriot army was given a respite to recruit its strength and to hold and consolidate the province of Santiago. People were very unhappy. Central Chile had suffered great losses in crops, cattle, and men, and there had been no trade with Peru and little with anyone else. The popular favorite, José Miguel Carrera, betrayed by the junto, was still in prison or perhaps dead somewhere to the south. Chile might still be subject to devastating punishment from the royalists. Other independence movements in South America were failing too—even in Buenos Aires, where there was fatal internecine political rivalry but good military leadership from the man who had emerged as the top general, José de San Martin, governor at Mendoza.

The junto, reviled on suspicion of having sold out the country, was surrounded by a large crowd and rescued by Juan José Carrera, at the head of the artillery, who pledged to carry out the will of the assembled people. Meeting *en masse*, they voted to expel the junto and install a new system led by a dictator who would rule on behalf of the Larrains. The names of Irissari and Lastra were proposed. On March 14, 1814, the people chose Francisco de la Lastra, thirty-eight, former governor of Valparaiso, as the supreme director of Chile. Lastra had once confessed to David Porter that he doubted whether independence was right for Chile; now, as head of government, he looked forward to talks with Captain Hillyar and others who might solve the problem of what to do with a semi-sovereign state that was retracting its revolution.

In its final act, the junto signed a decree declaring its own dissolution and requiring that all men in Santiago be issued weapons, and that all royalists be placed on board prison ships at Valparaiso. Lastra gave the job at Valparaiso to "a certain Captain Formas, who had been disgraced by Carrera for cowardice." In Santiago, Lastra ignored the resolutions of the junto regarding arming a militia and imprisoning royalists, but he eagerly proceeded with the ceremony in which he was invested with the title and powers of supreme director.

Poinsett had to recognize these events as the end of his mission. In acknowledging the demise of an independent Chile, he had to give up on his hopes for the liberation of the rest of Spanish America. In the absence of José Miguel Carrera, he drew close to Porter, the only other American official in Chile. Porter, for his part, told Poinsett that he was ready to escape. He too had given up—had abandoned, regretfully, his fantasy of knights errant jousting offshore, frigate to frigate, for all the glory in the Pacific. He had failed to sting the Englishman into combat. Disciplined and determined, terrified of failure and obedient to the Admiralty's ban on one-on-one frigate battles, Hillyar had maintained his strategy of inglorious containment while enduring the taunts and feints of the angry little American.

Concealing his intent, Porter shuttled back and forth to the wharves. Poinsett was a frequent visitor and confrere, and Porter sent ashore his purser, John Shaw, to act the part of a provision-dealer conspicuously offering a weeklong opportunity for trade. Poinsett and Porter had a lot to talk about, including the likelihood of a land-based royalist attack and the possibility of enough confusion that Porter might sneak off to sea. At the same time, Poinsett's contacts among the rebels were reporting rumors of the near approach of another British battleship.

Porter, the illusionist, let go of the illusion of victory. Knowing that he could outsail both of his tormentors, his escape was mainly a matter of proper timing and sleight-of-ship, of seizing the moment with a favorable wind and opponents who were too far to leeward to stop him when he jumped. His adventure would end, he knew, without the glory that he had sought in the Pacific, but the Atlantic was full of British frigates, and who was to say that he would not defeat one on his way to New York?

Chapter Twelve

Victory

Shortly before midnight on Sunday, March 27, 1814, one year after he had sailed from England, James Hillyar was awoken in his cabin and told what his lookouts had seen. He made a quick assessment and in a few minutes *Phoebe* and *Cherub* were surging downwind toward small dancing blue lights and then the white flare of rockets. Hillyar signaled repeatedly but was not answered, and by half past one he knew that he was chasing "the enemy's boats as a decoy." Not to be fooled further, he came about and spoke the *Cherub*, instructing Captain Tucker to follow him upwind toward the harbor, where he spied the outline of the tall spars of the sleeping *Essex*, still riding at anchor. The breeze was strong, much fresher than he had thought, and suddenly, with a noise like a gunshot, Hillyar's main topsail split. In a few minutes it was replaced and a triple-reef taken, and he prudently double-reefed the other topsails out of respect for the squall.

At dawn, Porter saw his British opponents, royals doused, sailing to windward of the Point of Angels, the headland beyond the western limits of the harbor. This was a disappointment, for he had hoped that *Phoebe* and *Cherub* might be to leeward, where Lieutenant Maury's blue-light boats had lured them the night before. Still, anything could happen on this day, which began cloudy, with light winds in the harbor promising to turn nasty offshore. Consul Poinsett, who had spent the night on board, spent the day with Porter discussing rumors and assessing possibilities. Poinsett, as it happened, was not ready to depart; he had been hearing reports from the south of massing armies and the possibility of a great victory for O'Higgins and the realization of Chilean independence. As the hours passed, Porter grew cheerful. The weather was making up from the southwest and had "increased to a strong gale." The *Essex* was a splendid heavy-weather sailer, and conditions were perfect for a race that Porter's ship would win—but he wanted to get a great start.

A few of his officers, ashore in town that afternoon to secure fresh provisions, were "in the midst of emptying a few bottles in the home of the Rosales family," staunch friends of Americans, when the sound of the cannon, Porter's signal, "made them all snatch up their caps and, without further goodbye than 'Farewell forever!' dash into their boat shouting huzzahs." They got on board at about three o'clock. With final plans made and his uppermost royal masts lowered, Porter hailed the *Essex Junior* to send a boat. About a half-mile away, Hillyar and Tucker came bowling in toward the anchorage area. They could not see Porter cut his port anchor cable and raise the starboard anchor. Poinsett left in the boat, Porter shouted his commands, and suddenly the *Essex* blossomed in canvas and charged off to windward, opposite the incoming British. A little late, Hillyar brought his vessels about and started the chase. He set his mainsail in the "fresh gales and heavy squalls," and he and Tucker each streamed their ensigns reading "God & Country, British Sailors' Best Rights, Traitors Offend Both."

Porter flew ahead of them, carrying a perilously heavy press of canvas; but he had done it before, in the desperate weather of Cape Horn, and he had seamen aloft to take in sail if ordered. His escape plan was working. He stepped back to inspect his flexing topmasts and straining topsails, and he muttered to the storm gods as the frigate crashed forward, groaning in the squall, surging along by the high bluffs at the head of the Point of Angels. A hundred yards from the open sea, she suddenly slowed amid the thunder of luffing canvas. Porter cursed violently. He had sailed too close to the cliffs and lost his wind; but the *Essex* rode along on momentum, and in a minute she would be in the clear. Astern were the British pursuers; aloft were the men on the yardarms; ahead lay the wide ocean and a clear path to America. Porter gave no orders, trusting to the strength of the *Essex*. As the vessel emerged from the unwanted calm of the shore, she caught the renewed force of the gale and the great ship leaped ahead, heeling so hard that the deckhands had to scramble as she buried her lee rail. And then there was a terrible noise as the main topmast and its tower of sails came crashing down and two men went screaming into space. In an instant, at the very verge of freedom, the *Essex* had broken.

But not David Porter. If he could get his ship back to the neutral zone of the harbor, all would be well. It was possible; it was certain. He gave orders to put her on starboard tack and to cut away the main topsail, fouled by the wreckage. Someone thought to toss over the wooden life buoy. Crewmen swarmed up and onto the yards and worked furiously, but the *Essex* could not get around in time to beat her pursuers to the anchorage—Hillyar and Tucker blocked her from whatever safety the harbor anchorage might have afforded, and the guns of the fort at Castello Viejo were silent. Captain Formas was not about to intervene on behalf of the arrogant American.

Porter panicked. He could not head out to sea; his vessel was injured, and Hillyar and Tucker would run him down like wolves. His best chance was to get near the shore and claim protection. Others on board thought Porter mad; the *Essex* was by far the fastest of the battleships, and they ought to keep going. A new topmast could be sent up and new sails bent on—the drills of a very long cruise had made the crew crackerjack at such things. Although *Phoebe* would gain during the process, *Cherub* was a "dull sailer" that would not keep up, and no vessel could carry full topsails and topgallants in the storm anyway. At close quarters the *Essex*, with twenty, thirty-two-pound carronade guns to a side, would devastate *Phoebe* in the first exchange and set up the chance for boarding or for pulling away.

For whatever reasons, David Porter did not consider this scenario, which was the only one that drew on the considerable strengths of his vessel and her armament. He had survived *Phoebe*'s first pass in February by maintaining his rights at anchorage, and now he thought of a spot along the coast about three miles distant. Hillyar, following, was incredulous when he saw Porter run the *Essex* into a cove, douse his sails, and anchor half a pistol-shot from the shore, more than a mile from the harbor's eastern fort, the Castello El Baron. Poinsett, ashore, had followed the action on horseback, first riding toward the old fort near the Point of Angels, then doubling back once the *Essex* had fallen off toward the north, across the harbor. With Samuel Johnston and a posse of Americans, he quickly closed the three-mile gap and arrived at full gallop calling for the commandant to defend his coastline and fire the guns, but the British battleships had already passed out of range. Poinsett demanded that the guns be turned over to him on carriages so that he could move them to the hillside to help defend the *Essex*; the Chilean commander, however, had received no orders and could not allow El Consul to strip his fort of its armament.

Rashly, Porter broke out the white pennants with their taunting mottoes. As they lifted in the breeze, he had his crew start to fix the damage. "In this situation," wrote Porter, "we considered ourselves perfectly secure." Actually, only he did, on the assumption that they occupied neutral waters. Many of his loyal men felt that he was dead wrong and had forfeited any claim of immunity by leaving the harbor at the Point of Angels. *Phoebe* and *Cherub* came on toward the motionless *Essex* lying head-to-sea, the perfect target for raking fire. With a numbing sense of dread, Porter's sailors watched the British battleships advance. They now had "no chance of success" and every chance of a bloodbath unless their ship was "run ashore, throwing her broadside to the beach to prevent raking." This would let them fight "as long as consistent with humanity, and then set fire to her." Stuck in a cove, far from the harbor anchorage and the possible protection of the three Valparaiso forts, they had already lost.

About ten minutes later, at 3:55, *Phoebe* glided into position and dropped anchor, and *Cherub*, under sail, set up opposite. On board the *Phoebe*, Lieutenant Ingram pleaded with Captain Hillyar not to conduct the assault in this fashion. War should be an honorable exercise, respectful of one's opponent and of one's own feelings as a gentleman: "Let us have no *Cherub* to help us, but with the *Phoebe* alone lay the *Essex* aboard, yard-arm to yard-arm, and fight like Britons." Hillyar, incredulous, turned on Ingram. Stupidity was the last thing he expected from his gallant chief. "It is our duty," he stated sharply, "to capture the *Essex* with the least possible risk to this vessel and crew. We will use whatever means are placed at our disposal to take the enemy—an enemy who has done so much damage to British commerce, and whose escape will be attended with the most serious consequences." Ingram took the blow, apologized, and returned to the duty of preparing his gunners for a shooting gallery.

Captain Tucker opened fire. The *Cherub* was quite close to the target and had many long guns and a few carronades. The *Essex* had a few long guns bow and stern, and most of the carronades uselessly pointing in the wrong directions. Porter's constant drilling now paid off, and the forward gun crews, with only four cannon, dealt out such punishment that *Cherub* soon moved away with Captain Tucker wounded.

Phoebe began her barrage to little effect, as many of her shots went wide and some flew completely over the *Essex*. Again the Yankee gun crews fired with fatal efficiency. A few carronades found their marks, putting seven thirty-two-pound balls through *Phoebe*'s hull along the waterline, while a twelve-pounder holed her under water and another lodged squarely in her mainmast. Porter prowled the deck, cheering on his busy men. He sent a boat's crew to set a spring line on the anchor cable in order to swing the *Essex* into position for broadsides, but the spring line was shot away, and so was a second one. The stationary *Essex* took a pounding, even as her gun crews and marines kept firing. On board the *Phoebe*, Lieutenant Ingram, the handsome idealist of war, had reconciled himself to the spectacle of a one-sided artillery drill and was coolly issuing commands when a cannon shot smashed the bulwarks and a log-sized piece of railing flew up and took off the top of his head.

At Porter's side, twelve-year-old Midshipman Gatty Farragut would play many roles in a fight that, for him, began with "the horrid impression" made by "the death of the first man: it was a boatswain's mate; his abdomen was taken entirely out, and he expired in a few moments." After this man's ghastly end, the boy's overall experience of bombardment took on a different cast. The crewmen "soon fell so fast around me that it all appeared like a dream, and produced no effect on my nerves." As Farragut stood next to Porter "just abaft the mainmast, a shot came through the waterways which glanced upwards, killing four men who stood by the side of their gun, taking the last man in the head, and his brains flew over us both, but it made no such impression on me as the death of the first man. I neither thought of nor noticed anything but the working of the guns." In this way, watching the men at the cannons, fetching and placing the powder, Midshipman Farragut was able to withstand visions of devastation and carnage that might otherwise have undone him.

For all the heroism on board, there was great frustration as the marines' musketry fell short and many guns remained silent, incapable of being aimed at *Phoebe*. But some did great damage, and the well-drilled cannoneers, supervised by Samuel Johnston at the long guns, fired truly, smashing the British decks and slashing the rigging so badly that after half an hour Hillyar felt that "appearances were a little inauspicious" and gave the order to make sail to get out of range. Then the cove fell silent except for the cries of the gulls and the wounded and the murmuring of the crowds that had gathered on the hillsides.

The men of the *Essex* had fought the enemy to a standstill. Although pinned near the shore, Porter's frigate remained intact and afloat, and most of his crewmen were eager for more. After weeks of insults and slogans, of fistfights on land and false alarms at anchor and at sea, they had reached a fever pitch in battle, stoked by the buckets of rum laid out for them. His men, Porter knew, would fight to the end—but what might that look like? Unable to use deception or outside assistance—the Chileans in the forts had failed him—Porter still had choices. He could certainly surrender now, having put up an honorable resistance in an indefensible position. He could order his men to abandon ship and set her on fire. He could stay at anchor and fight against a vastly superior foe, sacrificing many more lives in addition to the twenty or more of his brave men who had already been killed or badly injured. Because he was David Porter, he could also imagine getting the *Essex* under way and shooting down the masts of both opponents, or pulling alongside the *Phoebe* and taking her by storm.

The British warships came to anchor beyond the reach of their target's carronades but well within range of their own long guns. Then they resumed firing, and the *Essex* began to disintegrate. For the men on board, the missiles of death came randomly, in various shapes, out of the air or from the gut-level explosion of their own cannons. At one gun station, three separate crews—fifteen men—were successively wiped out while the same gun captain survived with only scratches. As Farragut described it, there was a surreal aspect to the experience of warfare on an unsailing ship. The sailors' and marines' combat training could not be fully applied to this encounter, in which they did none of the tasks of maneuvering under sail but became the occupants of an indefensible wooden fort. They never saw their opponents, let alone fought them. It all turned abstract early on, as missiles landed and blew things up, and men and material went flying. The main killers were the massive splinters of wooden railings and deck planks—the stuff of the men's own vessel.

Such a splinter killed Lieutenant James Wilmer while he was trying to release the sheet anchor. Farragut witnessed his end, but Wilmer's aide, young Henry Ruff, did not. When Ruff asked Farragut if he had seen his lieutenant, Gatty said that he feared the lieutenant had been killed, whereupon Ruff thought for a moment and declared, "Well, if he is gone, I will go too," and jumped out a gunport to his death. In another instance, Farragut and an old quartermaster, Francis Bland, were standing near the ship's wheel when the boy saw a flying cannonball "coming over the fore yard in such a direction as I thought would hit him or me, so I told him to jump and pulled him towards me at the same instant that the shot took off his right leg."

Porter, with a spring line now on the cable, moved his vessel a bit, but not enough. He imagined an epic reversal. In his vision *Phoebe* was wounded and *Essex* was a predator. Joyfully, he gave the order to cut the

The Victory

After months of sharing the neutral waters of Valparaiso Harbor, Porter and the frigate *Essex*, thirty-two guns, tried to break away from the British frigate *Phoebe*, thirty-six guns, and the sloop of war *Cherub*, eighteen guns. The *Essex*, a fast sailer, was headed for the open sea when her topmast collapsed. Porter moored her in a cove down the coast to make repairs, but the British attacked. Keeping their distance, they methodically poured hundreds of cannon shot into the helpless American vessel, whose captain's refusal to surrender cost the lives of ninety of his men. That Porter should title this illustration "The Victory" suggests the depth of his delusions, the magnitude of his spin-doctoring, or both. *(from* Journal of a Cruise made to the Pacific Ocean, *David Porter, 1815)*

cable and fall on the enemy, but the halyards for hoisting the sails were all cut and only a jib could be raised, not enough to take the ship far in the faltering breeze. Porter's maneuver failed, and his men were being slaughtered. Still, the *Phoebe* had again retreated a bit, to find a more comfortable and safer position from which to rain down her bombs.

Death on board the *Essex* was totally random. Two men would be doing the same thing, and suddenly one's head would blow off through no agency that could be observed. For most, their jobs became their battle; they focused on the repetitive tasks needed to keep firing the cannon toward vessels so far away and so enshrouded in smoke that it was impossible to know whether the shots were having any effect. Most were not; the carronades could not reach them, and their huge projectiles only tore up the waters of the cove. The men's fight, now, was not for the United States. It was for their captain, who would not surrender; it was for their messmates; and it was for "free trade and sailors' rights." After all the singing and posturing of the weeks before, this was the phrase that the men would call out to encourage each other, and it also served as their last words, like prayers, to give meaning at the moment of death. They had all once been sailors in the merchant service and had seen their country's commerce spread across the globe and carry its reputation to all nations. The men took great pride in that, and believed in their own cause—it was why they had enlisted in the navy. If they had to die fighting, it was good to do so under the banner of "Free Trade & Sailors Rights."

Porter remained on deck, directing the action, "brave, cool, and intrepid," setting a suicidal example so that "every man appeared determined to sacrifice his life." As they died horribly, in agony, with pieces of their bodies missing, the men called to Porter to keep fighting, as if there were some hope. Now, at the finale, the *Essex* could not stay where she was and he could not close with the *Phoebe*, so he would have to get the *Essex* ashore and destroy her. The ship was making progress toward the coast when the wind shifted and pushed her bow back toward the sea, so that she was again subjected to a horrific raking fire. One bow gunner, a young Scot, was hit full-on by a cannonball and had his whole leg shot off; calmly, he tied the stump with his handkerchief and then addressed his mates: "Well boys, I adopted the United States to fight for her, and I hope I have this day shown myself worthy the country of my adoption—I am no longer of any use to you or to her, and I will not be a burthen: So, goodbye!" He hiked himself onto the sill of the port, and went over.

Twice the men doused small fires on the *Essex*, and suddenly John Downes materialized, climbing aboard out of a boat from the *Essex Junior* to receive final orders from his captain. Porter had kept the smaller vessel out of the fight to give her a chance to survive and perhaps escape. The enemy continued to rake the *Essex*, which could not bring even one gun to bear. Most of her cannon had fallen silent through direct hits and the death and injury of the gun crews. Downes assisted in bringing the head of the *Essex* around, with hopes of setting her adrift on waters that had gone calm—but the hawser parted, and nothing more could be done. Through it all, the *Phoebe* and the *Cherub* poured heavy metal into the *Essex* with devastating results.

Farragut, like other midshipmen, ran errands during the fighting. At one point Porter gave him a pistol and ordered him to hunt down and shoot a man who had deserted his post—the boy did not find him. Later, coming up from the wardroom with priming tubes of gunpowder, Farragut was at the head of the ladder when "the captain of the gun directly opposite the hatch was struck full in the face by an 18-pound shot and fell back upon me"—the ultimate dead weight. "We both fell down the hatch together (and) I struck on my head, and fortunately he fell on my hips, whereas, as he was a man weighing about 200 pounds, had he fallen directly on my (upper) body he would have killed me. I lay there stunned for a few minutes by the blow; when, awakening, as it were, from a dream, I ran on deck. The Captain, seeing me covered with blood, asked me if I was wounded, to which I replied, 'I believe not, sir.' 'Then, my son,' said he, 'where are the tubes?'"

Porter's men kept firing, or trying, although it was hopeless and ghastly on board the *Essex*, a red cavern of pure carnage in which men exploded and limbs and heads rolled around on the blood-slick decks. The remaining officers, gallant to the last, now fell, and only Johnston, McKnight, and John Glover Cowell continued at their posts. In his spotless lieutenant's uniform, Cowell dodged around the deck, encouraging the men at their guns, moving from place to place to direct the crews and form new ones as the others were killed. He knew that two of his fellow Marbleheaders were dead, and two wounded, and he was determined to keep on.* After two hours in the thick of it, Cowell was hit and sent flying backward across the deck. When he came to, his right leg was wrecked. His men bore him down to the surgery in the cockpit, but he saw how busy the doctors were. Doctor Hoffman came over to confer, and after a heated discussion the surgeon applied a tourniquet to Cowell's thigh, and the lieutenant hobbled up the ladder and back to his station, greeting his men with a grimacing smile and saying that together they would see the fight through to the end.

Once again the ship caught fire as a stack of cartridges exploded in the main hatchway, and sailors came screaming up from below with their clothes ablaze. Their friends tried to strip them, and when they could not they yelled at the burning men: "Jump overboard! Jump overboard!" Above the din of bombardment, the cry spread through the ship like a command, and the crew thought the *Essex* must be about to explode. Although they were more than half a mile from shore and many of them could not swim, dozens of sailors and marines abandoned their posts and jumped into the water.

Porter could do nothing to stop or assist them, and he would not leave the *Essex*. When he called for his officers, he was stunned to find that

---

* Joseph Thomas, captain of the maintop, and Thomas Russell, seaman, were killed in action; Enoch Morgan Milay, quarter gunner, was badly wounded but would survive; carpenter's yeoman Benjamin Wadden was slightly wounded.

only Decatur McKnight answered the summons; the rest were dead, wounded, or swimming toward shore. In despair and defiance, Porter ordered that they torch the ship, but McKnight made a plea for the "brave companions lying wounded below." Porter thought again; the men should not be roasted, and the *Essex* might already be so badly damaged as to render her useless to the enemy. He took back his order and issued a new one: Lower the ensign. Even then, after sending the message of surrender, there was no relief. Amid the smoke and wreckage, the signal was evidently missed by the British. Although the *Essex* had ceased firing, the gunners of the *Cherub* and the *Phoebe* kept at their work, and more Americans were killed and wounded. Captain Porter stood at the mainmast, furious, half-mad, spattered with blood and brains, waving his sword and screaming into the maw of a war that did not hear him.

In the belief that Hillyar intended to kill them all, Porter ordered that the ensign be raised again so that they could go down fighting under the flag, but no sooner had he spoken than the deathly booming ended and the echoes died away. The thick smoke drifted off on the light southerly breeze, revealing the scene to the spectators on the hills. It was half past six and the beginning of another mild evening in the Valley of Paradise.

Of Porter's crew of 255, about 90 had died and an equal number were wounded—the worst slaughter in the history of the navy. The dead were silent, blown suddenly to smithereens or expiring below in the screaming cockpit as the blood-soaked surgeons kept slicing and gouging, amputating limbs that had been mangled and shredded, knowing that most had no chance. When the first British party came on board, they found twenty-three corpses on the spar deck alone. To one side, forty-four severed limbs were stacked in a pile. Not all of the dead died on board. A fair number had jumped overboard and drowned, although some made it to the beaches only to be shot down in the sand.

The living were the undead. The battle was over, and they, for no apparent reason, had not been killed. As wanderers in the chaos of destruction, they had emerged conscious and alive when so many others had not. The sights they had seen they would never forget; nothing like this would ever happen to any of them again. It had been an apocalypse, without hope of survival, and many of them were quite drunk, having made ample use of the buckets of rum. A few were so affected by the experience of extremity and so incredulous that they had survived that they decided a mistake had been made. Benjamin Hazen, a young sailor from a farm in rural Massachusetts, went below after the firing ceased. He washed his face and returned in a clean suit as if headed to Sunday meeting. "I don't know about you," he announced, "but I will never, ever, be made a prisoner of the damnable English," and he started trotting and then hopped the rail into the Pacific.

Gatty Farragut, like the rest of the survivors, had to deal with the aftermath. "The effect of excitement is astonishing," he found. "Accustomed to blood and death" early in the fight, he was amazed at the sudden change in his feelings, the rush of painful intensity, that occurred in the aftermath when he went below into the dark world of suffering and horror, full of "the mangled bodies of my shipmates, dead and dying, groaning, cursing, and expiring with the most patriotic sentiments on their lips. I became faint and sickened; my sympathies were all excited."

As the doctors went about their gruesome work, the boy "assisted to staunch the blood and dress the wounded as occasion required." In the carnage of the cockpit surgery, men cried out for water and writhed in agony, pressing and tearing at their wounds, knocking back liquor, waiting to go under the knife. One of Farragut's best friends, Lieutenant Cowell, sat quietly, face pale and eyes bright. Farragut was pleased and excited to find him, and asked how he fared. Cowell's shocking reply was, "Oh Gatty, I fear it is all up with me." The boy hastened to Doctor Hoffman, who, "with some assistance, laid him on the table, and found that his leg was shattered above the knee." The midshipman was taken aside and told that his friend might easily have saved his own life an hour before, during the battle. When Cowell had been brought below, the doctor had "proposed to drop another patient to attend to him," but Lieutenant Cowell had refused to pull rank, replying, "No, no, doctor—none of that—fair play is the jewel. One man's life is as dear as another's, and I would not cheat any poor fellow out of his turn."

Cowell was made of stern stuff. He survived the belated amputation and was taken ashore to recover. Many others joined him, and they were treated with the greatest care and kindness by the people of the town.

Porter was bereft when he went on board the *Phoebe*. The dream of glory was gone. His hopes for "something more splendid" had resulted in the loss of his ship and the slaughter of his men. He tendered his sword to his old friend Hillyar, who praised Porter for his bravery and assured him of liberal terms. The two captains soon got down to the business of surrender and possession, of prisoners and lodgings and transportation. Porter, subdued and perhaps shocked by defeat, did not at that time protest the legitimacy of the battle or raise the subject of neutral waters. Instead he quibbled about the outline of Hillyar's preliminary report and worked himself into a fury over precise sequences of events and minutes elapsed, insisting on his version as if it were still possible to achieve a victory.

There was no such discussion among the crewmen, exhausted survivors of a two-and-a-half-hour lifetime of horrifying mayhem. The victors felt relief and some elation, but it had not really been a fair fight, and some of their friends were dead because of it: a marine, three sailors, and the esteemed Chief Officer Ingram. Below decks, Phoebe's doctors had worked skillfully to save the lives of the seven wounded.

Those on board the Essex had been in hell. They had died by the dozens in the rigging or been blown apart while manning the guns or drowned in the water alongside. More than 200 cannonballs had struck the hull of their vessel, and many more had bounced off, hit their cannon, smashed spars and rigging, and skidded lethally across the decks. The men died singly and in groups, almost all of them heroic in their devotion to duty and to each other. As they lay dying, they had cheered for their ship, and they had cheered for the captain who had led them on a very long cruise into this last cove, and they had urged him to fight on.

Captain James Hillyar had carried out his mission without ever striving for personal fame or risky heroics or anything like glory. For nearly a year, since Phoebe had left Rio, he had tried without much hope to find his old friend and create the right conditions for victory. He sailed with a sense of duty and humility, carrying out assignments given by his superiors, avoiding any temptation to play the charismatic or the martyr. He had confronted his limitations many times along the way, and he felt truly blessed by God to have had the chance to fight and win. The consequences, otherwise, would have been too terrible to consider. Like all captains of British ships, he well knew that the Royal Navy had hanged one of its admirals for failing to perform to expectations. At their last meeting, when Porter said he could never approve of Hillyar's decision to attack a crippled opponent in neutral waters, tears came to Hillyar's eyes, and he took the American's hand. "My dear Porter," he said, "you know not the responsibility that hung over me with respect to your ship—perhaps my life depended on my taking her.'"

Hillyar was not aware that Porter, in his own long, scurrilous report, would accuse him of cowardice and cold-blooded murder and even of refusing to rescue the men who had fallen from the maintop. Later,

Hillyar would assert that Porter could not claim the protection of a neutral coast when he himself had violated the neutrality of Chilean waters on several occasions, as when he had burned the *Hector* in those very waters, and when he had sent out a flotilla of armed boats from the harbor to take the *Phoebe* by stealth, and when he had fired three shots at the *Phoebe* from a position much closer to the common anchorage than the one he had chosen in the cove. Finally, Porter had passed the Point of Angels into the open sea in his botched attempt to escape, and thereby had forfeited any claim to the protection of the Chileans.* Predictably, Hillyar was magnanimous in victory. He could afford to be; the defeat of Porter cleared the way for British domination of western South America and the Pacific, just as Hillyar's superiors had intended. He agreed to almost everything that Porter proposed. Porter and his officers and men could sail on board the *Essex Junior* as an unarmed cartel to New York, on parole, or word of honor, not to fight again until exchanged for British prisoners of equal rank. Hillyar would give them a passport so that any British vessel would recognize their right to enter an American port. Because they sailed on parole, they were not prisoners of war but trusted free agents. In his report to the British Admiralty, Hillyar made a point of lauding Porter. "The defense of the *Essex*," he wrote, "taking into account our superiority of force, the very discouraging circumstances of her having lost her main top-mast and being twice on fire, did honour to her brave defenders, and most fully evinced the courage of Captain Porter and those under his command. Her colours were not struck until the loss in killed and wounded was so awfully great, and her shattered condition so seriously bad, as to render further resistance unavailing."

Poinsett too felt the devastation of their loss. Having spent two years helping to create and fight for a republic in Chile, he had given all he had for the cause, and he was willing to give more. He had received word that the Carreras had escaped and might be headed for Santiago. On April 11, 1814, he wrote Porter a secret letter in which it appears that, "in the event of the defeat of the last forlorn hope of this country," he and Porter planned to go over the cordillera to the United Provinces. "I have

---

* Despite many complaints and much anti-Hillyar propaganda in American newspapers, the U.S. government did not lodge a protest with the British government, nor with Chilean officials, over the issue of neutrality, which may be seen as a gentleman's agreement—one that Porter, the chief beneficiary, was as willing to break as Hillyar. This was also the opinion of other captains of the U.S. Navy, none of whom seconded Porter's complaints, and some of whom later spoke admiringly of Hillyar and befriended him.

mules and everything ready," wrote the consul, "with the determination that, if things remain in this hopeless state until you sailed, of accepting your offer of a passage to the U.S.; but if things take a favourable turn my intention was to remain a few months until I could once more leave everything settled usefully for the U.S."

Poinsett was in "daily expectation of a decisive action" by the rebels, and so had not returned to Valparaiso from Santiago and environs. He told Porter that he could put "excellent guides and mules at your service to Mendoza, where you will meet with Captain Monson to accompany you to Buenos Aires." Hillyar was evidently willing to allow Porter to take this overland route—"Captain Hillyar can give you a letter to the Commander in the River" at Buenos Aires—as better than a sea voyage, for "the Cape at this season in a crowded ship will be very unpleasant." Poinsett was deeply concerned about the Carreras, captive at Chillan: "I confess to you that after all my labour it annoys me to run away, and leave all my projects defeated. The idea too of leaving my friends in prison with no one interested in their release distresses me." Yet he desperately wanted to return to America, and he had arranged for his vice consul, Blanco, "to deliver to you ten boticas of wine" to be drunk by Porter on his passage around the Cape, or, if they went together, "on our passage from Rio" home. Finally, Poinsett asked a favor: "[I]f you do not go in the ship, I wish you would send me the little singing bird, for a fair friend of mine, who is bird mad. I have been foolish enough to speak much in its praise. . ."

To the navy secretary, William Jones, Porter made his own lengthy report, full of the self-righteous rhetoric of one who was already planning to address the public directly through friendly newspapers that might soon be promoting his book. He discussed the condition of the ships, claiming that he had badly damaged the British vessels and inflicted much loss of life. *Phoebe* and *Essex*, he wrote, were both in a sinking condition, and he doubted that either could ever be repaired to make the trip around the Horn. None of his statements was true, and his prediction was no better. The three ships would get to England in good shape, and the *Essex* would join the Royal Navy as a forty-two-gun frigate.

Once, when the war was new, Porter had written his confidant, "I know this: I can never survive the disgrace of striking the colors of the *Essex*." Now the survivor could report to Navy Secretary Jones that "We have been unfortunate but not disgraced. The defense of the *Essex* has not been less honorable to her officers and crew than the capture of an equal force, and I now consider my situation less unpleasant than that of Commodore Hillyar, who, in violation of every principle of honor and generosity, and regardless of the rights of nations, attacked the *Essex* in her crippled state within pistol shot of a neutral shore, when for six weeks I daily offered him fair and honorable combat on terms greatly to his advantage. The blood of the slain must be on his head, and he has yet to reconcile his conduct to heaven, to his conscience, and to the world."

It was a striking piece of propaganda and a shocking disavowal of responsibility by a navy captain, even one who had gone rogue. As commander of the *Essex*, Porter was at least obliged to take the blame for the loss of the ship. This he would not do. He blamed Hillyar for cheating, and he blamed Hillyar for the deaths of so many men. After the first half hour of the battle, when Hillyar had ceased fire and drawn away, Porter could have surrendered; instead, for every minute of the next two hours, he had allowed the slaughter to continue.* But Hillyar was not the only one Porter faulted. Navy Secretary Hamilton, a man Porter had secretly and repeatedly vilified, had never approved or even been aware of Porter's Pacific intentions, was also disparaged. "If the *Essex* has been lost for want of suitable armament," contended Porter, "I am not to blame. Myself and officers applied to Paul Hamilton Esq. for a greater proportion of long guns which were refused us; and I now venture to declare that, if she had been armed in the manner I wished, she would not have been taken by the *Phoebe* and *Cherub*. With our six twelve-pounders only, we fought this action; our carronades were useless. What might not [we] have done had we been permitted to take on board a few long eighteens?" In fact, the carronades had done much damage in the first half hour; in fact, Porter had chosen to position the *Essex* so that her broadside guns could hardly be used; in fact, Hamilton had authorized

---

* In his magisterial work on the War of 1812, in the multi-volume *History of the United States of America During the Administrations of James Madison* (published 1889-91) Henry Adams was the first historian to write objectively about the performance of the U.S. Navy, and he was highly critical of David Porter. Adams derided his Nukuhivan adventure as an excuse for "amusing himself," "as though to make a voyage of discovery or to emulate the mutineers of the *Bounty*." Of Porter's decision to go for Valparaiso from Nukuhiva, Adams wrote, "Porter would have done better to sail for the China seas or Indian Ocean." Regarding battle tactics at Valparaiso, Porter "might have tried to run out at night, or might have fought, even after the loss of his maintopmast, under less disadvantage." Adams opined about the battle that "the carnage was frightful and useless" and "the loss of the *Essex*. . . was unnecessary." About Porter's allegations against Hillyar, Adams wrote scornfully that Porter knew "that he could not depend on Chilian protection," and that Hillyar "made no mistakes" in his conduct, especially "in regard to the neutrality of Chili, which was not even a recognized nation." Unlike many later writers, including those on naval matters, Henry Adams was neither an apologist nor a cheerleader in regard to American policy and performance in the War of 1812, and his works remain unsurpassed.

the transfer of a few long eighteens, which Porter had failed to procure. Far more damning, Porter had, during his long renegade rampage, captured twelve armed vessels that mounted more than one hundred guns. All of those cannon were in his possession for months before the showdown at Valparaiso, and at any time he could have re-armed the *Essex* in whatever configuration he might like. Once again, he had chosen to keep things exactly as they were.

At the funeral of Lieutenant William Ingram, conducted with military honors, the American crewmen joined the British and the local citizenry in paying their respects. Valparaiso's officials showed a cold contempt for Porter and his men, but "the neglect of the governor and his officers was fully compensated by the kind attention of the good citizens," wrote Porter. "When my wounded companions were brought on shore, they were borne to the place selected by me for a hospital by the kind Chileans. The ladies of Valparaiso took upon themselves the task of providing for their necessities and administering to the alleviation of their sufferings. At all times, women of the most respectable appearance attended at the hospital, who tendered their services gratuitously, to take care of the wounded. Without their aid, I have no doubt, many would have died, who now live to thank them."

As the lone officer among the wounded, Cowell had become the idol of Valparaiso, visited at the hospital by all the most gallant gentlemen and their beautiful ladies and by well-wishing sailors and marines of both sides. He was also remembered in family prayers and formal religious services, and attended around the clock by the "gentle humanity" of the nurses and by Glasgow Farragut. Infection set in early, but Cowell fought it with all his diminished strength, thinking of his wife and two small children at home in old Marblehead. Twenty days after the battle, he took a bad turn. Farragut stayed by his side, and the boy was there when, on April 18, "life went out, like a candle." Thus "died one of the best officers as well as the bravest of men," wrote Farragut, who had seen enough of death. The people of the city gave Cowell a hero's funeral, with orations and lamentations and the firing of minute guns, and a black parade of thousands following the cortege up the hill to the cathedral, where his remains were interred in view of the sea.

The *Essex Junior* sailed from Valparaiso on April 27, 1814. On board were 130 *Essex* sailors in cramped quarters, many still recovering, all thinking of lost shipmates. Barnewall and Johnston had survived and took their places on board. Johnston spoke for many when he wrote, "I shall only observe that this massacre of American heroes, under the guns of a battery which ought to have maintained its neutrality by chastising those who violated it, took place in consequence of the imbecility of Lastra" and his tool, Formas.

Porter had gone alone into the Pacific with dreams of Anson-like glory. Now he was coming out alone, without his prizes, money, or victory, guilty of the bizarre and bloody annexation of Nukuhiva and the loss of his ship in a protracted suicidal battle. He had run off with a battleship and 300 men, taken from a navy that could not spare a rowboat, and had spent fifteen months away from the theater of war, tying up government assets and pursuing his own interests. In the end he had given the enemy a new frigate and had caused the deaths of many brave men, including ninety of his own in battle, several Royal Navy sailors, two whalemen, and scores if not hundreds of Enana men and boys.

Twice, Porter had been poised to win the day and end his cruise in triumph. The first time was a matter of fate, in the proximity of an angry cannoneer holding a lighted match and a zealous young lieutenant who prevented the broadside that would have shattered the *Phoebe*. The historian Henry Adams wrote that "Porter probably regretted to the end of his life that he did not seize the opportunity his enemy gave him." In the second instance, Porter committed an error of seamanship and sailed too close to the Point of Angels, cutting off the frigate's wind, then emerging from its lee into the full force of a squall powerful enough to carry away the topmast. And even then he could have made choices giving him an excellent chance of escape or even victory over his pursuers. After all of his cruising and all of his hunger for fame, he had failed when it counted, and he never acknowledged it.

Behind him in Valparaiso, Porter would leave Consul General Poinsett with his "projects defeated," a man without a country to influence. Hillyar, in revenge for Poinsett's success in anti-British activities, had denied him a berth on the *Essex Junior*. In June 1814, Supreme Director Lastra, intimidated by a "violent letter" from the British high command at Rio, would summon Poinsett and inform him that he was an enemy of Chile and must depart immediately.

Behind him, too, Porter left twenty wandering crewmen, including a few who had already gone into the Chilean army* and two more lying in the hospital, unable to make the long passage around the Horn. One would soon die, and the other, William Call, who had lost a leg, would recover. Visiting on the eve of departure, Porter told Call that Consul Poinsett was still in town, and Lieutenant Gamble was due in from Nooaheevah in a month or two, and together they ought to scrape up a crew to continue the fight in the Pacific.

---

* In 1814, Porter listed thirty-one men, by name, as missing after the battle. Probably most of them drowned or were shot in the water. He went into the fight with 255 men on board; he sailed for home in the *Essex Junior* with 130 men. Of the other 125, probably 90 had died, and the rest remained in Chile, having served under Porter continuously for seventeen months. Most evidently stayed on at Valparaiso or went to Santiago to enlist as soldiers, for, although they are not mentioned in 1814 as being alive, Gamble refers to them in his account of events in Valparaiso after Porter's departure.

Chapter Thirteen

Consequences

Among the American prisoners at Valparaiso, the hawk-eyed Samuel Johnston kept a lookout on the new political landscape. "Shortly after the capture of the *Essex*," he wrote, "Commodore Hillyar left Valparaiso and repaired to the capital in order to settle the affairs of Chile." From there Hillyar went to Chillan to meet with the royalist General Gainza. "Nothing has yet transpired on the subject," reported Johnston, but "many people of judgment, even of the Larrain family, begin to feel the effects of their bad policy in not affording protection to the *Essex*. Their eyes are now open, and they see a large English force that may be turned against them at any time; whereas, if they had afforded to the Americans that protection which both justice and their crippled state demanded, Commodore Hillyar would have been thwarted, and the people of Chile could have carried on their war unmolested by British interference." It was galling to Johnston, a patriot of the republic, to realize that it was Hillyar, representing the policies and power of an imperial monarchy, who had made the difference in Chile.

Santiago had just learned that General Sir Arthur Wellesley (who was elevated from Marquess to Duke of Wellington in May 1814) had relinquished command in Spain to the adherents of Fernando VII. "This news," noted Johnston, "has added greatly to the influence the British had already acquired" over Lastra's "feeble government" and made it likely that "every plan proposed by Hillyar will be implicitly followed." Although Hillyar's negotiations had not yet produced results, Johnston foretold them: "Thus you see one of the finest countries on the globe, whose distance from the old world rendered it secure from conquest, invasion, or even the baneful influence of European power," subjected "by its own internal differences, and an insignificant British force, to the arbitrary will of the Vice-King of Peru."

Finally, Johnston discerned that Supreme Director Lastra, and men like him, had never wanted a republic or even a real revolution. They had held office quietly amid turmoil, plotting with the British, waiting for their chance to emerge from the shadows. "The intrigues of this man with the English have reduced the country to a state of dependence on, and placed them entirely at the mercy of," London, "whose emissary [Hillyar] will either deliver them over to the paternal embraces of their mother country, or take possession of their territory in the name of His Britannic Majesty, which, from the confused and presently exhausted state of Chile, I think would not be impossible for the British here to accomplish."

As he boarded the *Essex Junior* on April 27, 1814, Johnston noted that "Don Juan José Carrera, who made good his escape to the capital, has been banished from the country as a reward for his meritorious services as a statesman and a general, whose brilliant talents, it was feared by his loving kinsman Lastra, might eclipse his own." Banishment was not enough: Lastra had put Juan Mackenna to work writing a scurrilous report about the Carreras in order to discredit them and prevent their return to power.

Johnston had arrived in Chile as an adventurer and an idealist, hoping to contribute to the creation of a republic by the power of his printing press. He had come to love the country and its people and to admire Carrera as the George Washington of its revolution, and he had stayed to fight for independence. He had suffered betrayal, imprisonment, and defeat, and in the end all he had was memories: "The foresail of the *Essex Junior* is set, and a boat waiting to take this letter on shore. Neither Captain Barnewall, myself, or any other person belonging to the *Colt*, have received a farthing from the government for our services and sufferings in their cause. Adieu!"

At Fort Madison, Madison's Island—Porter's new name for Nuku Hiva—Lieutenant John Gamble, twenty-two, of the U.S. Marines, had command of Madisonville and four prize vessels: *Greenwich*, *Seringapatam*, *Sir Andrew Hammond*, and *New Zealander*. Lacking Porter's capacity for self-delusion, he could hardly be happy with his assignment. Upon his departure in December, Porter had told Gamble to hold the place as a refuge in case he and Downes returned for repairs. Gamble had suspected even then that the war maker was not coming back. In Nooaheevah, at Anna Maria Bay—Gamble refused to use Porter's names—there would be no new adventures. He was marooned, probably for months, in the drudgery and boredom of waiting, among natives who might not be so friendly if they were to discover how few men he really had.

Gamble could rely on his midshipmen, Clapp and Feltus. William Feltus, fifteen, had the makings of a top naval officer and had become Gamble's protégé early in the voyage. He was serious and brave beyond his years, and zealous in doing his duty. Benjamin Clapp, twenty-three, was bright and competent, although, like Gamble, not a mariner. He was a fur trader, and had sailed from New York in the *Albatros* bound for Astoria on the Northwest Coast. Astoria, however, had been sold, so Clapp had sailed with Captain Hunt and crew for Hawaii and then on to the Marquesas, where Clapp had joined the navy rather than go to China.

The remaining crewmen were not nearly so dependable. Twelve were short-timers, slated to sail away soon in the *New Zealander*, eighteen were former slacker crewmen of the *Essex*, and six were prisoners of war. To Porter, who had dumped them on Gamble, they were "a set of lazy, thoughtless fellows who would sooner risk a general massacre than arouse from their stupid apathy." Another two, Coffin and White, were roaming free on the island. It would not be easy to keep even the good men happy or busy, especially with all of the girls around. Gamble warned his young officers to watch everyone closely and immediately report any misbehavior. He did not have Porter's relationships with Gattenewa and Mouina or with the interpreter Wilson, whom he distrusted. On the other hand, Gamble could rely on George Ross and William Brudenell, the sandalwood traders—sober, sensible, and friendly with the native leaders.

Of Gamble's inherited *Essex* crewmen, the highest ranking, boatswain Thomas Belcher, was an Englishman, an older fellow plagued with syphilis, proud of his service in the 1770s with Captain Cook in the Pacific. The six prisoners were English too, and six more were English recruits from the whalers. Since America was at war with England, Gamble did not regard these men as he did his eight American-born sailors. At first he kept all of them gardening near the fort; then he ordered that hundreds of barrels of sperm oil be transferred from the other three vessels to the *New Zealander*.

The Taipi and Hapa'a, dropouts from "the great American family," assessed the situation right away: Opotee was gone, and his moon-troopers with him. Only a skeleton crew remained, too few to keep them from raiding the village. They had started by stealing pigs, setting fire to the brush above the wall, and running off with provisions. Gamble took a few hostages and strengthened his defenses, employing all hands in moving six guns from the *Seringapatam* up the high hill to the fort. The rainy season began, and Gamble had to deal with downpours, high winds, and securing his vessels moored in the bay. Despite illness among his men and unrest among the English prisoners who worked alongside them, Gamble got the *New Zealander* loaded with two thousand barrels of oil and sent her away under John King and a small crew, cheering as they sailed for America. Gamble and his men sorely wished they could have gone too.

Unavoidably, Ben Clapp and the boy Will Feltus were given much authority over the crewmen. In his journal, Feltus recorded his typical duties, which included inspecting the vessels to make sure that natives were not aboard. On a January 20 visit to the *Seringapatam*, he and Clapp broke up a raucous party, and Gamble "punished the men and also the women, and turned the latter on shore." Now distrustful of the crewmen, Gamble sent his middies to collect lances and harpoons from their vessels and to make an inventory of the stores and provisions. Discipline was maintained to an uncomfortable degree, with watches kept strictly on the ships and at the fort and village. Isaac Coffin, deserter, had been brought in by one of the sandalwood traders and put in irons in the *Sir Andrew Hammond* along with John Robinson, an Englishman caught stealing. Relations were not improved by the draining, on January 22, of "the last can of grog."

Running low on supplies, Gamble sailed off in the *Hammond* looking for swine and vegetables. After trouble at the island of Dominica, he and his crew went on to Cook's Resolution Bay at Christiana Island, where Gamble enjoyed several days of productive barter, all the while fielding questions about "when the ships were to leave the Bay, and when Opotee was expected to return." After nine days away, Gamble found "all things in proper order" back at Nooaheevah.

February came and went without any word from Porter. The rains continued, and some of the men grew desperate. Here, soaked each day, with the girls still beckoning, they were forced to drill and work under a couple of officious boys, for a master who was hardly more than a boy himself. The U.S. Navy had come to seem a foreign concept to men who only wanted to join the natives in their pursuit of happiness. Toward the end of the month, Gamble lost the excellent John Witter, who drowned in the surf, and early in March Isaac Coffin ran off again. That evening the lieutenant armed his eight best men and went off down the Teii valley. They found Coffin "dozing in the midst of a group of natives" and dragged him off to the beach to be flogged. When Gamble scolded the Teii, they retorted that Coffin had a right to visit and that his punishment, thirty-six lashes and confinement below, was "illiberal and unjust."

On the night of March 18, the watchmen of the *Greenwich* reported that a boat was missing along with muskets, cartridges, clothes, boards, tools, two compasses, a hat, five barrels of powder, and an English ensign. Also missing were Isaac Coffin, John Robinson, and John Welch, the latter of whom, after liberating the other two from their irons, had rowed over to the *Seringapatam* to take on one more, Peter Swook, an original crewmember of the *Essex*. Further, they had been careful to stave in Gamble's blue pulling boat, the fastest of those that might have been used to chase them.

Next morning at breakfast time, the deck watch cried out that the natives were about to attack on shore. Gamble hopped up on deck and saw a large crowd headed for the camp. He ordered the cannons primed with grapeshot and summoned the men ashore to come to the *Greenwich* with their muskets, but the natives were unarmed and carrying great quantities of breadfruit and bananas. Someone—Gamble suspected Wilson, the interpreter—had told the Teii that the American vessels would be departing in a few days and that Opotee would never return. The bundles of edibles had been given in gratitude at this splendid news.

The weather continued stormy, and on March 26 the *Seringapatam* parted her lower anchor cable and was headed for shore when the men on board the *Sir Andrew Hammond* hauled her back with spring lines connecting the two vessels. The storm kept up, and next morning the ships were driven toward the rocks. It was only "by indefatigable exertions [that] they were both drawn into deeper water, and soon secured." The day after, in a squall 4,500 miles to the east, David Porter made his fateful bid to drive the *Essex* out of Valparaiso Harbor and into the open sea.

In the rains of early April at Nukuhiva, Madisonville's buildings flooded and torrents went "rushing down the hills in beautiful cascades." Gamble suspected that Porter, gone for four months, had met with disaster. Gamble provisioned the *Seringapatam* and the *Sir Andrew Hammond* until they were loaded down by their sterns, and on April 14 he had the men commence the two-week process of rigging the ships for a long voyage. The *Seringapatam* was given an armament of ten long nine-pounders, four twelve-pound carronades, and four long six-pounders, while the *Sir Andrew Ham-*

mond was fitted with fourteen carronades. Lieutenant Gamble was under orders to remain at Madisonville for another seven weeks.

The Teii held an island-wide banquet as part of the festival of *coeeca*, which was protected by a powerful *tapu* forbidding harm or injury. Given this, several of Gamble's men were allowed to observe. At the grand public square, on the Teii's largest *paepae*, feasting and dancing went on for three days, and indeed it was an unforgettable Enana love-in.

But Gamble's misgivings did not go away. On May 3, he discovered that the boat's sail had been stolen by someone on board the *Greenwich*, probably the boatswain's mate, Thomas Belcher. Gamble asked around, and the next day was told that "most of the men were forming a scheme whether to mutiny or make their escape in one of the ships, and that Belcher and four of the prisoners of war were the chief instigators of the plan." Gamble continued his consolidation of arms, removing all pistols and muskets to the *Greenwich*. On May 6, the nature of the coming storm became apparent, as the conspirators could no longer hide their anxiety and determination to bring about "an awful explosion." Gamble might have moved at this point, destroying two of the ships and sailing away on the third with the men who were loyal, but he was twenty-two and had his orders, and so he stayed on, knowing that something terrible was likely to happen.

On May 7, the breeze was light and the weather clear. Gamble had some men caulking the decks, replacing rigging, and moving oil tanks on board the *Seringapatam*, the beautiful teak vessel built for Tipu Saib, the last unconquered sultan of India, in his doomed effort to fight off the British Royal Navy. After lunch, Clapp went over the side on a staging to paint her port topsides, Feltus watched the riggers, and Gamble supervised the placement of two oil tanks below. From the deck, he ordered a man to get cracking, and the Englishman defied him, saying he'd be damned if he did any more work on board the ship. "Scarcely had the words escaped his lips, when all the men on the deck threw down their hats and made the same declaration." One of them drew a large knife from his shirt, and cried for the rest to get hold of Lieutenant Gamble, who dashed to the railing. The men pulled him away and threw him back on the deck. "After struggling a short time and receiving many bruises," recalled Gamble, "I was prostrated and my hands and my legs tied."

"What do you mean by this treatment?" demanded Gamble.

"Say another word and I'll beat your brains out," yelled the caulker, Martin Stanley, making as if to bash him with his maul. "We've been your prisoners long enough in this damned place! We're not your slaves, and we will have our liberty!"

Trussed with his legs painfully crossed, Gamble was hauled to the hatch. "Then they threw me on the second deck," he wrote, "thence dragged me into the cabin and confined me in the run," the pitch-black crawl space under the cabin floor. The midshipmen were soon overpowered, trussed, and put in the run with Gamble.

The seven mutineers gave three cheers and hoisted their flag into the rigging of the *Seringapatam*, an English vessel once more. One party went on shore to spike the guns and take the powder of Fort Madison, while the other went to the *Greenwich* and *Sir Andrew Hammond* to spike their guns and carry off their small arms, muskets, and valuables. Then they sent for Robert White, who had been made a pariah by David Porter. As the ship got under way, the three prisoners yelled that they could not breathe. The two boys were allowed to crawl out and stay in the cabin. After a while, Gamble was freed and marched to the cabin and seated on a chest near the skylight, with two men guarding him "with his own pistols, loaded and cocked."

At about eight in the evening, the ship cleared the bay and entered the open sea, and just then one of Gamble's guards shot him. At the sound of gunfire, five muskets were pointed down through the skylight and the guards yelled, "Don't fire, don't fire!" which saved all the lives in the cabin. Gamble had been shot through the heel just below the ankle, and the boys did not know what to do. Soon they were untied, led up to the spar deck, and told that "a boat was in readiness to receive them." Gamble protested that they could not be sent away without arms to defend themselves against savages—it was "wanton barbarity." The thirteen mutineers agreed with Gamble and gave him two muskets and a powder keg and sent him and his men over the side, where they found William Worth and Richard Stansbury sitting in a half-swamped boat.

Night had fallen when they shoved off from the steep sides of the *Seringapatam*, Gamble's own prize, so brilliantly captured in the Galápagos. Now, under short sail, she moved away by the light of the rising moon, under the king's flag. A face appeared at the stern railing. Feltus saw that it was the boatswain's mate, old Tom Belcher, who "called out to Lieutenant Gamble and several others to witness that he was obliged by the mutineers to stay." Perhaps it was true.

Several miles off Nukuhiva, the castaways made their way across the peaceful nighttime sea. Clapp bailed, Gamble steered, and the other three rowed hard. After many hours they stood on the deck of the *Greenwich*, where the five remaining Americans, including the very ill John Pettenger, happily greeted their officers as men returned from the dead. They were informed that the interpreter Wilson, Porter's great friend, had been the chief fomenter of the uprising and had already led the plundering of the *Sir Andrew Hammond* and the pillaging of Madisonville. Gamble got his wound dressed, then passed out from exhaustion and loss of blood.

When he awoke next morning, the young lieutenant found himself in a nearly hopeless situation. Where was Porter? No word had come from Valparaiso. Although the six months had not yet passed, it was time to go. The *Hammond* was fittest for a sea voyage, so Gamble had all hands move sails and other items from the *Greenwich* and rig her for sailing. He sent some of his men inland to recover the items that Wilson had taken, and he urged Ross and Brudenell, the traders, to come away with them. For much of the day, the men moved goods from the fort and the village down to the beach.

After sunrise on May 9, the day of departure, Feltus and Clapp and the men went ashore to raft the material out to the ships. With help from the Teii, they loaded up and arrived at the *Greenwich* for breakfast at eight. An hour later, they were back on shore when Brudenell came running down, saying that the natives had his muskets and Wilson was at his house and they'd better come quick if they wanted to catch him. With one musket between them, seamen Worth and Coddington went off after Wilson, but soon they reported that he had escaped to a distant tribe. Feltus received Gamble's permission to lead a party to Wilson's house to recover the stolen items, especially the barrels of gunpowder. The Teii had said that Wilson would receive no protection from them. Feltus and Brudenell, promising to be quick and stay alert, set out in the boat with four seamen and three muskets. On the final day at Nooaheevah, they wanted revenge on Wilson.

Gamble stayed in his cabin, in agony and fever from his gunshot wound; he had acting Midshipman Clapp stand on deck and scan the beach. At half past noon, Clapp shouted that the boat was in the surf with a crowd of natives. Gamble hobbled up the hatchway and had Clapp and two seamen take him to the *Hammond*, whose guns were intact. On their way, Clapp spied a wild scene: some of the natives were in the boat, and many more were plundering the goods. From the *Hammond*, Gamble fired deadly grapeshot and had just ordered a second round when two white men appeared in the surf, waving in distress, then plunging in. Clapp and the two seamen jumped into their leaky boat and began rowing for the shore. As they did, three Enana canoes turned their prows toward the *Hammond*. Alone on deck, Gamble loaded the cannon and fired away, driving back the canoes and giving cover to the rescue boat. Clapp and his men pulled out the swimmers, Coddington and Worth, and returned to the ship. Coddington was bleeding at the ears from a fractured skull. Worth, with a broken leg, said that there had been a massacre—Feltus, Brudenell, and the sailors Thomas Gibbs and John Thomas were dead. George Ross, barricaded at his trading house, might also have been killed.

Gamble was devastated. It had not been necessary to make the last trip, and he should not have allowed it. He had lost three more men, and he had lost Will Feltus, whom he loved like a brother. He hobbled back to the guns and kept firing at Porter's island, at the burning village and at the fort, where the flag still flew over Massachusetts Bay and where Wilson could be seen directing the Enana to unspike the cannon. Worth somehow got aloft and bent on sails until the sun went down. Finally, Gamble ordered that Pettenger be brought from the *Greenwich* and that she be set on fire.

"All things being in readiness, the cable of the *Sir Andrew Hammond* was cut, and with a fine breeze from the land, she stood out of the bay. The night was dark, and the course of the ship was guided chiefly by the flames of the *Greenwich*."

From the beaches, the Enana watched. Some of the moon men had been killed and others had sailed off in their ships, but now all of them were gone, and Gattanewa could rest. He had endured a difficult siege, which he had not thought he would survive, and now he suffered the pains and anxiety of a curse laid on him by one of the Hapa'a. His solution was to place himself and his tribe under the protection of the warrior Mouina.

Gattanewa, wrinkled and tattoo-blackened scion of the first-comer Teiki'nui'ahaku and of five hundred patriarchs since, whose names he sang in his cracked falsetto, had commissioned the making of a beautiful canoe in which to join them in the life to come. This much he had learned from Opotee, that death was not far away, and he welcomed it, as the surf through which he would be launched on his voyage to paradise.

The United States and its champion, José Miguel Carrera, had lost, and Great Britain, friend of rebel and royalist alike, had won. It was easy for Hillyar to complete his mission. Everyone involved was now a monarchist, looking to bow to a king and a king's representative. As Johnston had noted, Hillyar moved around quickly after his victory, shuttling between the dicta-tor Lastra at Santiago and General Gainza at Talca. Gainza had been facing defeat when Hillyar came riding into camp with the astounding news that the war was over, the rebels had given up, and Fernando had been restored to the throne of Spain. It hardly seemed possible, but Hillyar assured Gainza that it was true, thanks to the British armies under Wellington, and that, even as they spoke, 2,000 battle-hardened Spanish soldiers were on their way to Callao to serve Viceroy Abascal. The war, said Hillyar, was truly ended in Chile just as it was in Spain. After twenty years of fighting, the English had prevailed, and the world would now follow the lead of Great Britain. In Chile, an armistice would be proclaimed, and the people would cheer. Gen-eral Gainza would call for a peace conference at Lircay, just outside Talca, and Generals O'Higgins and Mackenna would be pleased to meet him there.

Gainza and Hillyar proceeded to the banks of the Rio Lircay, and there O'Higgins, on behalf of Supreme Director Lastra and his junto, hand-ed over the independence of Chile. The treaty had a preamble and sixteen articles, amounting to a restoration of government and society as it had been before the uprising in 1810. The preamble identified the indepen-dence movement as having been an attempt to destroy "the kingdom of Chile," to delude its people and desecrate its traditions. In the provision for exchanging prisoners of war, O'Higgins specified a secret side agreement in which Luis and José Miguel Carrera, captive at Chillan, were to be sent to Rio de Janeiro to be imprisoned. All traces of the republic were to be erased: nothing would remain of the constitution or the congress, of free public schools, civil rights for Indians, and freedom for the enslaved. Thousands of lives had been sacrificed for nothing. Only one innovation survived the treaty's brutal retrogression: Chile's ports, opened proudly to the world in 1811, would remain open to foreign trade, limited exclusively to vessels fly-ing the flag of Great Britain.

Gainza was to withdraw rapidly from Talca to Concepcion and em-bark his troops for Callao. The viceroy of Peru was to recognize a royalist government at Santiago. And Chile was to send a couple of delegates to the legislature of Spain. All parties at Lircay pledged their loyalty to Fernando VII, Rey de Espana, and with the signatures of O'Higgins and Gainza, on May 3, 1814, the fate of Chile was sealed.

Hillyar had closed out London's business in the Pacific. Two more British frigates arrived, and the *Racoon* returned from the Northwest coast to report that the Americans there had already departed. In the Santiago parade celebrating the restoration of law and order, Hillyar marched in the robes of a friar, smiling and waving, blue eyes merry, as crowds cheered the *mediador* who had brought peace to Chile. Once the treaty was sent to Abascal for ratification, Hillyar was free to go.

At Valparaiso, Hillyar conferred with his colleague, Captain Thomas Tudor Tucker of the *Cherub*. Tucker, healed from his wounds, would stay on in the Pacific. He soon sailed for the Galápagos to recover three British whalers that Porter was alleged to have concealed at the Encantadas or perhaps the Sandwich Islands. Hillyar also conferred with David Porter. Porter would be allowed to command the *Essex Junior*; stripped of her guns and sailing as a cartel, she was to carry the 130 American survivors to New York, where they would be exchanged for an equal number of British captives. Two officers, Lieutenant S. Decatur McKnight and acting Midshipman James R. Lyman,* were to board the *Phoebe* to go to British naval headquarters at Rio and submit affidavits about the capture of the *Essex*. Out of courtesy, Hillyar had agreed that Porter and his other officers were not prisoners but gentlemen on parole, bound by their word of honor to fulfill the repatriation agreement. On May 30, 1814, Captain James Hillyar stood on the quarterdeck looking out at the harbor of Valparaiso and saw English merchant vessels riding at anchor, but no Americans—and so it would be, he thought, for a long time. The *Phoebe* received the salutes of the three forts as she moved through the peaceful waters, past the house of the governor and then past the Point of Angels, bound homeward for England.

At Chillan, General Gainza had no intention of honoring the treaty, just as he assumed that O'Higgins had no intention of allowing Chile to revert to its colonial status. Gainza proceeded to free 300 patriot prisoners, retaining only the Carreras. José Miguel, still being tried for treason, had won the respect of all in the military tribunal for his dignified bearing and his insistence that his actions as head of state and general of the armies were "right and necessary to sustain freedom in Chile." It seemed odd to Gainza that O'Higgins had made no effort in their diplomacy to ransom the Carreras, heroes of the republic; it made him think about those who were expendable, and why—the kind of thing that occurs to a general whose luck has been bad.

---

* James R. Lyman of Connecticut had sailed on a merchant vessel (perhaps the *Colt*) that had been sold in Chile after a voyage to the Northwest coast.

On May 11, the Carreras were set at liberty with the warning that they should beware of the junto, and especially of Mackenna, "your worst enemy." Carrera thanked his hosts for his nine-week stay, assuring them, somewhat ungraciously, that "wherever we find vassals of Fernando and the defenders of Spain, we will raise our swords—our hatred is eternal." With money and pistols, they set off that night through the rain with three soldiers and a guide, headed for a safe house. Gainza had smiled and told them to stay away from their liberty-loving amigo O'Higgins at Talca, but he did not mention that he had already sent a message to O'Higgins announcing the distressing escape of the wily Carrera brothers.

The *Essex Junior* had a rapid, uneventful voyage out of the Pacific. Porter drove her hard around the Horn and through the South Atlantic. He obsessed about arriving home in time to get command of a new warship and take her across the ocean to engage the *Phoebe* and the *Essex* in the English Channel.

That sort of job was already being done by Secretary Jones's new sloops of war. The navy's five remaining frigates—only Porter and the late James Lawrence had lost theirs—were bottled up in port. Their place was taken by hundreds of privateers, useless at fighting the Royal Navy but superb at preying on British merchant shipping throughout the Atlantic and the Caribbean. The frigates were too large to be used effectively for that purpose, and too few to threaten the British ships stationed on blockade duty. And the frigate duels of the early part of the war, which had won such renown for American captains and crews, were now forbidden by order of the British Admiralty.

The new sloops of war had proved perfect for their roles as destroyers of commerce. Unlike the privateers, they were in the business of sending vessels and their cargoes to the bottom, which meant that they could stay out on long cruises with full crews, unreduced by having to man prizes. The three sloops of war built at Baltimore and Washington were trapped by the British blockade, but the other three, *Frolic*, *Peacock*, and *Wasp*, were able to carry the fight into the Atlantic.

Frolic, launched at Boston in February 1814, went hunting in the Caribbean and sank two British merchantmen and a Spanish privateer before being captured by a British frigate. The proud *Peacock* cleared New York in March 1814. Six weeks later, off the Bahamas under Commander Lewis

Warrington, she defeated the Royal Navy brig of war *Epervier* and sent her into Savannah with $128,000 in specie. From Savannah the *Peacock* went to the coast of Ireland and sank fourteen merchant vessels before heading home via Spain and the West Indies. On her final cruise, Warrington entered the Indian Ocean and took three valuable prizes and a naval vessel before learning of the war's end.

The twenty-gun *Wasp* proved a superb performer upon sailing from the Merrimack River in May 1814. In many ways Commander Johnston Blakeley, thirty-three, achieved what David Porter had only hoped for. Twice, in equal combat, he and the men of the *Wasp* defeated British naval vessels, and he terrorized the English Channel and inflicted great damage on British merchant shipping, sinking four vessels, including a large ship, and sending in a fifth as a cartel with thirty-eight prisoners. Once at sea, Blakeley had no intention of interrupting his rampage by returning to the United States. He dealt with the blockade by staying away and taking food and ammunition from his prizes.

On June 28, off the west coast of France, the men of the *Wasp* encountered the Royal Navy sloop of war *Reindeer* under Captain William Manners. With eighteen fixed guns and a shifting twelve-pound carronade, *Reindeer* was manned by a 118-man crew "said to be the pride of Plymouth." At a quarter past one, Blakeley began a two-hour tacking match that ended with the two ships sixty yards apart. The *Reindeer* opened fire with grapeshot from her shifting gun and fired four more times before the *Wasp* could get in position to respond, mainly with muskets and pistols. After Captain Manners was killed, the *Reindeeer*'s lieutenant ran her up against the *Wasp* for boarding, but his men "were repulsed in every attempt." Then the Yankee crew charged over the rail, "and at 3:45 the enemy hauled down his flag." Twenty-five brave Englishmen had fallen dead, and forty-two were wounded. Of the American crew, five died that day, four more the next.

According to Blakeley, the *Wasp* had taken a pounding. "Six round shot struck our hull, and many grape; the foremast received a 24-pound shot which passed through its centre, and the rigging and sails were cut up." However, "the *Reindeer* was literally cut to pieces in a line with her ports, and her upper works, boats, and spare spars were one complete wreck." After the lengthy process of removing the wounded and their baggage, the *Reindeer* was "set on fire, and in a few hours blew up"—fireworks for an early Fourth of July.

Blakeley put in at Lorient in France, hospitalized his wounded, freed the British seamen, and sailed away. He left a report that caused a sensation in America. Thrilled at his victory by boarding, Congress bestowed "suitable honors and rewards on those gallant men whose noble achievements" had won the day. Secretary Jones, noting that "all that skill and valor could do was done quickly," promoted Commander Blakeley to the position of captain, but America's new hero had a war to fight, and he remained at large in the Atlantic, a terror to British shipping.

Porter's vanquished crew missed the Fourth of July, but on July 5 they arrived off Sandy Hook, New Jersey, and were intercepted by the British frigate *Saturn*. Having read Hillyar's written pledge to respect these men as "on parole," Captain Nash permitted the *Essex Junior* "to pass freely to the United States without any impediment." He sent them into New York along with a gift of oranges and fresh newspapers for Captain Porter. But then there was a problem. Two hours later the *Saturn* forced *Essex Junior* to heave to, and a boat's crew came over with a boarding officer. Captain Nash, he said, had some concerns, and would need to detain the *Essex Junior* in order to review passports. Porter flew into a rage, insisting "that even the smallest detention would be a violation of the contract" and surrendering his sword, by God. The British officer declined the sword and promised to confer with Captain Nash. Upon his return, the officer advised that the *Essex Junior* would spend the night "under the lee of the *Saturn*." Porter histrionically declared, "I am your prisoner; I do not consider myself any longer bound by my contract with Captain Hillyar. Tell your Captain Nash that if British officers have no respect for the honor of each other, I shall have none for them." As they pulled away in their boat, Porter called out, "If detained all night, I will consider myself at liberty to effect my escape!"

His officers and midshipmen stood by in amazement as their hot-headed captain worked himself into a blind fury. More than any outrage he felt toward the British, Porter had cracked under the pressure of guilt and dread he felt in coming home to face the consequences of his actions in the Pacific. Since first making the decision to round Cape Horn, he had been wrestling with his conscience and worrying about the reaction of his superiors. He knew he had acted beyond his orders, and he had never stopped telling himself, in his journal, that only a resounding success would justify his long stay in the Pacific. By any measure, Porter had not been successful. He had done much that was questionable and perhaps unforgiveable, and he had, of course, lost the navy's frigate and led dozens of men to their deaths. He knew that he must face a formal inquiry or a court martial, the outcome of which might well see him cashiered from the navy or even hanged from the yardarm. His men looked on as he stormed around, spitting with rage, cursing the demon British. Subsiding at last, he went into a funk. His best hope, he decided, lay in New York and a hero's welcome. A big parade might affect the navy's decision-making. Already his friends, naval and journalistic, had begun campaigning, claiming that defeat by a superior force was as noble as victory over an equal. He was the avatar of American valor, fighting to the last against great odds and a ruthless and dishonorable opponent. Giving an envelope to John Downes, Porter instructed him to hand it to Captain Nash in the morning, and not to worry about Porter's whereabouts.

Shortly after dawn, a launch settled into the water alongside the *Essex Junior*, and Porter and a few sailors started northward toward Long Island, forty miles away in a fogbank. He had a fast boat, a hard-rowing crew, plenty of arms and ammunition, and a suicidal attitude. He "was determined to make a desperate fight if pursued." They were "nearly a gunshot" away before the lookouts raised a cry. "At that instant," wrote Porter, "a fresh breeze sprang up, and the *Saturn* made all sail after us. Fortunately, however, a thick fog came on, upon which I changed my course and entirely eluded further pursuit. During the fog, I heard a firing; and on its clearing up saw the *Saturn* in chase of the *Essex Junior*." Downes had made a break for it, Porter-style.

Downes had the unarmed *Essex Junior* bowling along toward Sandy Hook for three hours before being overtaken. A senior officer came on board, with the request that Downes muster his crew. The officer tallied the sailors against the passport list, looking for a rumored English deserter. No such man existed. The officer regretted the inconvenience, and sent them in to New York. On the way they passed a permanently moored store ship, perhaps invisible in the fog; it was the *Alert*, captured almost two years before, the first and only naval victory of Porter's war.

The *Essex Junior* encountered another British warship, the frigate *Narcissus*, whose captain waved them onward to the Hook by about eight o'clock on this "dark and squally" evening. "We could not procure a pilot," wrote Gatty Farragut, "so the captain took her in by his chart. When we got opposite the small battery in the Horse Shoe, we hoisted our colors with a lantern, clewed up our sails, and sent a boat ashore with a light in it. By accident the light was extinguished, and the fort immediately commenced firing on us." In the last hour of her long passage, the *Essex Junior* was going to be sunk by American gunners in the outer harbor of New York City. "But the ship was not struck by a single shot," noted Farragut, "which convinced me it was not as awful a thing as supposed to lie under a battery."*

Rowing and sailing, Porter and his boat's crew went on for sixty miles until finally landing in heavy surf on Long Island, where the people of Babylon took him into custody as a British officer of the sort that he so liked to impersonate. The militia gathered and Porter "was closely interrogated; and, [his] story appearing rather extraordinary, was not credited." At last he produced his certificate as a navy captain, and the people raised three cheers and fired off a twenty-one-round salute from a swivel gun. They gave him a feast, and next day they gave him a horse to ride to New York and a cart and pair of oxen to carry his boat.

When Porter arrived in Brooklyn, he reported to the commanding officer there, and then rode a hack into Manhattan, where crowds turned out in the streets. "There," reported Farragut, "the mob took the horses from the carriage" and pulled it by manpower "all over the city, thereby showing that his countrymen had esteemed his defeat not less than he had."

Porter acted out the final scene of his long drama to the applause of the New Yorkers. In the middle of a patriotic holiday, the derring-do of his whaleboat escapade thrilled the public and persuaded the editors. Porter did not even have to rouse his author friends James Paulding and Washington Irving, for this was a great story that would sell newspapers.

The *Essex* had been defeated with the sacrifice of many lives, and the enemy had played dirty. The world now knew that, under the right sort of commander, Americans, with "determined, unconquerable courage," would sacrifice their lives by the scores even without hope of victory.

Porter's return "created in the hearts of his fellow citizens a kind of melancholy joy scarcely ever equaled on any similar occasion. We are rejoiced once more to clasp the hand of a hero whose bravery stands pre-eminent in the naval records of our country; but . . . we dare not ask him how fares the brave little *Essex* and her gallant crew. Alas! She is no more." In fact, the *Essex* was accompanying her twin, the *Phoebe*, across the Atlantic at that moment to take up her new career as a forty-two-gun frigate in the Royal Navy.

---

* Farragut would apply this lesson fifty years later on the Mississippi in the Civil War.

Everyone wanted a piece of Porter. He was treated to banquets, tributes, and gifts. Several families named newborns "David Porter," and at least one vessel owner christened a privateer by that name. In Philadelphia he was given another grand parade, and there Sindbad met with Washington Irving, now editor of the *Analectic Magazine*. Irving and others had been plying the newspapers for a year with praise for Porter in the Pacific; now, the famous author was drafting a nineteen-page "biographical memoir" with a portrait of Captain Porter, curly-haired and indomitable, whose last cruise was "conducted with wonderful enterprise, fertility of expedient, consummate seamanship, and daring courage."

In Washington, he was invited to dine with President James Madison and Navy Secretary William Jones at the White House. That was a great relief to Porter, who regaled them with tales of the South Pacific. Madison was entertained but not impressed, for he had no interest in annexing Pacific islands, nor did anyone else in government. That was fine with Porter. Somehow Nooaheevah and Gattanewa and Gamble had become unreal, and the whole Marquesan matter was not worth pressing. Even the most violent events had faded after the apocalyptic battle of Valparaiso and its still-vivid scenes and terrifying chaos. Still, the island interlude made for great reading in Porter's forthcoming book, already being typeset from his journal, with engravers working to turn his own drawings of giant tortoises, battling frigates, and half-naked island girls into illustrations worthy of a best-seller.

Back in Boston, William Bainbridge, Porter's former commander, sent him a message indicating that all was forgiven. Rendezvous with him at the navy yard soon, he wrote, and Bacchus "shall overflow you," and Bainbridge "will drown you, in lieu of hanging."

Chapter Fourteen

Rancagua

J osé Miguel Carrera and his brother Luis, freed at Chillan and warned to
stay clear of Bernardo O'Higgins, proceeded directly to Talca and walked
right into army headquarters, where the Spanish flag was flying. O'Higgins looked as if he had seen a ghost. Confronted by the person of his old
comrade in arms, he stepped to José Miguel and gave him an unsmiling
embrace. In private, he begged Carrera not to take to the streets and resume
the war. Carrera responded, "You know I never do favors that demean me.
I have nothing to hide. I miss my friends in the capital, and I will do what I
have to, by negotiation or by bayonet." O'Higgins made no reply. They had
a brief lunch, and the Carreras were given rooms in the barracks. That night
they slept with their pistols close by, and next day they departed for Santiago, with two cavalrymen to protect them and a third to keep them under
surveillance. O'Higgins sent a messenger to Lastra, who posted a reward for
the Carreras' capture.*

On May 19 they arrived at their father's ranch outside Santiago and
notified Lastra that they would be asserting their rights as citizens. Having
thrown down the gantlet, they withdrew toward the Andes and thought

---

* The description of the Carreras' betrayal and imprisonment at Chillan, and of their journey to Talca and
Santiago and their revolution against Lastra, is taken from José Miguel Carrera's diary, kept faithfully from
March 1813 through October 1814. After José's death, the diary descended in the family and was first
published in 1900 as the *Diario Militar de José Miguel Carrera*. It remains the only dependable day-by-day
account of the Carreras and their activities, and of many of the events relating to the effort to create and
sustain the republic of Chile.

about going to Mendoza to fetch their banished brother, Juan José. Finding the passes blocked by snow, they returned and sent messages to their old friends in the officer corps and government, nearly all of whom slipped out of the city and went up into the mountains to meet with the Carreras, assess the condition of the country, and brainstorm the elements of a rebellion. On June 18 the Carreras' father, Ignacio, was arrested by Lastra. Two weeks later, José Miguel came down from the hills and met secretly in Santiago with his adherents over the course of a week. Then Luis came to town accompanied by twelve riflemen. José Miguel wisely removed his headquarters to a suburb, but Luis was betrayed and captured on July 9. Mackenna, in the capital with Lastra, was completing his long report about the "execrable" Carreras and their crimes. He sent off a note to O'Higgins suggesting that Luis be sent across the continent to prison in Montevideo. O'Higgins concurred, but first Luis was put on trial for treason.

José Miguel Carrera had done all he could to revive the national independence movement. He could not be sure that he had succeeded, but his father and brother were in prison, he was being hunted, and he had no time left for organizing. On July 23, at three in the afternoon, the revolution began in downtown Santiago. By the hundreds, infantrymen marched into the central plaza, and cannon were trundled down the streets and placed at every intersection. A few of Lastra's officers were arrested, and it was over. Accompanied by Rivera and his cavalrymen, José Miguel Carrera, wearing a brightly colored poncho, rode into the square. The capital resounded with the cheering of ecstatic soldiers, followed by the jubilation of the general populace, who came flooding into the streets to celebrate.

Mackenna and Irassari, abandoned by their adherents, were soon captured—Mackenna in a haystack, Irassari in a sewer. Supreme Director Lastra was taken from the palace and imprisoned, and Luis Carrera was set free. As Arteaga's "Birth of a Nation" battalion stood by, a new three-man junto was sworn in to run the national government, with José Miguel Carrera at its head. The flags of Spain came down, and the tricolor banners of the republic of Chile were unfurled over the capital.

President Carrera immediately revoked the Treaty of Lircay, then turned his attention to military resources. There were none. Under Lastra, the Santiago defense force had dwindled to 600 men in the barracks, with 200 operable rifles and no money in the treasury. He met with the soldiers and ordered the mint to pay them, and he set in motion the process of intense recruitment of troops and the fabrication of 4,000 new uniforms. With 900 men, Luis Carrera marched to Valparaiso and threw Formas in jail. José Miguel Carrera proceeded with the banishment or imprisonment of eighty-five monks and seventy Larrain adherents. He advised Roberts Poinsett, in exile at Buenos Aires, that he had resumed authority in Chile and that El Consul would do him a great honor by returning as his advisor and comrade. Poinsett replied with congratulations but regretted that he must return to his own country and help to win its war with England. In the meantime, Poinsett made arrangements for the shipment of 500 rifles—maybe a thousand—and ammunition to Carrera.

Carrera sent José Miguel Infante south to Talca to confer with O'Higgins. On August 2 Carrera had the pleasure of sending Mackenna, Irassari, and five more of his bitterest enemies into exile in Mendoza, noting in a letter to San Martin that he had been generous toward men who had not been so to him, and who had neither honor nor love of country. Carrera sent Joaquin Larrain and four other former government officials into exile in the north. In mid-August, Carrera's emissaries met with O'Higgins, who was reminded that Carrera had once resigned his generalship of the army in order to save the country and that O'Higgins now had the same chance to put Chile ahead of his own ambitions. It was not too late to join forces against General Gainza at Chillan; after victory, their quarrels could be settled at the ballot box.

O'Higgins opted for civil war and kept his men marching northward.

Carrera had not had time to organize a real army—most of his followers were militiamen, and most had no weapons. Many had not fought for Carrera's officers, and some had not fought at all. On August 19, Carrera deployed his brother Lucho in command of the second division vanguard, heading south toward Paine, about thirty miles from Santiago, to slow O'Higgins at the pass. Other former patriot officers of Carrera were in the countryside trying to raise new fighters. Colonel Diego Benavente and 200 horsemen followed Luis, and four days later Colonel J. M. Portus reported with a huge corps of 1,200 cavalrymen, most armed with lances.

O'Higgins proceeded toward Santiago despite having received, two weeks earlier, the alarming news of an invasion at Talcahuano by a large force sent from Lima under General Mariano Osorio to combine with Gainza. O'Higgins kept the news to himself, and on August 26 his troops, scouted by Lucho's retreating outriders, arrived on the outskirts of Santiago at the Plains of Maipu. There, at noon, the battle commenced.

For two hours the nationalist armies clashed, with Luis Carrera's division slowly gaining against O'Higgins' infantry. Finally, José Miguel deployed Portus's cavalry, which charged into the center and split the enemy force in two. The rout was on, but the men largely refrained from killing. Carrera's troops took 400 prisoners, captured thirteen officers and two guns, and achieved total victory. At nightfall, Carrera learned of Osorio's invasion and sent a proposal to O'Higgins that they unite to defend the capital. O'Higgins had only 800 fighting men left, with 250 good rifles. To the south were thousands of well-armed, well-disciplined Spanish troops, fresh from the battlefields of Europe. His old comrade Bernardo repented in tears to José Miguel, who assured him that all he wanted was "a sincere reconciliation in order to exterminate the tyrants."

On September 4, 1814, seven weeks after the coup, O'Higgins placed himself and his army under the command of José Miguel Carrera with the understanding that he, O'Higgins, would lead the vanguard into battle. Osorio's army, in good health and good spirits, about 3,500 soldiers strong, had been marching north without opposition and had already reached Talca, fifty miles from Santiago. Carrera, deprived of the chance to draw Osorio into a series of battles, had done his best to gather an army but had not had time to organize, equip, or train it, and his men had expended most of their ammunition and much of their energy in the battle at Maipu. The Carrera-O'Higgins troops, very recently fighting each other, would be at a severe disadvantage, with no room for failure. One bad defeat, and there would be nothing to keep Osorio from taking the capital.

On September 23 the preternaturally slow *Cherub* arrived at Valparaiso, returned from her foray into the western islands. Tucker made a point of taunting the American-friendly people of the port by entering under the ensign and pendant of the United States, with the captured banner of "Free Trade and Sailors Rights" at his foremast head. On board were American prisoners John Gamble and his men, who were "extremely disappointed at seeing the old Spanish flag displayed in the forts." Gamble wondered if all had been lost, but "a boat soon came alongside, with the agreeable intelligence that the patriots were still advancing in their great work, and intended shortly again to hoist their own flag."

Although a prisoner, Gamble was allowed to visit in Valparaiso. There were still twenty sailors from the *Essex* in town—and a few more who had gone off with the rebel army—according to Vice-consul Blanco, Poinsett's successor, who "received him in his arms as a father, and entertained him in the most friendly manner." To Blanco, Gamble told the sad story of the uprisings and the massacre at Nukuhiva and its aftermath.

With his wounded and broken crew, Gamble had sailed on through the Pacific night after barely escaping the furious Enana. "Our situation was deplorable," he related, "inasmuch as we were at sea in a leaky ship without either boats, anchors, or hands to navigate her, having only two sound men out of seven." They had no charts and no hope of getting upwind to Chile or to some island where they would be safe from the British. "In this situation," he had thought that the only possible means of "escape from death, was to run the trade winds down to the Sandwich islands, a distance of 1,800 miles. No time was lost in bending the necessary sails for this purpose, which we accomplished by means of a windlass and capstan." Under heavy canvas, but with no experience in navigating a large vessel over unknown seas, they had accomplished the amazing feat of making landfall two weeks later, on May 23.

"To our great joy, we discovered the high land of Hawaii, the windward island of the Sandwich group." These islands were known to be inhabited by the Kanaka people, with a few British and American traders and beachcombers. After encounters with islanders in canoes and a nighttime brush with breakers, Gamble and his crew had found some Boston traders who were waiting out the war. Unable to make the trip to Chile without acquiring naval supplies, Gamble had shipped nine new men at the bay and taken off to visit the storehouse of Tamaahmaah, the king of the islands, at Hawaii.

John Gamble and his men began to think they might survive this adventure in paradise and return to Valparaiso, but at dawn on June 13, as they approached Hawaii, a strange vessel appeared dead ahead. Gamble first supposed her to be the *Albatros*, then thought of the *Seringapatam*. His mind, he feared, was playing tricks, but he had no spyglass and could not be sure. At eight in the evening, in perfect calm, the stranger hoisted American colors. Suddenly Gamble perceived her as "a ship of war, and an enemy." Horribly, a large, white pennant was unfurled, emblazoned with the words "Free Trade and Sailors Rights," and she fired a shot at the *Hammond*. Gamble had no choice but to surrender. Taken on board, he found that he was the guest of Captain T. Tudor Tucker, commander of the Royal Navy sloop of war *Cherub*, cruising for American whalers ten weeks after having helped to defeat an American frigate at Valparaiso.

For Gamble, the terrible news about the *Essex* had been the start of a new nightmare. With Porter defeated, there was no hope of Gamble and his crew being set free or getting home. They had been held prisoner for several weeks, during which Tucker had captured two American vessels and tried to lure Americans out from their island hideaways. Finally, Tucker and *Cherub* had sailed for Chile, trailed by three American prizes.

José Miguel Carrera and Bernardo O'Higgins had little time to prepare a proper strategy or coordinate their meager assets. Their armies were poorly provisioned and desperately short of ammunition and weapons. For three weeks, throughout September, they tried to organize and arm their forces, but only about half the men had rifles that still fired. Still, there was no time left, and they marched south to meet the enemy. Above the Maule River, at the Pass of Paine nine miles north of the town of Rancagua, Carrera found good high ground to hold, but O'Higgins had already deployed his division of 850 men below, near the Cachapoal River, and would not budge. Carrera warned him that he was too far forward and his men too exposed. Carrera wanted to fight a decisive action with the full weight of both armies thrown against each other, and O'Higgins's salient would prevent that, but O'Higgins was adamant. And so on September 21, Carrera sent his brother Juan José in command of a division of 750 men to join O'Higgins south of the Cachapoal, and meanwhile moved 700 men of the National Guard—184 of whom were armed with rifles and the rest with lances—farther down the road that led to Rancagua. José Miguel kept the third division, with 1,300 militiamen under Luis Carrera, in reserve, as the last line in the defense of Santiago.

When Osorio and his large army reached the Cachapoal River, O'Higgins was badly intimidated and immediately fell back to a new position in Rancagua. There his men quickly turned the main plaza into an Alamo of logs, rocks, and cattle hides, with snipers on the roofs and cannons in the walls. Juan José Carrera, taking a seat in a priest's house, turned over his troops to God and O'Higgins. On the afternoon of September 30, under cover of artillery, Osorio hurled a first wave of men against fortress Rancagua. They were thrown back. The Spanish regrouped and sent more than 3,000 men and twenty cannon across the plain and into the town, completely surrounding the rebel position. Two more assaults, however, could not penetrate the inner perimeter.

That night, O'Higgins dispatched a messenger up the road to tell José Miguel Carrera, "Send ammunition and the third division, and all will be accomplished." The president, without ammunition, replied, "It will have to come in the form of a bayonet charge. You are completely surrounded, and must break out your men to the north." At dawn, Osorio began a barrage, and soon the town was bombed into a hell of burning buildings and stone rubble. O'Higgins now fought under a Chilean flag cinched with a black ribbon, the symbol of a battle to the death, without quarter given or expected. As before, the Chilean defenders, with little ammunition, held off Osorio, suffering with large losses. One gun crew, out of grape shot, primed its cannon with doubloons. Hundreds fell dead and wounded as they fought on through the morning. At eleven o'clock, they heard from a lookout in the church tower: "¡Viva! ¡Viva la patria!" Luis Carrera and José Miguel Portus had arrived in the distance at the head of 900 men from the third division.

Inside the perimeter at Rancagua, O'Higgins ordered an assault on three fronts. His bravos poured yelling over the barricades, charging and firing, but they did not break out to the north, and Luis Carrera's division could not fight through the forces that barred their way. Portus's hussars were repulsed several times, and still they tried to force their way in on side streets, but the Spanish army, fighting from behind fences and from trenches and houses, was too strong. For four hours the third division and the National Guard tried to break through, but finally their lines began to crack, and José Miguel Carrera ordered a retreat to Paine. "The ruin of Chile seemed decreed by Providence," wrote Carrera. "All was blindness and error."

Late on the second day at Rancagua, after thirty-six hours of continuous fighting and bombardment, the troops of O'Higgins and Juan José Carrera made a desperate thrust through Osorio's soldiers and escaped northward to Paine. Night had fallen, and chaos ensued. With a Spanish army of 3,500 coming toward his milling mob of perhaps 1,800, José Miguel Carrera ordered them to withdraw, but the retreat became a rout as hundreds of terrified men, no longer an army, poured into the capital.

After burning government documents and gathering wagonloads of specie from the mint, the Carreras and hundreds of their followers fled to the north, hoping to regroup and renew the fight. O'Higgins and his adherents did not follow, but fled east *en masse*, looking over their shoulders as they started up the foothills toward the high passes of the cordillera, shedding money, supplies, and weapons as they went; and they did not stop until they crossed over to Mendoza, in Argentina. José Miguel Carrera's remaining officers and troops would not go north to Coquimbo—panic had set in, and the army had completely dissolved. Accepting the totality of the disaster, Carrera turned toward the eastern mountains.

The forlorn hope was over. The nation that they had fought for—the visionary republic of Chile—was not to be.*

On the night of November 2, the new royal captain-general of Chile, Mariano Osorio, began his reign of terror. Forty of Chile's leading citizens were dragged from their homes and hauled into the Santiago prison yard to be transported to the coast and shipped 200 miles to the island of Juan Fernandez. Hundreds more patriots would be hunted down throughout the country and incarcerated hundreds of miles away at Valdivia and in prisons built at Valparaiso and Santiago. With a stroke of the pen, Osorio reinstated the old order exactly as before, from slavery to church fees to exclusion of foreign commerce. Large numbers of Spaniards arrived to fill the offices of the bureaucracy and to rule the Chileans as a captive population forbidden to own a pistol, walk with a cane, or go abroad in the streets at night.

At Mendoza, of the six revolutionary heroes—O'Higgins, Mackenna, Manuel Rodriguez, and the three Carreras—just two would be alive by the autumn of 1818, and only one would see Chile again.

On October 14, 1814, José Miguel Carrera and the remnants of his army arrived at Uspallata, the pass through the mountains that led to Mendoza. General San Martin was waiting for him. Since the victory at Maipu in early September, Carrera, as head of state, had banished many of his rivals over the Andes to Mendoza, where they had deluged San Martin with accusations against Carrera and his fellow officers, confirmed by San Martin's new friend, the exiled general Juan Mackenna. San Martin was an Argentinian and a soldier. He loathed politics and stayed away from the capital city of Buenos Aires as much as possible, because its juntos were hardly worthy of the brave freedom fighters he commanded on the frontiers. It was easy for him to conclude that Carrera was the same sort of divisive and self-absorbed politician, especially since San Martin had already clashed with General Juan José Carrera during the latter's banishment by Lastra while his brothers were in prison. Resentful of San Martin's patronizing attitude and his assumption that independence could not be achieved by Chileans, Carrera had warned

---

* From this time forward, the period of the Chilean revolution and struggle for independence would be known as La Patria Vieja, roughly "the old homeland" or "the first nation."

San Martin to stay out of Chile, saying that it was not his war to fight, that brother José Miguel was commander-in-chief, and that Chilenos would liberate themselves, perhaps with San Martin's help but not at his command.

José Miguel Carrera now found himself in a hellish exile, surrounded by "intrigue, ignorance, vengeance, and power." The disaster at Rancagua haunted everyone. O'Higgins blamed the Carreras for not fighting their way in, while the Carreras blamed O'Higgins for disobeying the order to withdraw.* Beyond Rancagua, there was the larger and more tragic decision that O'Higgins had made in marching on José Miguel Carrera at Santiago rather than making common cause to drive Gainza out of Talca. At Mendoza, in the misery of defeat and the bitterness of old feuds and new recriminations, there was little chance of reconciliation. Those whom Carrera had defeated at Maipu were now San Martin's favorites, and the agents of the dictatorship, Lastra and the Larrains, were treated with respect. Carrera's victories and his many sacrifices were of no interest to San Martin—it was all moot now, part of a failed movement, a history that had led to a dead end on the wrong side of the Andes.

San Martin regarded himself as "the instrument of justice and agent of destiny," fated to conquer all of southern Spanish America and to rule from the throne of the viceroy's palace at Lima. He had already decided that O'Higgins, so useful to the former Supreme Director Lastra, was the perfect figurehead for Chile in the new order he envisioned.

In the meantime, something had to be done with Carrera and his men. San Martin moved them away from Mendoza into separate barracks and placed them under Colonel Balcarce. Carrera requested passports for Coquimbo. San Martin ignored him and offered Carrera's soldiers the opportunity to join the army of the United Provinces, but they scoffed at him and said they would only fight under the flag of Chile. Erupting in fury, San Martin had Balcarce evict the soldiers from their quarters and throw their possessions in the street. He then arrested José Miguel and Juan José Carrera and their colonels. José Miguel, defiant, was told to behave. "Behave?" said Carrera. "I make the Spanish behave, in shackles, in my prisons." The four officers were kept under guard until they were sent east with an escort of thirty dragoons.

---

* Carrera would always contend that O'Higgins, having formed a square inside Rancagua and thereby allowed his force to be surrounded, had a duty to fight his own way out, and that it would have done no good for the third division—the only reserve corps left to Carrera—to have fought its way into Rancagua only to become part of that square, crushed on all sides by a larger, better-armed force.

At Buenos Aires, the capital of rebel Argentina, Carrera conferred with his lieutenants Manuel Rodriguez, Diego Benavente, and Julian Uribe; his brothers Lucho and Juan José; and other officers and adherents. A few days after arriving, former General Luis Carrera, twenty-three, crossed paths with former General Juan Mackenna, twenty years older, and challenged him for grossly abusing his family in the report written for Lastra. Mackenna replied that he had told the truth and that indeed the Carrera family had been the cause of all of Chile's problems. In a duel the next day, November 21, Carrera shot and killed Mackenna.

José Miguel Carrera, banished president of a country that no longer existed, did not give up on his vision of the republic of Chile. In his imagination, the tricolor flag would once again wave over Santiago, and he would liberate his father and the other political prisoners. After all the battles, political triumphs, imprisonment, escapes, and betrayals, Chile's future remained his only concern—and he remained Chile's only hope for an independent republic. But he had no money and no political base, and San Martin intended to use O'Higgins for the reconquista.

There was no time to lose if Carrera wanted to start a new liberation movement. Having listened to Poinsett for two years, he knew what was needed: a navy and a formal alliance with the enemy of O'Higgins's friends the British. It was not too late to liberate his people, if only he could make his way to the paradise of all nations, the United States of America.

Chapter Fifteen

Reverberations

In the roasting heat and thick haze of midsummer 1814, British warships sailed on the Chesapeake Bay below Baltimore unopposed, as they had for more than a year. So common a sight were they that no one noticed the arrival of several transports, and lookouts were slow to spot the large British army that landed and began marching south from the Patuxent River toward Washington.

On August 19, 1814, David Porter was in New York working on his book, plying the newspaper editors, playing with friends, staying away from his wife and children, and trying to stay calm while attending the navy's court of inquiry into the loss of his ship. He was not unduly anxious, for he had already been promised a large frigate under construction and nearly completed at the Washington Navy Yard; the forty-four-gun *Columbia* would be renamed *Essex*. Porter opened an envelope from Navy Secretary Jones and responded by taking out a newspaper ad: "Free Trade and Sailors' Rights. To the crew of the old *Essex*: Sailors, the enemy is about attempting the destruction of your new ship at Washington and I am ordered there to defend her. I shall proceed immediately, and all disposed to accompany me will meet me at three o'clock this afternoon, at the Navy agent's office." This seemed like a good idea to their captain, but not to those who had survived long service with Porter.

Money, as much as fame and obsession, had driven Porter into the Pacific, pursuing whalers when so much else might have been done. The calculations he had made while competing with the memory of Anson had proved to be fantasies. His projected $2.5 million for captured vessels and sperm-whale oil came to a grand total of zero—every one of the ships he had taken, and all of their oil, went back to England. The Royal Navy had retaken all of them except the _Seringapatam_, which was sailed from Nukuhiva to London by her English captors. Worse still, Porter actually doubled the amount of sperm oil that got back to Britain, for nearly all of the ten American whalers that had been trapped at Talcahuano, hoping for the convoy that Porter never provided, were captured in the Atlantic before reaching port.

As his crewmen had long discussed, Porter could have avoided Hill-yar altogether and chosen a very different way of concluding their Pacific adventure. He could have sailed west from the Marquesas, sold his prizes and oil in Asia, and perhaps returned to the United States as a proud captain with his ship and a full crew, and not as a paranoid captive on board a cartel of shattered survivors. The navy was kind enough to purchase the _Essex Junior_ for the handsome price of $25,000, which was the only prize money Porter's men would receive. Divided according to the rules, it paid Porter $3,750 and the deckhands or their widows about $100 apiece.

The survivors of the _Essex_ had further reason to regret serving under Porter, for they were forgotten as soon as they went ashore. Within ten days at New York, still unpaid, they were all strapped for cash. On July 20, Enoch Milay of Marblehead and six other crewmen "without one cent in our pockets" sent a letter to Porter at his mansion on the Delaware. "It gives us extreme pain," they wrote, "to be under the necessity of intruding on the quiet you are about to enjoy with your family, and which you are so justly entitled to after your well earned laurels, but merely to request that you will see that justice done us, which we, who have in our station equally defended the honor of our country, deem ourselves entitled to." Out of patience and out of confidence, they asserted that they were "men, sir, who tho' not in so high a station in life as you are, have some feelings of pride about us, and cannot bear to be dependent on strangers." They concluded by asking, "Is this the reward, sir, we expected to meet from our country, the conduct for men to receive who have been at all times willing to shed their blood in defense of that country's rights?" Navy Secretary Jones soon heard from Porter, and on July 25 he made $30,000 available to the long-suffering crew of the former American frigate _Essex_.

Lieutenant Edward Barnewall, Doctor Richard Hoffman, and some of his men joined Porter at half past three on August 20 as he headed south to turn away the enemy and save his new ship. Secretary Jones and other Washington officials waited in vain for the arrival of John Rodgers, Stephen Decatur, and David Porter. On August 22, Jones rode to the riverbank and watched six British ships slowly ascending the Potomac, grounding in the mud from time to time, shifting their cannon, and then moving on. Jones ordered Commander John O. Creighton to take a fast gig and a crew to reconnoiter and ascertain whether the enemy had transports and troops. In the meantime, Captain Joshua Barney, commander of the much-harried American flotilla on the Chesapeake Bay, had abandoned his vessels and marched his men toward Washington to meet the fast-moving English army under General Robert Ross. Porter, with a small force, arrived at his hometown of Baltimore and placed himself under Commodore John Rodgers. Secretary Jones tried to find them on August 23, with orders to proceed to Bladensburg, Maryland, where Barney and the local militia general, William Winder, were massing their troops "to preserve the national capital and its invaluable establishments from the ruthless hands of a vengeful foe."

The British had already won the world war. With Napoleon in exile, America became the target, and London sent some top generals with 20,000 veteran troops across the Atlantic. The invasion of the Chesapeake was the first of three operations intended to finish things off and commence a global Pax Britannica. On August 24, General Ross and his army routed the local forces and rolled into Washington, from which President Madison, Vice President Gerry, Secretary Jones, members of Congress, and all the others who, two years before, had declared war on Great Britain fled into the countryside. Ross had his men set fire to most of the federal buildings, including the Capitol and the White House, and take possession of the Washington Navy Yard with its new vessels and its many tons of material and ammunition. Captain Tingey, the yard's commandant, was too quick for them and torched the whole place, destroying property worth $417,000, including the new *Essex*.

On the run and without navy vessels on the Chesapeake Bay, Secretary Jones could do little to save Baltimore or to stop the British armada. On August 27, Royal Navy bomb ships caused the destruction of Fort Washington on the Maryland shore, below Washington, which now lay undefended on the river, as did the prosperous seaport of Alexandria on the Virginia side. There, merchants had scuttled twenty-one vessels to the river bottom to prevent their capture and form a barrier to the wharves. Possessing only two cannon, Alexandria's citizens were terrified that their city would be sacked and burned like Washington. As the Royal Navy frigate *Seahorse* came gliding in to the town's main anchorage, Mayor Charles Simms welcomed her commander, Captain J.A. Gordon, and readily agreed to refloat the merchant vessels, replace their sails and furnishings, and fill each one with produce and goods.

The U.S. Navy had done nothing to prevent Gordon's long, slow parade up the Potomac, but Secretary Jones hoped to improvise some batteries on the heights "to annoy or destroy the enemy on his return down the river," an assignment given to Rodgers to be executed by him or by Porter. Rodgers responded by sending Porter with 100 men to Washington, mainly to prevent looting. Rodgers declared that he would stay at Baltimore, where the people had "patriotic spirit" and a feisty militia general, Samuel Smith. Perhaps they would do better than the militia had at Washington. If not, Philadelphia was next.

The navy men focused on stopping Gordon. He had two frigates, three bomb ships, a rocket ship, and the merchant vessels. His fleet, twice the size of Porter's in the Pacific, was an easy target, but the Americans had no guns and no ships. At Alexandria, the British picked up the pace with the hope of sailing by the end of August. Porter was to build batteries and earthworks downriver at White House Point, opposite the battery of Captain Oliver H. Perry, still without cannons.

Porter and his new friend Creighton crossed on horseback to the Virginia side of the river, along with a Lieutenant Charles Platt, and headed for the newly constructed battery downstream. The two captains were furious at having lost their new vessels in the Navy Yard fire—they could not stop talking about it—and now, in striking distance of the enemy, Porter had the crazy impulse to lash out at the British in Alexandria. Somehow he and his friends would wreak terrible vengeance on these invaders. Neither Creighton nor Platt understood the suicidal nature of Porter's mania, or, if they did, they were too afraid to oppose him. Before they knew it, they were galloping down a dirt road into the city, then charging down a cobblestone street toward the waterfront. Creighton, large and powerful, was the one who first spotted British Midshipman John Went Fraser, not much bigger than Gatty Farragut, busy on a wharf while his boat's crew waited in the dock.

It was a strange moment in the history of warfare, as two naval captains on horseback charged murderously onward through the middle of a city held by the enemy. Alexandria, defenseless before a squadron of

British battleships, might be blown apart and burned down for any provocation. Creighton, charging onto the wharf, leaned down and grabbed
the uniformed teenager by his collar and yanked him stunned across the
pommel. They rode back up the street with the boy bucking and struggling
and Creighton grasping him by his neckerchief. Suddenly it came unknot-
ted, and Fraser fell from the horse, regained his feet, and lit out for the
waterfront. The Americans tried again, gave up, and rode off through the
suburbs, across the fields, and into the woods leading toward White House
Point, still furious, still unavenged.

It was by luck alone that Fraser was not killed and that Porter and
Creighton, designated leaders of a major operation against an enemy flotilla, were not captured. It was by something other than luck that the city of
Alexandria was preserved from destruction. Hearing of the brutal treatment
of his midshipman, Captain Gordon immediately raised his battle flag on
the *Seahorse* and had his drummers beat the crew to quarters. Fortunately,
Mayor Simms was on site and pleaded for a chance to explain. As he wrote
to his wife, Nancy, safe at a farm, "your fear that something might occur
to provoke them to fire the town was not unfounded." The "naval officers
rode into town like Saracens and seized on a poor unarmed midshipman,
a mere stripling, and would have carried him off or killed him had not his
neck handkerchief broke. This rash act excited the greatest alarm among
the inhabitants of the town, women and children running and screaming
through the streets, and hundreds of them laid out[side] that night without
shelter," thinking that their houses would be destroyed. As Simms prepared
a message to Gordon, "one of the captains rushed into the parlor with the
strongest expressions of rage on his countenance, bringing with him the
midshipman who had been so valiantly assaulted by those gallant naval officers." Despite Porter and Creighton, Simms saved his city.

Porter, Creighton, and Pratt arrived at the Virginia battery on
White House Point that evening, September 1, and were joined by Secretary
of State James Monroe and two militia generals. On the heights above the
river, militiamen were chopping down trees and building earthworks atop
a cliff, but no big guns had arrived. An eighteen-gun British brig sailed past
and fired a broadside up toward the men. With two small four-pounders,
Porter opened "a brisk fire" on the brig, which continued to blast away and
made a leisurely escape down the Potomac. Porter did not tell Secretary
Monroe about his earlier adventure in Alexandria. The battery consisted
of three long eighteens and two long twelves in addition to six six-pound-

ers and the two four-pounders, but most of the cannons were not properly mounted in carriages.

Only David Porter could believe that such a force could withstand the concentrated power of bomb ships, rocket ships, gunboats, and four battleships with a total of sixty guns to a side. He did not have long to wait for the test. Captain Gordon's squadron left Alexandria on September 3, headed downriver on the fifty-mile trip to the bay. It was slow going, as before, with several groundings. Commodore Rodgers sent some barges and fire ships against the flotilla, but all were parried without damage. On the morning of the fifth, Gordon's vessels came under fire from both sides of the Potomac. Oliver Hazard Perry's battery at Indian Head was of "too small caliber to make much impression on the enemy," so he withdrew. Off White House Point, Gordon anchored his frigates so the gun crews could perfect their aim, and they blasted away at Porter's earthworks with calm, lethal efficiency, assisted by the bomb ships. Porter called for the militia to advance to "the woods upon the heights" and lay down musket fire, but the Virginians' commander held back, realizing that he would be sacrificing men who could not stop the enemy from passing down the river.

Porter alone stayed at his post with a hundred men, including several veterans of the *Essex*, to face "the vast quantities of shot, shell, and rockets which were showered upon the hills." His battery had no effect on the ships below, while the gunnery of the British squadron made a Rancagua of the cliff top, a chaos of explosions, shrapnel, and slaughter. As before, Porter stood unscathed, but Lieutenant Barnewall received his third wound and Doctor Hoffman was bleeding at the head. Noticing that thirty men lay dead or wounded in the killing pit, Porter ordered the discharge of a few more pointless shots, his last in this war, and then sounded a retreat to a hill nearby, entreating the survivors to be ready to "charge the enemy if he should land to spike our guns." It was a final fantasy, and by eight o'clock, those guns were silent.

Slowly, the ships and brigs and schooners and sloops of the convoy passed down the peaceful river. It was a sight never seen before: a few British warships leading twenty-one proud trading vessels, safe from every army and every navy in the world, in a majestic parade toward the bay and the horizon beyond, where Britannia ruled the waves from the Americas to Europe and Africa, from Arabia and India to the far reaches of the Orient, and on into the vast Pacific.

The British army that had captured Washington next began to advance on Baltimore, accompanied by a flotilla in the Chesapeake Bay. David Porter could not get through enemy lines, but his hometown had no need of him anyway. Samuel Smith and the militia defeated the British regulars at the Battle of North Point. On September 14, the British withdrew, just as they did in New York State, where MacDonough's naval victory at Lake Champlain caused General Prevost to retreat to Canada.*

For Porter, the war remained an opportunity for career advancement. War was his business, without which things would be slow and boring. Porter's new frigate had gone up in smoke, and the other battleships were blockaded in port. Still, he was inspired by the success of the Baltimore privateers, and he proposed the formation of a fleet of fast navy vessels to raid Britain's commerce in the Caribbean. To his surprise, Secretary Jones authorized it, and Porter got to work.

Madison addressed Congress on the state of the union on September 20. He had not approved or even recognized Porter's embarrassing annexation of a Pacific island, but Porter was popular, and Madison was his president. At last, things were going well for the United States in its war effort, so in his speech Madison could afford to note a couple of disappointments. After acknowledging the capture of the frigate *Chesapeake* and the heroic death of Captain James Lawrence, he stated that "on the ocean, the pride of our naval arms has been amply supported. A second frigate has fallen into the hands of the enemy: but the loss is hidden in the blaze of heroism with which she was defended. Captain Porter, who commanded her, and whose previous career had been distinguished by daring enterprise, and by fertility of genius, maintained a sanguinary contest against two ships, one of them superior to his own, and other severe disadvantages; till humanity tore down the colors which valor had nailed to the mast. This officer and his comrades have added much to the rising glory of the American flag; and have merited all the effusions of gratitude which their country is ever ready to bestow on the champions of its rights and of its safety."

Porter's stock stayed high. His friend Washington Irving, famous author, excerpted Nukuhivan passages from Porter's journal in his *Analectic Magazine* for October and November 1814, advising that "those who

---

* John Glover Cowell's father-in-law, Captain Joseph Lindsey, forty-six, served as sailing master on board the schooner *Ticonderoga* in the battle and was cited for "coolness, skill, and bravery."

have hitherto admired Captain Porter only as the hero of Valparaiso, will doubtless be pleased to see our American Anson in another character: like [Captain] Cook, observing and describing the manners and habits of newly discovered savages."

The Federalists of suave old Salem, builders of the *Essex*, responded with outrage at Porter and his actions. The editor of the Salem *Gazette* flogged him for committing mass murder and traducing "the character and honor of this country." In conclusion, the editor quoted Porter's own shameless description of the Taipi valley as he was leaving it: "When I had reached the summit of the mountain, I stopped to contemplate that valley which in the morning we had viewed in all its beauty, the scene of abundance and happiness. *A long line of smoking ruins now marked our traces from one end to the other*: the opposite hills were covered with the *unhappy fugitives*, and the whole presented a *scene of devastation and horror*." The editor closed abruptly with "Reader! Are you an American? Then, here stop and cover your face!"

In Albany, a well-informed reader using the penname "Las Casas"* reacted incredulously to Irving's Anson-Cook apotheosis of Porter. It was not Porter's candor that bothered him, but the ruthless brutality, the "hostile aggression" toward "defenseless natives (for they knew not the use of fire arms)," as if Porter had been eager to "slaughter" these people. Las Casas felt shame for America when he contrasted Porter's "prompt interference in the quarrels of these petty tribes" with the behavior of others—Cook, Vancouver, Pelouse—in these same remote waters where cross-cultural encounters tested the values of both parties. Brilliantly, Las Casas went on to relate Porter's adventures to the condition of the United States, which, two years into the war, now found its ports blockaded, its countryside overrun by British armies, its borders invaded by counterattacking Canadians, and its national capital smoldering in ruins. In a way, America had brought on the devastation that the Taipi had never asked for, the Taipi in whom, as he read Porter's narrative, Las Casas saw virtues that were scarce in America: "On reading the fate of these noble barbarians, or rather of these exalted patriots, what person will not admire their heroism and lament their fall with mingled emotions of astonishment, grief, and indignation?" In one day of extreme violence, Porter had arguably created "a dread and horror of civilized Americans throughout all Polynesia," and subjected American mariners to years of reprisals.

---

* Bartolome de Las Casas was a conquistador in Central America who had a revelation and became an advocate for the peaceful and respectful treatment of native peoples.

Las Casas saw all this and deplored the coarseness that war had unleashed in his formerly rational and polite republic. As war tainted everything, and as the nation's president, burned out of his house, acted and spoke out of fear of a general collapse and total defeat, it was easy to extol the warlord, praising the results and ignoring the means, whether in the Pacific or at home. In closing, Las Casas offered little hope. Andrew Jackson, Indian slaughterer, and David Porter, Polynesian killer, were made heroes in the public prints, and President Madison could only praise them "with no emotion of concern for our own barbarities." Las Casas asked, "And shall such tragedies pass before us unminded as the idle wind? On hearing of these things, the man of serious and devout meditation"—the old-school American trying to live in peace and justice with his neighbor—"will be apt to start, and inquire anxiously, What has become of the moral sense of this country?"

Desperate to get into battle before the war ended, Porter spent weeks and then months on the logistics for the new naval force for the Caribbean, and finally had to admit that he could not bring together enough ships and supplies and men to make it happen. Instead, he predictably proposed a cruise to the Pacific. Secretary Jones approved, putting him in charge of a three-vessel squadron, but his last chance to outdo Anson was thwarted when his friend Captain Stephen Decatur refused to serve under him.

Getting home was no easy thing for Consul General Poinsett. While stuck at the Argentine capital from June 1814 onward, he continued to compose messages to Secretary Monroe, just as he had done all along, without any response. Unaware of the victory of Osorio and the exile of the Carreras and the rest of the patriots, Poinsett summarized "the present state of Buenos Ayres and Chile in order to enable you to judge of the probable result of the revolution of these colonies." Regarding Argentina and its main city Buenos Aires, he described the supreme director, Posadas, as well advised, intent on vesting all of the region's power in the capital, and determined to fend off Spain, primarily by means of a close alliance with England. "In the prosecution of their plans to free themselves from the yoke of Spain, they endeavour by every possible means to interest Great Britain in their favour, and, in order to accomplish, as far as concerns them, the guarantee given by that power of the integrity of the Spanish monarchy, have determined to send deputies to Spain and proffer their allegiance, but at the same time to insist on a free commerce, and election of their own rulers, and to be allowed to keep on foot a small standing force—conditions which secure their future freedom and the enjoyment of their rights." Poinsett believed that their trade with Britain was "the principal resource of Buenos Aires," producing "great advantages from expanding their commercial spirit" to the benefit of London and the detriment of "the jealous colonial policy of Spain." As he would note later in this report, the leadership's preference for Britain was not at all shared by the people in general, who favored the United States as friend and ally.

The Buenos Aires leaders, whose armies were led by San Martin, were vigorously opposed by José Gervasio Artigas, chief of the Banda Oriental (much of modern Uruguay), who was also committed to an independent federal union and backed by many of those from the interior who felt that the capital had too much power and was too ready to make deals with the royalists at Montevideo and Rio. In this, the Artigas party resembled Paraguay, which, with two presidents and a large congress, was determined to preserve "itself free from the influence of Buenos Aires." Both parties in Argentina, observed Poinsett, "affect great reverence for the constitution and government of the United States," and people generally felt very positive "toward their brethren of the north; and it is certain that, whatever may be the disposition of the raging factions, the popular sentiment is so strong against the English that they will never gain a permanent footing in these countries."

Regarding Chile, Poinsett had less to say, perhaps because of the trauma of the events that had led to his banishment. With an analytical distance that disguised his own deep involvement and partisan behavior in the highest levels of the revolution, he identified Chile's greatest problem as the prevalence of "violent and irreconcilable factions, as at present the Carreras and Larrains—the former, active and daring, influenced with the love of glory and anxious to advance the welfare of the country—the latter, equally ambitious but more timid, have, by intrigue and cunning means, taken possession of the command, and have been again immediately dispossessed by their more enterprising adversaries, who now govern the kingdom already so weakened by their dissensions that it will probably fall into the hands of the royalists."

Poinsett had lost his idealism and could no longer see any clear prospect of independence in South America, concluding that "it is difficult to form a correct opinion what may be the result of the revolution. It has hitherto been marked by rapid and continual changes of rulers and measures, than which nothing can be more destructive to the progress of a state, and denotes a character that would bear them through a revolution only under the most favorable circumstances. If, however, at the presence of imminent danger, all parties unite in the common defense, the power of Spain will not be sufficient to subdue them unless she purchases subsidies and assistance from Great Britain by yielding her commercial privileges in the colonies, which, from the present temper of the Court of Madrid, does not seem probable.

"Should they struggle through all their difficulties and succeed in establishing their independence, it is much to be feared that, harassed at the frequent failures of their legislative experiments, and having found that all parties—as they alternately fill the seat of government in order to secure their power—trample on the sacred rights of liberty, they will despair of obtaining that inestimable blessing, and terminate the struggle by a military despotism."

Like Consul Poinsett, John Gamble, the marine lieutenant, had begun to wonder if he would ever get home to America. In October 1814, at Valparaiso, he was put on board the *Cherub*, bound for Brazil with two prizes, one of them Gamble's own former command, *Sir Andrew Hammond*. Limping onto the wharf in Rio on November 30, Gamble was permitted "to lodge in town"—the other *Cherub* prisoners were required to stay on board—and "he had the pleasure to meet with several American gentlemen, not a few of them, like himself, extremely desirous to go home." Gamble met with Thomas Sumter, still the minister in this Portuguese port, who was trying to charter a cartel for the sixty American prisoners there. Gamble's friend Benjamin Clapp soon came ashore, and they did some horseback touring while Sumter negotiated for a transport. The deal was done, the passage was granted, but on February 8 Dixon, the British admiral, reneged.

Two weeks later a brig from England brought news of the peace treaty. Gamble was too sick to sail at first, having relapsed in the dust and sweltering heat. Impatient at the non-appearance of American ships, Gamble booked passage on the Swedish ship *Good Hope*, which cleared for France on May 15, more than five months after his arrival. She was "deeply laden, and withal, a dull sailer" whose "general progress through the water varied from two to four knots." One night those on board were treated to a natural spectacle when "the surface of the water had a grand and brilliant appearance, and the wake of the ship, as far as the eye could see, seemed like one vast sheet of fire." At the end of July, approaching the coast of France, the *Good Hope* fell in with an American vessel. "I left the Swede and went on board of this ship," the *Oliver Ellsworth*, bound to New York, wrote Gamble. He was treated kindly, and on August 27, "after encountering a dreadful gale," he had "the inexpressible joy to come once more within view of his native land, after an absence of two years and ten months."

Gamble's former *Essex* shipmates Lieutenant Stephen Decatur McKnight, eighteen, and acting Midshipman James R. Lyman, formerly of the ill-fated *Colt*, had also hitched a ride from Rio with a Swede, Captain Jan Gabriel Mollen, and were well along on a voyage to England when overtaken by a strange vessel from which a warning shot was fired. She flew an English ensign, and the boarding officer wore an English surgeon's uniform. After some shuffling of papers, it was revealed that this was the U.S. sloop of war *Wasp*, with 150 men and twenty-two guns, under Captain Johnston Blakeley.

The *Wasp* had been busy. On the evening of September 1, she had fallen in with the eighteen-gun Royal Navy brig of war *Avon* and defeated her in a battle of broadsides. Moving on, Blakeley and crew had captured two merchant vessels, which they had scuttled, and on September 21 they had cut off a valuable Royal Navy eight-gun brig, *Atalanta*, and sent her for the United States. Then came the mid-ocean interception of the Swedish vessel and the happiness of McKnight and Lyman in transferring to a ship of the U.S. Navy, one that had, in four months of cruising, won three victories over the Royal Navy and destroyed nine merchant vessels. The two young men had a chance to reflect on Johnston Blakeley's record. Without leaving the Atlantic, the *Wasp*, sometimes cruising right up the English Channel, had done more damage to enemy shipping and morale in the month of September alone than anything even attempted by Porter and the *Essex* in more than a year in the Pacific.

Captain Mollen and crew bade them all farewell as the handsome warship stood for the equator, hoping to overtake a British convoy bound for the West Indies in hurricane season.

The *Wasp* and her gallant men were never seen again.

Poinsett waited a while longer for a ship to carry him homeward, but the British were unwilling. As long as there was a war on, they wanted him on the sidelines, under observation. One night in November he arranged for an open boat to carry him down the Rio de la Plata to Montevideo, where he was able to get a berth on a Portuguese brig. Transferring to a schooner at the Brazilian port of Bahia, he found himself headed for the coast of North Africa and the island of Madeira, 400 miles out to sea, where he learned that the war was over. He spent some weeks at Funchal, observing and making a report on yet another foreign culture. At last he booked passage for the United States, and at the end of May 1815, he arrived in Charleston, too late to become a hero.

Poinsett had not meant to go to South America. When he had returned from Europe in 1810, he had hoped for fame and glory fighting the battles of his country. Instead he had taken the assignment that the president had offered, giving up a large part of his life and risking his career to represent the United States among revolutionary movements in Spanish America. It was a dangerous and solitary mission, one that had taught him a great deal about the power of culture to influence the political development of a people, and a great deal also about how much any one man could accomplish.

He came away feeling that the South American provinces were likely to separate from Spain but not to form republican governments, largely because of the outsized influence of the self-interested upper classes, with their bitter rivalries and their inveterate recourse to military force as a means of governing or changing governments. It gave him a profound respect for the unique qualities of the American revolution of 1775–83 and the remarkable process by which an eight-year war of independence had united the colonies and produced a new country.

It was, evidently, as impossible to adapt the American republican model to the rebellions of Spanish America as it was pointless to have imposed annexation on the people of Nukuhiva. Neither nation-building nor imperialism, as undertaken by two Americans in 1814, had led to reasonable outcomes.

Although ruling every sea, England was not quite ready to celebrate its takeover of the planet, for Napoleon escaped from his exile on the Mediterranean island of Elba and raised a huge army. This forced London to resume the costly role of savior of Europe in addition to fighting an unwanted land war in North America. The United States would be the best postwar market for Britain's industries, and London wanted to stop killing and start selling. The defeats at Baltimore and on Lake Champlain convinced the king's ministers to push their negotiators, and the Treaty of Ghent was signed in December 1814 to close out an Anglo-American conflict that had, in general, made prophets of its detractors.

The Battle of New Orleans, fought in January 1815 before news of the treaty reached Louisiana, was won by Andrew Jackson's superior artillery and was by far the biggest American victory of the entire war. Conveniently, it gave everyone a chance to celebrate and to congratulate President Madison, living in a boarding house, for having led them to triumph. London, too, celebrated the end of the brief American conflict and the final defeat of Napoleon, whose army was crushed by Wellington's allied forces at Waterloo. In mid-June 1815, the terrible world war, after twenty-one years and millions of deaths, was finally over.

Earlier, Madison had identified British interference with American shipping as the primary cause for war. That practice, a consequence of the Anglo-French conflict, vanished from postwar seas. America's maritime commerce resumed trading in most old markets and several new ones, especially in Brazil. Nantucket and New Bedford led the world in whaling, and foreign trade thrived until the worldwide depression of 1818. On the frontiers of America, where the Indians had been minimally supplied by the British, white expansion continued as if the war had never ended. Canada came away a winner, its borders intact.

The war had produced epochal consequences, mostly unintended, in the United States. Cut off from the usual supplies of overseas fabrics, American entrepreneurs had launched a homegrown textile industry that would proliferate under the protection of the 1816 tariff. The Federalist Party was disgraced and destroyed. In a country that had created the necessity of fending off a powerful invader, the party's consistent anti-war position was ultimately fatal. Finally, the war, in all its madness, bloodshed, improvisation, and heroism, served to give the United States, formerly a plural collection of regions and states, a patriotic new identity as one nation, indivisible.

Of all the vessels that had gone whaling in the Pacific, and all that Porter had captured, only the 370-ton *Seringapatam* pursued a westward course across that ocean. On May 7, 1814, the fourteen Englishmen who put Gamble and company in a leaky boat made off with the ship.

First they stopped at Tahiti, where the nature of their brief adventures may be imagined. Then they sailed a long leg south and west to New South Wales (Australia), arriving at Port Jackson with many colorful stories to tell. No one really believed them, but an agent helped them claim salvage rights at the Admiralty Court in Sydney, which passed the buck to London. It happened that Captain Eber Bunker, fifty-three, "the father of South Seas whaling," was ashore just then and could be persuaded to sail for England with this rum crew. Formerly a resident of Nantucket, Bunker had been sailing London whalers for the Enderbys since the 1780s and had been among the first to transport British convicts to the new colony at Botany Bay, Australia. In 1791, he had led the inaugural whaling expedition in Australian waters, followed by some sealing at New Zealand. He had just begun an ambitious sheep-ranching operation when the governor asked him to take command of the suspicious vessel.

Captain Bunker sailed *Seringapatam* into the Indian Ocean, then west to the Cape of Good Hope, and then up the coast of Africa and on past Spain, Portugal, and France. Upon boarding a pilot to bring her up the English Channel, he learned that the great war had ended and that they were all under a Pax Britannica. He delivered her to the Admiralty authorities, who arranged for the long-missing vessel to be sold back to her smiling owners, a firm of British merchants who had eagerly reopened a lucrative commerce with the postwar world.

David Porter began a new manic phase. By January 1815, he had published the first war story ever written by an American officer and was distributing copies of his two-volume *Journal of a Cruise Made to the Pacific Ocean* to friends and influentials, starting with President Madison. Sales were slow. Not everyone wanted to read about a war that had not gone well, and some were made uneasy by the allegory of a runaway ship with a loyal crew trapped on board, month after month, season after season, following the leader toward some conclusion that might prove disastrous.

In the White House and in the state and navy departments, readers must have fixed on some of the more disturbing issues raised by a navy captain acting like a self-serving renegade. For more than a year, Porter had divorced himself from the larger aims of the United States in its war effort and its relations with the Pacific world, aims that had been so well represented by Consul Poinsett. No doubt these matters came up for animated discussion within the U.S. Navy officer corps as well.

In written criticism, Porter was faulted chiefly for his boasting and his candor, if not rawness, and for his monstrous brutality in dealing with the Taipi. Americans of the book-buying class welcomed a bit of titillation, but not orgies and slaughter. Porter's memoir was unique and provocative in showing the American war spirit in action. Decatur or Bainbridge, knights of the sea, would have written of their adventures with much greater refinement, but a truthful account of the actions and attitudes of Andrew Jackson, for example, would have ripped away the complacency of the American gentry and made Porter seem tame. Some did see the book as a revelation, and not a good one. They had assumed that officers were adhering to a code of humane and gentlemanly honor through the temptations and ambiguities of wartime, immune to the violence, lust, and bigotry that Porter exemplified.

Porter was also faulted for his style, "strongly marked with a kind of bombastic verbosity, alike disgraceful to the hero and the man of education." One Philadelphian opined that, "interesting as that journal is, it is surely disgraced by invidious comparisons and by calculations which will hardly bear the test of truth"—to say nothing of the "reprehensible" "mistaken pride" that had led him to destroy the Taipi homeland. No one cited Porter's total absence of warmth toward others, his obvious alienation from his own mental-emotional life, his lack of religiosity, and his incapacity for reflection, moral struggle, or insight.

Porter, at least, was honest about who he was and what he had done. If his behavior, as described in his book, did not comport with genteel expectations, it was because most serious readers came from a privileged class that had little understanding of the rough forces that were carrying America forward onto the frontier, into industrial manufacturing, and over the seas. They had not stood on the deck of a trading vessel as a friend was shot while repelling a British boarding party, nor had they returned from a day of squirrel hunting to find the corpses of scalped parents and siblings. Extraordinary violence saturated the lives of many ordinary Americans, as did enslavement, poverty, illness, and ignorance, but these things were not addressed in Congress or even discussed in taverns. And the war itself, the pervasive reality of war, added a new and darker layer to the whole, affecting the entire culture and not just those engaged in the constant violence of carrying it out.

His admirers generally agreed that Captain Porter had produced a well-illustrated book full of thrilling material that needed better editing. At the *North American Review*, Boston's foremost intellectual publication, the reviewer quoted copiously from Porter's work and praised his depiction of the "uncivilized state of mankind" in the Pacific. He appreciated the explanation of *tapu* and the engraving of Mouina, "a very fine figure most curiously tattooed. The beauty and fancy of the lines and ornaments are very striking . . . ." The reviewer ignored "the conflicts with some of the tribes" except to say that the fight with the Hapa'a was "perhaps justified," but the war with the Taipi was "a great errour of judgment."

The reviewer wrote that "a striking feature in the composition of this journal is the frankness with which it [is] written. The author has narrated everything, and, as he has not disguised anything that others would have suppressed, he has laid himself open to those who are disposed to judge him harshly." Porter had written as a warrior who dealt in hard truths of real experience, on the edge of violence and death, without resorting to fiction or finessing the shameful parts.

Captain Porter did not need a best-seller. In the spring of 1815 he was appointed one of the three members of the Board of Navy Commissioners—a board that had not existed before and that would, at last, put navy men in positions of authority at the Navy Department. Porter celebrated by hiring his old friend, the writer James K. Paulding, as secretary to the board, and then he opened fire on the new secretary of the navy, Benjamin W. Crowninshield, a merchant and former shipmaster from Salem. One of the largest wartime lenders to the federal government and the primary owner of the nation's most successful privateer, the 600-ton battleship *America*, Crowninshield had no intention of being torpedoed by Captain Porter and his friends, and he took his case to the president. After a while, Madison had to tell the board members that they were not there to run the navy, but to advise its secretary.

Although it did not pay well, sitting on the Board of Navy Commissioners was a high honor, and Porter had finally made enough money from government settlements that he could afford to purchase a fine 157-acre tract near the White House. There he built his own mansion looking down on the president's. At "Meridian Hill," he became a lion of Washington and hosted grand soirees, although he and Evelina did not get along. Captain Porter turned into Farmer Porter, on the model of George Washington and Thomas Jefferson, and engaged in agriculture of the most advanced scientific sort, which made his hillsides a kind of spectacle of experimentation that attracted the skeptical public as well as audiences of astonished farmers and hustling real-estate men.

Most of his innovations were as expensive as they were unproductive, which forced him to take out enormous loans. How would he repay them? The answer, as before, was for the navy to send him to the Pacific. He would lead a squadron to Japan, an island nation that everyone had heard about but very few had visited. It was an interesting idea, but Navy Secretary Crowninshield did not see Porter as quite the right man for the job, and the proposal was shelved.

With no Japan in his future, Porter thought about the world he had seen, and where it was that he might make himself useful and rich. The more he considered it, the more he wondered if he had not missed a great opportunity on the coast of Chile.

Chapter Sixteen

Minute Guns

José Miguel Carrera, tall, confident, and handsome, came ashore in America after a sixty-three-day voyage, arriving at Annapolis, Maryland, in mid-January 1816. Navy Commissioner Porter set up a lengthy interview with Secretary of State James Monroe and an informal audience with President Madison, who had recently forbidden the export of arms and ammunition to South America. Neither made commitments, but both were impressed. It was a good start, and it got better.

The newspapers tracked the travels of the charismatic hero of Chile as he went here and there, addressing patriotic societies and military men, impressing them with his genial dignity and arousing an interest in Chile and the importance of an independent republic. In private, to potential investors, President Carrera laid out the plan for winning back his country with a naval squadron, a corps of officers, and military supplies for a people's army. To invest in his nation-building program was to help secure the future of the United States in the Pacific and Spanish America, with a high return on investment and prompt repayment projected from the sale of Chilean government bonds and duties on foreign commerce.

Roberts Poinsett did not meet with Carrera until July 1816, in New York. Poinsett was a changed man. His idealism had not survived his experiences in Spanish America and his missed opportunity to serve stateside in time of war. The news of Osorio's re-conquest had depressed and embittered him, and he had little hope that Carrera, now on the outside, could unite Chile's factions and restart the movement. Observing the realities of the postwar United States, he had come to appreciate its pragmatic politics and its lack of interest in the affairs of other nations or regions. In 1815, the government had recognized Fernando VII as king of Spain, and Secretary of State Monroe—soon to become president—had to dismiss any thought of recognizing Chilean independence, let alone committing to military intervention.

Denied other opportunities, Poinsett had begun a political career in his home state of South Carolina. He would do no more for Chile unless the federal government adopted a formal policy of "emancipation of the colonies" and authorized him to intervene, preferably as general of an invading army. He was weary from his years in the field and planned to make a grand tour of the American West that summer, including a meeting in Kentucky with House Speaker Henry Clay, expert in South American affairs and partial to Juan Martin Puerryedon, the ruthless French-Irish governor of Argentina, and Bernardo O'Higgins in Chile. Poinsett, bucking for preferment, opined to Clay that O'Higgins's love of the English had been exaggerated and that he was, in fact, a better republican than Carrera. True, Carrera possessed "more intellect and more vigour of character" and might be the only person "capable of carrying the revolution to a successful termination," but his republicanism was mainly "due to my ascendant over him, and I found on that subject he was difficult to govern." By contrast, O'Higgins was "a well-disposed man" whom "a skillful agent can render subservient to all his views." As for Carrera's mission to America, Poinsett was willing to introduce the Chilean leader to some expatriate military officers who had served Napoleon, and to arrange with a Philadelphia merchant house to provide munitions. That was it: Poinsett would keep in touch with Porter and would advise Carrera when he could.

Carrera often stayed with the ever-growing Porter family at Meridian Hill. Porter saw a chance for big money in Chile, and considered heading up its navy. He helped his guest learn to speak English fluently so as to impress congressmen, senators, and potential investors. In Baltimore, Porter's hometown, there was great interest in the potential of South America. Many of its swells had made their fortunes in wartime Caribbean privateering and had a strong desire to continue to make money in that direction. Porter's friend John S. Skinner, a Baltimore newspaper publisher, admired Carrera and agreed to lend him large sums at high rates. Another Porter connection, Baptis Irvine, "a fanatic of liberty" and New York editor-publisher, opened doors to merchants and reformers who liked the idea of a free Chile, or at least of supplying the armies. In his writings and promotions, Irvine countered Clay by promoting Carrera as the true George Washington of Chile.

Chile

José Miguel Carrera's American tour went on too long, as Porter and his connections slowly assembled money, men, and materials. Shortly after Thanksgiving, at the end of eleven months of speech-giving and deal-making, Carrera was ready to begin his own fateful cruise to the Pacific. With many of his new friends and investors, he stood on a wharf in New York and surveyed his fleet: the twenty-eight-gun sloop of war *Clifton* and the schooner and brigs *Davey*, *Adeline*, and *Patriot*, with full crews, forty soldiers, thirty officers, a couple of printing presses, and a dozen teachers and artisans, together with enough weapons, ammunition, and uniforms to equip an army. It was December 5, 1816, and time to begin the liberation of Chile.

Bound for Valparaiso, the squadron first put in at Buenos Aires to acquire provisions and take on troops. On February 22, George Washington's birthday, a band on the *Clifton* struck up martial music and each ship fired a national salute, returned thunderously by the port's batteries. At Baxter's Hotel, Americans dined and drank to the memory of their first president, concluding with a toast from Carrera—"The generous North Americans, to whom this country is in gratitude eternally bound"—to which all glasses were raised "to General Carrera: Under his auspices may the Chilean flag wave in triumph over that of Old Spain!"

Even then, Carrera knew that his tricolor flag might never wave again. José de San Martin's Argentine army, with a division under O'Higgins aided by one other Chilean officer, had already departed to engage the royalists in Chile. If the Argentines won, Carrera would have no cause and no country. By early February, San Martin's Army of the Andes had descended from the summits and begun skirmishing with the Spanish-Peruvians of the new captain-general of Chile, Casimiro Marco. On February 12, outside the town of Chacabuco, O'Higgins showed San Martin an ideal salient and wished to begin the battle with his vanguard. San Martin objected, but O'Higgins moved out with his men and smashed into Marco's army with irresistible force. Before San Martin had fully deployed the rest of his troops, the enemy was on the run, and the battle was over. A day later, the Army of the Andes entered Santiago in triumph, and San Martin made

O'Higgins the new supreme director of Chile. The royalists crowded onto ships at Valparaiso and escaped to Callao, and San Martin started overland for Buenos Aires to recruit forces for an invasion of Peru. Neither he nor O'Higgins realized that in the south of Chile, where the royalists remained strong, General Mariano Osorio had an army of 5,000 soldiers and was marching toward Santiago.

General San Martin arrived at Buenos Aires exhausted from his battles. He met with Governor Puerryedon, and they reviewed the state of Argentina and the threats to its stability, which were many. Its eastern army had been defeated by Artigas, and some provincial leaders were opposing the government. San Martin and Puerryedon discussed the presence of José Miguel Carrera and his surprising American fleet. Buenos Aires needed more munitions, and San Martin's puppet government in Chile could be made safe by removing the only serious threat—Carrera, who had just placed himself in their hands. If they stopped him, there might be fallout from the United States, but probably not enough to stir any formal opposition. They made some decisions, and San Martin rolled away across the pampas, bound for Chile. At the end of the month, a company of Buenos Aires soldiers seized the *Clifton* and captured Carrera and his men, while the other three vessels were allowed to go home to America, although many of the passengers signed up to fight for Argentina.

Moved from jail, Carrera was imprisoned on a brig moored in the river. His brothers Lucho and Juan José got word to him there that the royalist army of their old enemy, the implacable Mariano Osorio, was on the march from Concepcion toward Santiago to overthrow Supreme Director O'Higgins. By mid-March 1817, San Martin was in Chile at the head of 4,000 men east of Santiago, near Cancha Rayada. On the evening of March 16, Osorio launched a surprise attack. In the darkness and confusion, San Martin had trouble finding his officers. The battalion commanded by O'Higgins bore the brunt of the assault, and in the thick of it, O'Higgins was shot in the arm and nearly killed when his horse went down. San Martin's Army of the Andes lost most of its artillery but eventually made an organized retreat. Victorious, Osorio went south to await reinforcements and supplies with which to renew his campaign and capture Santiago.

By the fall of 1817, David Porter and some of his friends, deeply invested in the success of José Miguel Carrera, had formed a pressure group in Washington advocating for direct American intervention in Buenos

Aires and Chile in order to restore Carrera's presidency. John S. Skinner, now postmaster of Baltimore, wrote a series of "Lautaro Letters" directed at Speaker Clay and widely reprinted in the newspapers. He argued that the United States must intervene to rescue the region's one republic, Carrera's Chile, and work from there to bring about the creation of other, similar republics. If it did not, the continent would be lost to anarchy, dictatorship, and Great Britain. "Recognize the independence of the republic of Chile," Skinner predicted, and the United States would "shatter to atoms the British intrigues of Buenos Aires, by means of which the fine country of Chile is at present held, for commercial purposes, as a province of that City." Further, "the real, most sincere, and efficient of the Patriots," like Carrera, could overcome "the corrupt intrigues of Britain" and return to Chile and create "a Spanish American Republic, from thence to aid in the liberation of the whole New World." The overwhelming benefit to the United States would be "to open [South America] to our commerce, and prepare it as our ally against the Legitimates of the other Continent."

James Monroe, the new president, was being pressured by Clay to do something with regard to the South American rebels. No policy had been formulated or even discussed by his new secretary of state, John Quincy Adams, who focused on Spanish-American issues in Florida and Mexico.* Adams and Monroe created the new position of commissioner for Spanish America to manage issues for that region, and they agreed that the best man for it was Roberts Poinsett. Monroe offered him the job, but Poinsett was too busy in South Carolina. Hoping to win Monroe's support against Clay, who continued to favor O'Higgins and San Martin, David Porter and John Skinner wrote letters and speeches insisting that Carrera was the only leader favorable to American goals in the region, that "the interests of the U.S. are jeopardized by the machinations of England," and that "we are the natural allies of South America [and] that unless we aid them they will throw themselves into the arms of our worst enemy."

Their campaign backfired. Now that Americans were aware of the existence of two contenders for leadership of an independent Chile, no one wanted to fund a war between them. The Porter-Skinner effort had one other major result: it blocked Henry Clay's push to recognize O'Higgins in Chile and Puerryedon in Buenos Aires. As a result, Clay, the most powerful

---

* The Monroe Doctrine—which recognized existing European colonies while pledging U.S. intervention should European powers attempt to interfere with states in North and South America—was not promulgated until the end of 1823.

legislator in America and the best friend of the independence movements, turned away from Spanish America altogether.

In Buenos Aires, José Miguel Carrera's brothers, with Manuel Rodriguez and others, had grown desperate. Argentina had made Chile its colony, and nothing had happened to change that. No American fleet had arrived, and no force with Porter or Poinsett intervened in the name of republican solidarity. There was not even a protest against the incarceration of the president of Chile. Clearly, the Americans had lost interest, and now or never, the brothers must head for the mountains. Rodriguez would lead his guerillas into the countryside, and the Carreras were to go to Santiago and raise their old army units against O'Higgins and San Martin. They got word to José Miguel Carrera, who urged them to wait; the time was not right, he said, and they lacked sufficient resources. But he was in prison, unable to lead or dissuade.

"Disguised in the apparel of muleteers," Luis and Juan José Carrera and their friends set out across the pampas. Near Mendoza, Manuel Rodriguez rode off to raise recruits for his Legion of Death, while the Carreras started their ascent to the cordillera. Betrayed by an infiltrator, both were captured and imprisoned by San Martin's men at Mendoza. On the morning of April 8, 1818, San Martin's secretary, Monteaguda, arrived in Mendoza and signed their warrant, and at six o'clock Luis and Juan José were led out of the jail and seated on a bench in the public square. The two liberators, once the chiefs of the army of the Chilean republic, embraced, and Argentine soldiers shot them down.

In Chile, hearing of the executions, people realized that San Martin and O'Higgins were willing to rule by terror. Many now felt "fear of the party that so wantonly" employed violence. Over time, that fear would deepen "into horror against some of the individuals" who "became so intoxicated with power that, with the name of freedom on their lips, they oppressed and murdered."

Three days later, west of the Andes, at Maipu, just south of Santiago—where Carrera's soldiers had once scored their great victory over O'Higgins—Osorio brought his army into battle array under the flag of Spain. Having been harassed by Manuel Rodriguez's rebel guerillas all the way from San Fernando, he looked forward to a real fight. The enemy was close by, with a force no larger than his own. Osorio had defeated this same army before and knew that he could do it again and reclaim his position as captain-general of Chile. His troops held a ridge as the shelling began. The cavalries engaged on the right and left, exchanging the advantage. He sent

Mendoza, Argentina, showing the marketplace and the Andes beyond. Like everyone else who traveled overland from Buenos Aires to Chile, U.S. Consul Poinsett passed through Mendoza, the last stop before the ascent of the Andes. This desolate town proved to be a graveyard of the revolution—site of the executions of several Chilean revolutionary leaders and the place to which Poinsett and the shattered remains of the revolutionary army retreated in 1814 after their defeat at the Battle of Rancagua.

his infantry division into the center, and the enemy fell back. San Martin's reinforcements counterattacked ferociously and broke Osorio's main line. Osorio withdrew, but his lieutenant, Ordonez, regrouped the army and made a strong stand until San Martin's artillery opened up. At the end of the battle of Maipu, 2,000 royalist soldiers lay dead, and Chile belonged to Argentina.

O'Higgins was assigned by San Martin to go to Santiago and take over as supreme director, but there was a problem: Colonel Manuel Rodriguez and his Legion of Death. Having learned of the execution of the two Carreras, Rodriguez had ridden straight into Santiago and raised an insurrection, demanding an end to "Argentine interference." He ruled for thirty hours, until O'Higgins showed up with an army. Rodriguez was captured and taken to the town of Til Til, and there, on May 26, he was executed, and his corpse desecrated. In America, Porter was astonished when the news arrived. These men had been his friends, leaders of independent Chile and enthusiastic admirers of the United States, and America had not come to their aid.

O'Higgins would remain supreme director for five years, until he was deposed by his comrade Ramon Freire in the spring of 1823. He thought about moving to Ireland but instead went to Lima, where Simon Bolivar, rather than San Martin, had brought about the independence of Peru. O'Higgins lived in obscurity for another seventeen years, never seeing Chile again.

On January 1819, the United States frigate *Macedonian* arrived at Valparaiso, commanded by none other than John Downes, now holding the rank of captain. At last an American battleship had been sent to Chile as an instrument of policy, to protect American commerce. Although ignored by Downes, the most active seagoing trader was Captain Richard J. Cleveland of Salem, formerly a smuggler along the coast of Chile and a proselytizer for republicanism, returned to his old haunts in a last effort to recoup his once-great fortune. Freighting cargo and trading goods, Cleveland, in command of John Jacob Astor's ship *Beaver*, finessed both the Chileans and the Peruvians for many months, recovered much of what he had lost, and sailed homeward for the last time, in triumph.

At Santiago, Downes presented the compliments of his government to Supreme Director O'Higgins and arranged to meet Admiral Lord Cochrane, a British nobleman, head of the Chilean navy, very successful in encounters with Spanish warships and funded by a large loan from London. Downes and Cochrane became friends. Downes had learned a few things from his frustrating days under David Porter, who, for all his pursuit of wealth and glory, had not seen that Anson-like plunder was still available and that all things were possible in the name of protecting American trade. For a full two years, without once engaging an enemy or harassing the locals, Captain John Downes patrolled the west coast of South America. Thoughts of José Miguel Carrera and the old republic never troubled him as he bullied his way into ports large and small and set himself up as a floating bank-fortress and smuggling emporium in a highly successful effort to promote American commercial interests, his own foremost.*

---

* Downes is believed to have amassed about $2 million while stationed on the South American coast, a very small part of which he would lend, from time to time, to the always-strapped David Porter.

Mendoza

José Miguel Carrera, escaped from prison at last, crossed the Rio de la Plata to Portuguese-held Montevideo in 1818 and raised forces against the government of Buenos Aires. With San Martin away in Peru, civil war had broken out in Argentina. Carrera became a warlord, unmoored from any home, living in the hills and sleeping in the open, cut off from his wife and five young children, giving up everything for vengeance. In the process, he lost his ideals and some of his humanity. Inhabiting a permanent war zone, he allowed his men to engage in terror and atrocities, plundering the towns they passed through and fighting other groups in an endless campaign of nihilism and death.

Living in the bush, Carrera thought about his martyred brothers and the Patria Vieja and continued to dream about the liberation of Chile. He battled on for months and then years without any outside assistance, but he got no closer to Mendoza and the pass in the Andes that led to Santiago. He never stopped hoping that the Americans would come to his rescue. When he made his will, he ordered that his little son be sent to America to be raised by David Porter. In the spring of 1821, after a string of brutal victories, his army had shrunk to about 500 men. He was heartened to see that Spain had once more sent land and sea forces against Chile, but the dictator O'Higgins was holding firm with his large army led by San Martin and supplied by the English, and with his navy commanded by Lord Cochrane and manned mainly by British sailors. Still, there was some chance that the Spanish would succeed in destabilizing the province of Santiago. Then the people might look once more to the hills for a smiling man in a beautiful poncho, descending from the Andes as the herald of liberty.

William Yates, one of Carrera's devoted lieutenants, wrote that his commander had captured many of his enemies over time, but had too much compassion and idealism to be much of a killer. He could not bring himself to execute an opponent "however criminal he might be." Even "assassins who had murdered our soldiers" could expect mercy "at the expense of justice itself." Perhaps, wrote Yates, Carrera "believed that by treating his enemies with kindness and loading them with obligations, they would become his friends," but "if that were his idea he was miserably deceived, and proved himself in a great measure ignorant of the character of his country."

Finally arrived at the outskirts of the fatal town of Mendoza, José Miguel Carrera was closer to the border of Chile than he had been in a long time. He and his guerillas fought and defeated a much larger force, but his men were desperate enough to believe that he intended to abandon them and go to the United States. They mutinied and took him and his officers into Mendoza. There, in prison, Carrera lived quietly, thinking and wondering, tired of living like a beast, tired of violence. He wrote at length to his friends and family, and to posterity: "I ask future generations to reclaim my name, for I die like a bandit in a strange land."

On the morning of September 5, 1821—seven years after he and O'Higgins had merged their warring armies and turned to face Osorio—Carrera had a visit from the local officials, and he scoffed when they spoke of a reprieve from San Martin. Priests gathered in the square. "He heartily despised all friars," wrote Yates; "however, they thronged round him . . . in order to re-convert him, that he might die a good Christian. Passing through the plaza, they employed all their logic in proving the existence of hell, and the torments of the damned." Carrera knew all about hell, and "he reprimanded them for their insolence in offering and imposing their unasked advice." He "continued steadfastly to view the troops, and make his observations on the strength of the town to the officer who guarded him"—as if he were in command.

They had him sit in a chair, but he wanted to stand. The padres "renewed their suit for the safety of his soul, which he told them was his care, not theirs." And he refused to forgive his enemies and the enemies of his family, and of Chile. He removed his poncho and his watch, vestiges of a former life, and then he sat, "but when the executioner came to tie his arms, he stood up rather indignantly, and ordered him to retire." The man did as he was told, and Carrera reproved the commander: "Since when does a ruffian get to tie up an honorable officer?"

He would not have his eyes covered, but sat calmly and placed his right hand over his heart, and directed the soldiers to proceed. They fired, and he fell over dead in the dirt. Most of his remains were given to his mother-in-law to be interred in the tomb of his brothers, but President Carrera's killers placed his head on a spike over the door of the town hall and nailed up his right arm under the clock.

Charleston

In 1821, after a stint in the state legislature and as the head of road-building and other internal improvements in South Carolina, Joel Roberts Poinsett, forty-two, was elected to Congress by his fellow Charlestonians. He was finished with Buenos Aires and Chile, having written a final report about those places at the request of the president. In Congress he memorably spoke against sending an American commissioner to Greece, whose people were fighting the Turks for their independence. Poinsett, thinking of Chile, insisted that the United States not become involved unless it was willing first to recognize Greek nationhood.

In 1822, after several failed attempts at revolution, there was a revival of nationalism in Mexico, from which Agustin de Iturbide, leader of the insurgents, emerged as emperor. Whether he had the strength and vision to establish a permanent government was a matter of great interest to President Monroe, who prevailed upon Congressman Poinsett to undertake a mission to Mexico. His predecessor, William Shaler, had carried out his consular assignment in support of the Mexican nationalists until their defeat by the Spanish in 1813; now Shaler was minister in Algiers, and Mexico was again independent. After traveling for three months in almost every Mexican province, Poinsett wrote a detailed report concluding with the belief that Iturbide would not be able to hold on to power there—and in fact the news of his overthrow by fellow Mexicans arrived in Washington just before Poinsett himself, who proceeded to publish the report as *Notes on Mexico*, the first American book on the subject. David Porter, among others, read it eagerly.

In 1823 Poinsett, still a bachelor, was reelected to Congress. Although a firm supporter of Andrew Jackson, he was chosen by the new president, John Quincy Adams, as minister to Mexico—America's first. Poinsett arrived at Mexico City in May 1825 at a time of great turmoil in a country nominally a republic but actually an oligarchy run by aristocrats and leaders of the military and the church. It was all too familiar. He was importuned by republicans plotting for a change in government. Sympathetic, Poinsett dispensed information but not advice. He was determined not to take a partisan role. He found the British there well advanced toward a pact on commerce. His efforts to co-opt the process met resistance, which he attributed to Mexican concerns about American designs on Texas and other northern parts of their country, but which mainly arose from a secret non-aggression and protection pact that the brilliant British diplomats had made with Mexico in 1823.

At last there was a revolt against the government. Poinsett's house, among others, was on one of the main streets down which the rebel forces marched, and it was known that Poinsett had given shelter to some Spaniards, including the former viceroy's widow. As the mob tried to smash in the door, Poinsett, with his usual courage, presented himself above them on the balcony, dramatically unfurling a large American flag and extemporizing a speech about the republic that it symbolized and the asylum that was offered to all who sought its protection. The crowd fell silent and then charged off down the street to resume its violence elsewhere.

Incredibly, David Porter came sailing back into Poinsett's life, and once again he was caught up in a fatal swirl of paranoia and revenge. As a fighter of pirates in the Caribbean in the early 1820s, Porter had done a splendid job for the U.S. Navy, but on one expedition he had gotten carried away and landed some men on a Puerto Rican beach. Puerto Rico belonged to Spain, which, in light of the new Monroe Doctrine, had every right to retaliate against the United States and the countries and islands that relied on American protection. When the subsequent court martial resulted in a one-year suspension from duty, Porter decided to quit the navy and even the United States.

In the summer of 1825 he contacted Minister Poinsett in hopes of finding work in the Mexican navy, such as it was, with one frigate, two brigs, a schooner, and some gunboats. French and Spanish naval forces were active in the Caribbean, menacing the ports of Cuba and Mexico, so the Mexican government authorized Poinsett to signal an interest in Porter's services, to which Porter responded, "I think I see before me a bright field of glory." He entered into negotiations toward becoming Mexico's first admiral. Despite his total ignorance of the country's politics and culture and his inability to speak or understand Spanish, Porter arrived in Mexico in the spring of 1826, impressed its leaders, and in July took command of the navy. Of course he soon argued with his superiors and his Mexican officers, whom he disparaged and largely replaced with Americans, including a nephew and two of his sons. He further insulted his employers by insisting on being made a brigadier general in the army.

In December 1826, Admiral Porter and his Mexican fleet put out to sea in search of the enemy and his shipping. After some success in capturing Spanish merchantmen off Cuba, Porter's navy was chased east by a superior Spanish fleet under Angel Laborde. In contravention of international law, the Mexican Admiral Porter holed up at Key West, Florida, and went off to New Orleans to recruit more sailors and ships. In his absence, his men attacked an American merchant vessel, and U.S. naval forces were on their way to Florida to expel him when Porter escaped to Mexico. There he misrepresented his achievements, made claims for payment of $13,000 per month, and demanded that the Mexicans build him a steam frigate.

The Mexicans pointed out that, although he had harassed Spanish shipping, he had scored no naval victories. Admiral Porter put back out to sea in 1828 but lost his largest brig in a fight with a Spanish frigate. Returning, he went on the attack against Mexico's treasurer, which alienated most of Porter's defenders, including the newspaper publisher. His inability to use the language continued to hurt him, as he was powerless to spin public relations as he had in America. Poinsett tried to elicit better behavior from Porter, who complained, "I am tormented to death with attempts to thwart and injure me." After General Santa Anna stepped in to support a presidential candidate, Porter became uncontrollable. Poinsett received a letter from the admiral confessing, "I would not have any more scruples about shedding Mexican blood than any other blood." Poinsett cautioned him to stay neutral, but Admiral Porter dove deeper into presidential politics, which earned him such enmity that twice he had to fight off assassins. Finally he was placed under arrest, and in September 1829 he was allowed to leave the country.

Poinsett was not badly damaged by his connection to Porter, but he too became controversial. His encouragement of a certain type of Freemasonry led to his undoing when the fraternal society was seen as allied with the revolutionaries against the government. He was successful in negotiating a boundary treaty, but his treaty of commerce was not ratified because Mexico refused to agree to return fugitive slaves to American owners. Poinsett found it difficult to stay current with the ever-changing cast of strong men and power brokers in Mexico, and his good relations with the British turned sour. He took pleasure in collecting manuscripts about Aztec and Mayan ruins, and he sent cuttings of various plants and trees back to his estate in Charleston. One of the flowers, of the genus *Euphorbiaceae*, had bright green and red leaves that made it popular as a Christmas plant, now known as the poinsettia.

Returning to the United States in 1829, Poinsett became embroiled in another near-revolution. This one, centered in Charleston, was arguably the greatest challenge to American nationhood between 1815 and 1861. The 1828 federal tariff had been bitterly opposed in the South and had led many South Carolina politicians to contend that federal duties on incoming cargoes need not be paid. The nullification movement, claiming to nullify the primacy of federal laws over state laws, turned virulent and threatened to lead to secession.

State Senator Poinsett, among the leaders of the state's Union Party, courageously opposed the sometimes-violent "nullies" for three years. In 1832 the state legislature passed a law upholding nullification and bidding defiance to the federal government, which had the effect of a revolution, as the state devoted an enormous sum to arm its citizens to fight federal forces.

President Jackson sent in warships and troops, and Poinsett became the head of the central commission coordinating state activities with the federal military leaders. He told the president, "I fully concur with you in your views of Nullification. It leads directly to civil war and bloodshed and deserves the execration of every friend of the country." Poinsett urged Jackson to send a large army to South Carolina, and went so far as to lead an armed party of union men into the streets of Charleston to oppose a mob of nullifiers. Having skirted actual warfare several times, the two factions, led by Poinsett's Union Party and by the State Rights Party, finally compromised and resolved the crisis late in 1834.

With peace restored to South Carolina, Poinsett, fifty-six, finally married a long-time widow, Mary Izard Pringle, and retired to her plantation, White House, to enjoy his books and become a rice grower and horticulturalist, raising plants that he imported from around the world. His unionist politics had estranged him from most of Charleston society, but he found a refuge in the Charleston Literary and Philosophical Society, to which, as its president, he presented a very interesting essay in 1834 on "the natural progress of the human race from barbarism to civilization" based on his observations of the peoples of wild places that he had visited in Asia and South America. Poinsett remained well known and highly regarded by those in top circles of the federal government, to which he was called by Jackson's protégé and successor, President Martin Van Buren, to become secretary of war in 1837.

Service in Van Buren's cabinet was the culmination of Poinsett's long-held ambitions. Although he never had a chance to fight in the uniform of the United States, he now directed its entire military establishment, army and navy. He did the bidding of Congress and the president with regard to the enforced removal of Native Americans westward across the Mississippi, and he was required to oversee the wars that were fought between federal troops and the Seminoles and some of the other tribes. At the same time, he improved the department's business operations, reorganized and upgraded the artillery based on European models, and completely revised the procedures for cavalry combat based on the French system, which he had employed while directing the patriot army of Chile.* Perhaps recalling the proposals of his former colleague Porter (now marooned in Istanbul), and certainly thinking of his own connection to the Pacific while consul general in Chile, Poinsett commissioned the first Pacific exploring expedition ever undertaken by the United States. Led by Lieutenant Charles Wilkes—three other commanders had turned down the appointment—it involved six navy vessels, including two large sloops of war, hundreds of sailors, and many naturalists, biologists, ethnographers, and other scientists, artists, and collectors. Wilkes proved unfit for the job, and the United States Exploring Expedition had many dark moments, including an incident in Polynesia in which eighty natives of Fiji were murdered and two villages incinerated. In the tradition of Porter and Downes, it had proved impossible for a U.S. Navy officer to encounter island cultures without resorting to slaughter.† Poinsett's lifelong interest in art and literature blossomed in Washington, D.C., to the benefit of the nation. Long a member of the Columbian Institute, he planned and organized the transition of that organization into a new one, the National Institute for the Promotion of Science and the Useful Arts, founded to conduct research and present exhibits in its museums. Its success was such that in 1846 it would form the basis of "an establishment for the increase and diffusion of knowledge" now known as the Smithsonian Institution.

In 1841, at the end of Van Buren's term, Secretary Poinsett retired to his plantation, where for ten years he lived happily with his wife, Mary, reading, gardening, running the farm, and coming out of retirement for one more cause: the founding, at Washington, of the National Gallery, opened in 1850, the year before his death, on December 12, in his seventy-third year.

---

* "Poinsett's Tactics" were published in 1841 and remained the standard guide for cavalry procedures for years, including during the U.S. Civil War

† Downes, commanding a battleship in 1832, had attacked the bamboo village of Kuala Batu in Sumatra while carrying out what was to have been an inquiry into the circumstances of an episode of violence involving a Salem merchant vessel the year before. He killed more than 200 people and destroyed their town.

Nukuhiva: Like Shadows

After Nukuhiva had suffered many more visits from white men with their diseases and their weapons in the 1820s and 1830s, a French fleet arrived in 1842 and took permanent possession of the Marquesas for King Louis Philippe and his empire. David Porter, far away in Turkey, knew nothing about it. The long-time consular official had endured a twelve-year descent into paralysis.

In that same year, 1842, at Nukuhiva, a couple of young American whalemen decided to jump ship and explore the island. One of them, Herman Melville, would write a picaresque account of their adventures, and his novel would get him off whalers and into the salons of New York. Unlike Porter's book, Melville's *Typee* was a best-seller. In it he relates his adventures humorously, as two American sailors try to stay on the good side of the Taipi tribe, among whom they live in loose captivity, making friends, partying, sightseeing, and nosing around in villages for evidence of cannibalism. They encounter the Enana talents for beauty, artistry, happiness, and love.

Melville wrote, "During my whole stay on the island I never witnessed a single quarrel, nor anything that in the slightest degree approached even to a dispute. The natives appeared to form one household, whose members were bound together by the ties of strong affection. The love of kindred I did not much perceive, for it seemed blended in the general love; and where all were treated as brothers and sisters, it was hard to tell who were actually related to each other by blood." This was as true of the Taipi as of any other tribe on the island; however, the French, their new lords and masters, were given fair warning: "By many a legendary tale of violence and wrong, as well as by events which have passed before their eyes, these people have been taught to look upon white people with abhorrence. The cruel invasion of their country by Porter has alone furnished them with ample provocation; and I can sympathize in the spirit which prompts the Typee warrior to guard all the passes to his valley with the point of his leveled spear, and, standing upon the beach, with his back turned upon his green home, to hold at bay the intruding European."

But for all his sympathy, even Melville could not see what was coming. The Enana were overwhelmed by French weaponry and the persistence of French priests and waves of venereal disease and other illnesses first introduced by Porter and his crew. The Taipi held out longest, but they too were brought under French rule, consolidated with the rest under a puppet king, none other than Mouina, the Teii veteran of Porter's campaigns. As "le roi de Noukaheva" he covered his splendid tattoos with a "military uniform, stiff with gold lace and embroidery, while his shaven crown," wrote Melville, "was concealed by a huge *chapeau bras*, waving with ostrich plumes. There was one slight blemish, however, in his appearance. A broad patch of tattooing stretched completely across his face in a line with his eyes, making him look as if he wore a huge pair of goggles; and royalty in goggles suggested some ludicrous ideas."

The degradation of the Enana had begun in earnest, and there would be no more comic novels about this doomed island, the saddest place on earth. Forty-five years later the Scottish writer Robert Louis Stevenson, thirty-eight, very sick and willing to go anywhere to find a sanctuary where he might survive, chartered a schooner in San Francisco and took his family to Nukuhiva to see if it might be the right place. It was not; rather, it was one vast grave. Islanders had been disappearing at a rate of twelve dead for every one born, falling before the overwhelming diseases of the white men. By the 1880s, with hundreds left where tens of thousands had lived, most of the villages and towns had been abandoned, and anyone hiking on the steep hillsides would encounter the "melancholy spectacle" of houseless stone platforms.

Still, Stevenson wanted to make contact, as Porter had. On a sultry, cloudy day, he and a schoolboy guide went up into the highlands, where "drenching tropical showers succeeded bursts of sweltering sunshine." They followed the green pathway of the road far into the bush, looking for the great platform where the feasts had been held and the religious ceremonies performed, as when Opotee had witnessed the dead warriors laid out with such palpable intent.

At last man and boy came to the spot: "As far as my eyes could pierce through the dark undergrowth, the floor of the forest was all paved. Three tiers of terrace ran on the slope of the hill; in front, a crumbling parapet contained the main arena; and the pavement of that was pierced and parcelled out with several wells and small enclosures. No trace remained of any superstructure, and the scheme of the ampitheatre was difficult to seize." Stevenson envisioned the spectacle on "the high place [that] was sedulously tended. No tree except the sacred banyan was suffered to encroach upon its grades, no dead leaf to rot upon the pavement. The stones were smoothly set, and I am told they were kept bright with oil. On all sides the guardians lay encamped in their subsidiary huts to watch and cleanse it.

"No other foot of man was suffered to draw near; only the priest, in the days of his running, came there to sleep—perhaps to dream of the ungodly errand; but in the time of the feast, the clan trooped to the high place in a body, and each had his appointed seat. There were places for the chiefs, the drummers, the dancers, the women and the priests. The drums—perhaps twenty strong and some of them twelve feet high—continuously throbbed in time. In time, the singers kept up their long-drawn, lugubrious ululating song; in time, too, the dancers, tricked out in singular finery, stepped, leaped, swayed, and gesticulated, their plumed fingers fluttering in the air like butterflies."

Neither priest nor shaman was able to stop the plagues, for, as Stevenson found, the people had resigned themselves to the death that "reaps them with both hands." In these end-times, he wrote, "the Marquesan beholds with dismay the approaching extinction of his race. The thought of death sits down with him to meat, and rises with him from his bed; he lives and breathes under a shadow of mortality awful to support; and he is so inured to the apprehension that he greets the reality with relief." By hanging and by poisoning, the Enana sought escape. Stevenson wrote that "this proneness to suicide" accorded with "the widespread depression and acceptance of the national end. Pleasures are neglected, the dance languishes, the songs are forgotten."

Sailing to Byzantium

David Porter, U.S. chargé d'affaires to the Sublime Porte of the Ottoman Empire, had no interest in returning to the United States. He had been rejected there many times, and had made terrible mistakes.

After his disaster in Mexico, Porter found it impossible to live with his wife, Evelina, and their children—some were not his, he claimed—and he became obsessed with money. He demanded payment from the Spanish, the Cubans, and the Mexicans as well as the federal government of the United States. Nothing happened. In desperation, he went to the new president, Andrew Jackson, a fighter of wars and a taker of territory. Jackson felt sorry for the forgotten hero and found him a job in the Department of State, one that would send him far away. A position in Tripoli fell through, but then one was discovered at Istanbul—the old Constantinople, once the capital of Christianity in the east and now the epicenter of the Ottoman Empire. Porter packed up and sailed away, leaving his family behind.

Porter found that he had little to do there, but the execution of his modest duties was punctuated by vicious fights with underlings. He pursued literary renown, but in writing, as in war, Porter could never get clear of the British. Long before, in 1822, responding to a lengthy assault by an English reviewer, he had put out a new edition of his *Journal of a Cruise* minus some of the raw passages and with the addition of a sustained counterattack in the preface. It too had drifted out of public view without much notice. He tried again in 1835, with the publication of *Constantinople and Its Environs*, a temperate work that was soon eclipsed by a beautifully illustrated British volume on the same topic.

As a connoisseur of Pacific expeditions, he must have read about Poinsett's Wilkes expedition with jealousy, and he may have read the book by the English naturalist Charles Darwin, *Journal and Remarks 1832–1835*, popularly known as *Voyage of the Beagle*. If so, Porter would have been surprised to find himself mentioned in a way that would eventually have epochal consequences. Darwin, in this account of the scientific voyage of HMS *Beagle* to the Galápagos, gave credit to Captain Porter, that close observer of the giant tortoises, as the first to have speculated about their variations from island to island and what that might mean about the origin of species.

Importing nephews as his assistants, carrying on long-distance feuds with family members, and battling through heart attacks and various illnesses and prostrations in the early 1830s, Porter subsided into virtual retirement. His body, exhausted by years of stress and violence, had given out. Sometimes, for months, he could barely walk and could not talk at all. For the last two years of his life, he was an invalid. No one in the United States noticed. The business of the American ministry was done by dragomans and Porter relatives, and the opium kept moving out on American vessels, bound for China and Sumatra to create and sustain Asia's addictions. Porter's amazing signature, once as marvelous as a Marquesan tattoo, had collapsed into an illegible blotch.

After suffering terribly in his final months, Porter enjoyed five days of peace, lapsed into a coma, and died on March 3, 1843, at age sixty-three, having left five last wills and ten children in America, most of whom detested him. At his direction his body was to rest under Old Glory in a crypt at the foot of the embassy's flagpole. "A deep grave was accordingly dug, which was lined and bricked, and a flooring of oak laid to prevent the effect of dampness." His corpse was buried like a pharaoh, in a succession of sarcophagi: outside was a "strong lead coffin," within which was a walnut casing marked with his initials, enclosing "an inner coffin of lead, made air tight and filled with rum."

The secretary of the navy, believing that Porter "stood conspicuous among the distinguished men who have done honor to our country," sent a brig of war to fetch the body of the man who had conquered Nukuhiva and lost his ship. On April 24, President Tyler, who happened to be planning a major annexation of his own—the part of Mexico called Texas—directed "that the flags be hoisted at half mast; that this order be read and thirteen minute guns be fired at each navy yard and naval station, and on board every vessel of war in the U.S. Navy, at noon, on the day after the receipt of this order; and that the officers of the navy and marine corps wear crepe on the left arm for the space of thirty days."

Porter's remains would be buried three more times and end up under a monument donated by the owners of a cemetery in Philadelphia. His legacy to the navy was most impressive, all things considered: his ward Gatty, David Glasgow Farragut—"damn the torpedoes, full speed ahead"—and his son David Dixon Porter were indispensable leaders during the Civil War, and were, respectively, the first and second men ever to hold the rank of admiral of the U.S. Navy.

Torpoint

Word of Porter's death was copied in some of the English papers and perhaps reached Torpoint, near Plymouth, as the spring flowers were blooming around the grounds of Tor House, home of retired Rear Admiral of the White, Sir James Hillyar, KCB.

After returning from Chile, Hillyar had supervised the refitting of the *Phoebe* and commanded her during peacetime until he was paid off at the end of forty-four years of service. He and his family went abroad to live, and returned from the Continent in 1830, when, at sixty-one, he took command of the *Revenge*. After a couple of years he was given the ship of the line *Caledonia* and ordered to the coast of Portugal, where he found a spot on the Tagus River to occupy for a quiet year. He was knighted in 1834 and again in 1840, and between those years was advanced to the rank of rear admiral, from which he was pensioned from the Royal Navy at a salary of 300 pounds.

In retirement Hillyar followed the news of Britain's imperial activities around the globe and especially its ascendancy in Chile. After the Chileans' defeat of a Peruvian-Bolivian force in 1839, Valparaiso became the largest seaport in the Pacific, running steamships along the coast and exporting huge quantities of wheat and copper all the way to China. With its own English newspaper and dozens of British merchant houses, Valparaiso had 5,000 Anglo residents and strong transoceanic relations with New Zealand and Australia. Well might Admiral Sir James Hillyar think that he had done his part to change the world.

On July 10, 1843, Hillyar died in his house by the sea in his seventy-fifth year, surrounded by friends and family. He had been thinking about his funeral and had had time to plan it out. There would be no delegation from London and no pomp or circumstance. His remains were interred at the local churchyard in a modest ceremony. The onlookers were the people and parishioners of Torpoint, and the mourners were the members of his family, including two sons who would themselves become admirals.

The pall containing the remains of their gallant captain was borne by four old warrant officers from the *Phoebe* who had served with him on that famous day, long since and a world away, when they had finally brought an end to the Pacific rampage of David Porter and the American frigate *Essex*.

Selected Sources

The events of Captain David Porter's improbable voyage into the Pacific world would probably never have been known except for the fact of Porter's having kept a journal, remarkable for candor if not for honesty, which he published in 1815 as *Journal of a Cruise Made to the Pacific Ocean*, when his adventures were fresh. I have used this version—he sanitized it in an 1822 edition—to inform my narrative and to try to understand a brave and baffling man. Porter's *Journal* is a seminal work of American literature. It is the first American book about war published by a participant; the first account of American conquest of a foreign people; the first extended description of the Pacific by an American; and the first relation, in English, of the lifeways of the Marquesas Islanders. It is also the first scientific treatment of the Galápagos Islands, and it served as grist for some of Herman Melville's best writing. Porter had hoped it would be a best seller, but it failed to reach a wide audience, and it caused a scandal for the rawness of the events it portrayed, unprecedented in the writing of American naval officers and even of all Americans.

Porter's journal stands as an indictment of its author, not just for what he admits to having done and for what he failed to do, but for shutting us out of his interior life, the concerns of mind and heart that might have redeemed him. As published, the *Journal* is all exterior, full of surface action but empty of reflection or emotion: here, in hundreds of pages, he records no dreams or personal insights or instances of friendship; he betrays no yearning for home or thoughts of wife and children, and very little admiration for officers and men who loyally followed him across the seas and seasons. Porter admits to anxieties, but only those relating to nature's harshness and the absence of the British prey that would justify his having gone rogue into the Pacific. God and man are of little interest: a deity is entirely absent, and the longest passage about a person is a rant directed at someone he had never met. When a favorite young lieutenant is killed in a duel, there is no mourning, and no punishment of the killer. In other cases, men who die on board ship are not buried but dumped into the sea in sight of land. Porter was no anthropologist—his observations of other peoples and cultures are singularly unenlightened—and he wholly lacked the methodical qualities of a first-rate explorer, but his acuity as a scientific observer was impressive, and it is a great irony that the book about his Pacific cruise proved to have its highest value, many years after it had been forgotten by the public, for an Englishman named Darwin.

Other sources for the events related in Mad for Glory follow.

Chapter 1

Chandler, Charles Lyon. "The Life of Joel Roberts Poinsett," The Pennsylvania Magazine of History and Biography, Vol. LIX, No. 1. Philadelphia: Historical Society of Pennsylvania, 1935, pp. 1-31.

Long, David F. Nothing Too Daring: A Biography of Commodore David Porter, 1780–1843. Annapolis: Naval Institute Press, 1970.

Paris, Francklyn Wynne. "The Three David Porters: Captain, Commodore, and Admiral, and Their Delaware Roots," Delaware Genealogical Society Journal, vol. 1, Nos. 1-3. Wilmington: Delaware Genealogical Society, 1981-82.

Porter, David. Journal of a Cruise Made to the Pacific Ocean. Philadelphia: Bradford and Inskeep, 1815.

Porter, David Dixon. Memoir of Commodore David Porter, of the United States Navy. Albany, NY: J. Munsell, 1875.

Shaler, William. "Journal of A Voyage Between China and The North-western Coast of America Made in 1804," American Register, No. 3. Philadelphia, 1808, pp. 137-175.

Chapter 2

Gallatin, Albert. Letter to James Madison, August 15, 1810, Founders Online, National Archives (http://founders.archives.gov/documents/Madison/03-02-02-0600 [last update: 2015-06-29]). Source: The Papers of James Madison, Presidential Series, vol. 2, 1 October 1809–2 November 1810, ed. J. C. A. Stagg, Jeanne Kerr Cross, and Susan Holbrook Perdue. Charlottesville: University Press of Virginia, 1992, pp. 486-488.http://hdl.loc.gov/loc.mss/mjm.12_0554_0556

Jameson, J.F. "Correspondence of John C. Calhoun," in *Annual Report of American Historical Association, 1899*, Volume II. Washington: Government Printing Office, 1900.

Madison, James. Letter Albert Gallatin, August 22, 1810, Founders Online, National Archives (http://founders.archives.gov/documents/Madison/03-02-02-0617 [last update: 2015-06-29]). Source: *The Papers of James Madison, Presidential Series*, vol. 2, *1 October 1809–2 November 1810*, ed. J. C. A. Stagg, Jeanne Kerr Cross, and Susan Holbrook Perdue. Charlottesville: University Press of Virginia, 1992, pp. 500–502.

Monroe, James. Letter to Joel Roberts Poinsett, April 30, 1811. Quoted in Frederic L. Paxson, *The Independence of the South American Republics*, Second edition. Philadelphia: Ferris and Leach, 1916, p. 113.

Chapter 3

Cowell, John Glover. Letter to U.S. Navy Secretary Paul Hamilton, September 24, 1812. *Miscellaneous Letters received by Secretary of Navy*. Washington, DC: Naval Records Collection of the Office of Naval Records and Library, National Archives.

Feltus, William M. Diary entry, November 23, 1812, in William S. Dudley and Michael J. Crawford, eds., *The Naval War of 1812: A Documentary History*. Washington, DC: Naval Historical Center, Department of the Navy, 1985; electronically published by American Naval Records Society, Bolton Landing, New York, 2011.

Harris, Thomas. *The Life and Services of Commodore William Bainbridge, USN*. Philadelphia: Carey Lea & Blanchard, 1837.

Mahan, Alfred T. *Admiral Farragut*. New York: Appleton & Co., 1892.

McKee, Christopher. *A Gentlemanly and Honorable Profession: The Creation of the U.S. Naval Officer Corps, 1794–1815*. Annapolis: Naval Institute Press, 1991.

Porter, David. *Journal of a Cruise Made to the Pacific Ocean*. Philadelphia: Bradford and Inskeep, 1815.

Porter, David Dixon. *Memoir of Commodore David Porter, of the United States Navy*. Albany, NY: J. Munsell, 1875.

Chapter 4

Cleveland, Richard J. A *Narrative of Voyages and Commercial Enterprises*, Vol. I. Cambridge, Mass.: John Owen, 1842, pp. 165–225.

Long, David F. *Nothing Too Daring: A Biography of Commodore David Porter, 1780–1843*. Annapolis: U.S. Naval Institute, 1970.

Porter, David. *Journal of a Cruise Made to The Pacific Ocean*. Philadelphia: Bradford and Inskeep, 1815.

Reynolds, Jeremiah. "Mocha Dick, or the White Whale of the Pacific," *The Knickerbocker, or New-York Monthly Magazine*. Vol. 13, No. 5, May 1839, New York: John Allen, pp. 377–392.

Chapter 5

Clissold, Stephen. *Bernardo O'Higgins and the Independence of Chile*. New York and Washington: Frederick A. Praeger, 1969.

Collier, William M., and Cruz, Guillermo F. *La Primera Mision de Los Estados Unidos de America en Chile*, uso exclusivo de VITANET, Biblioteca Virtual ano 2004.

Felstiner, Mary L. "Kinship Politics in the Chilean Independence Movement," *The Hispanic American Historical Review*, 56.1, 1976.

Galdames, Luis. *Estudio de Historia de Chile*. Santiago: Editorial Universitaria, 1906.

Johnston, Samuel Burr. *Letters Written During a Residence of Three Years in Chili*. Erie, Penn.: R. I. Curtis, 1816.

Poinsett, Joel Roberts. Letter to Secretary of State James Monroe, September 15, 1814. Poinsett Papers, Library of the Historical Museum of Pennsylvania, Philadelphia.

Porter, David. *Journal of a Cruise Made to the Pacific Ocean*. Philadelphia: Bradford and Inskeep, 1815.

Vilches, Patricia. "Not a Fox but a Lion: A Machiavellian Reading of Chile's First President, José Miguel Carrera," *The Journal of the Midwest Modern Language Association*, Vol. 44, No. 1 (Spring 2011), pp. 123–144.

Chapter 6

Irarte, Tomas de. *Biografia Del Brigarier General D. José Miguel Carrera*. Privately printed, 1863.

Poinsett, Joel Roberts. Letter to Department of State, September 10, 1814, quoted by Parton, Dorothy M. *The Diplomatic Career of Joel Roberts Poinsett*. Doctoral dissertation, Catholic University of America, 1934.

Porter, David. *Journal of a Cruise Made to the Pacific Ocean*. Philadelphia: Bradford and Inskeep, 1815.

Chapter 7

Feltus, William M. Diary entry, March 26, 1813, in William S. Dudley and Michael J. Crawford, eds., *The Naval War of 1812: A Documentary History*. Naval Historical Center, Department of the Navy, Washington DC, 1985; electronically published by American Naval Records Society, Bolton Landing, New York, 2011.

Fitzgerald, Nathaniel, and "Justice." "A Tribute" and "Poinsett and the Whalers," *Nantucket Inquirer & Mirror*, September 7 and September 14, 1872; August 9, 1824.

Hoffman, Richard K. Letter to John M. Gamble, April 15, 1824, in Gamble, John M. *The Memorial of Lt. John M. Gamble, of the U. S. Marine Corps, to Congress 1828*. New York: George F. Hopkins & Son, 1828, p. 7.

Johnston, Samuel Burr. *Letters Written During a Residence of Three Years in Chili*. Erie, Penn.: R. I. Curtis, 1816.

Poinsett, Joel Roberts. Letter to Secretary of State James Monroe, August 5, 1813 (1814 sic). Poinsett Papers, Library of the Historical Museum of Pennsylvania, Philadelphia.

Poinsett, Joel Roberts. Letter to Joseph Johnson, September 2, 1813. Poinsett Papers, Library of the Historical Museum of Pennsylvania, Philadelphia.

Porter, David. Letter to Viceroy Abascal, March 26, 1813, in Porter, David. *Journal of a Cruise Made to The Pacific Ocean*. Philadelphia: Bradford and Inskeep, 1815.

Porter, David. *Journal of a Cruise Made to the Pacific Ocean*. Philadelphia: Bradford and Inskeep, 1815.

Chapter 8

Dixon, Manley. Letter to J. W. Croker, June 21, 1813, in William S. Dudley and Michael J. Crawford, eds., *The Naval War of 1812: A Documentary History*. Washington DC: Naval Historical Center, Department of the Navy, 1985; electronically published by American Naval Records Society, Bolton Landing, New York, 2011.

Dixon, Manley. Orders to James Hillyar, July 1, 1813, in William S. Dudley and Michael J. Crawford, eds., *The Naval War of 1812: A Documentary History*. Washington DC: Naval Historical Center, Department of the Navy, 1985; electronically published by American Naval Records Society, Bolton Landing, New York, 2011.

Feltus, William M. Diary entry, June 25, 1813, in William S. Dudley and Michael J. Crawford, eds., *The Naval War of 1812: A Documentary History*. Washington, DC: Naval Historical Center, Department of the Navy, 1985; electronically published by American Naval Records Society, Bolton Landing, New York, 2011.

Montgomery, Alexander M. Letter to John M. Gamble, July 15, 1813, in Gamble, John M. *The Memorial of Lt. John M. Gamble, of the U. S. Marine Corps, to Congress 1828*. New York: George F. Hopkins & Son, 1828, p. 8.

Neumann, William. "United States Aid to the Chilean Wars of Independence," *The Hispanic American Historical Review*, vol. 27, No. 2 (May 1947), pp. 204–219.

Porter, David. Letter to Secretary of the Navy Paul Hamilton, July 2, 1813, in William S. Dudley and Michael J. Crawford, eds., *The Naval War of 1812: A Documentary History*. Washington, DC: Naval Historical Center, Department of the Navy, 1985; electronically published by American Naval Records Society, Bolton Landing, New York, 2011.

Porter, David. Letter to Edward Cary, July 23, 1813, in William S. Dudley and Michael J. Crawford, eds., *The Naval War of 1812: A Documentary History*. Washington, DC: Naval Historical Center, Department of the Navy, 1985; electronically published by American Naval Records Society, Bolton Landing, New York, 2011.

Porter, David. *Journal of a Cruise Made to the Pacific Ocean*. Philadelphia: Bradford and Inskeep, 1815.

Spears, John R. *David G. Farragut*. Philadelphia: George W. Jacobs & Co., 1905.

Tagart, Edward. *Memoir of the Late Peter Heywood, R. N.* London: Effingham Wilson, 1832.

Chapter 9

Dening, Greg. *Readings/Writings*. Melbourne: Melbourne University Press, 1998, pp. 159–178.

Farragut, David Glasgow. "Some Reminiscences of Early Life," in William S. Dudley and Michael J. Crawford, eds., *The Naval War of 1812: A Documentary History*. Washington DC: Naval Historical Center, Department of the Navy, 1985; electronically published by American Naval Records Society, Bolton Landing, New York, 2011.

Farragut, Loyall. *The Life of David Glasgow Farragut*. New York: D. Appleton & Co., 1879.

Melville, Herman. *Typee*. New York: Wiley and Putnam, 1846.

Porter, David. *Journal of a Cruise Made to the Pacific Ocean*. Philadelphia: Bradford and Inskeep, 1815.

Stevenson, Robert Louis. *In the South Seas*. London: Chatto and Windus, 1908.

Zinn, Howard. *Howard Zinn on History*. New York/London/Sydney/Toronto: Seven Stories Press, 2001.

Chapter 10

Porter, David. *Journal of a Cruise Made to the Pacific Ocean*. Philadelphia: Bradford and Inskeep, 1815.

Chapter 11

Barnard, Charles H. *Narrative of Sufferings and Adventures of Captain Charles H. Barnard*. New York: J.P. Callender, 1836.

Downes, John. Statement regarding Lt. William Ingram, RN, in *Niles' Weekly Register*, August 20, 1814.

Ingersoll, Charles J. *History of the Second War between the United States of America and Great Britain*. Philadelphia: Lippincott, Grambo & Co., 1852.

Johnston, Samuel B. *Letters Written During a Residence of Three Years in Chili,* Erie, Penn.: R. I. Curtis, 1816.

Porter, David. *Journal of a Cruise Made to the Pacific Ocean.* Bradford and Inskeep, Philadelphia, 1815.

Chapter 12

Adams, Henry. *History of the United States During the Second Administration of James Madison,* vol. II. New York: Charles Scribner's Sons, 1921.

Cowell, John G. Log Book of USF *Essex,* in William S. Dudley and Michael J. Crawford, eds., *The Naval War of 1812: A Documentary History,* vol. III, part 6 of 7, Washington, DC: Naval Historical Center, Department of the Navy, 1985; electronically published by American Naval Records Society, Bolton Landing, New York, 2011.

Farragut, David Glasgow. "Some Reminiscences of Early Life," in William S. Dudley and Michael J. Crawford, eds., *The Naval War of 1812: A Documentary History.* Washington, DC: Naval Historical Center, Department of the Navy, 1985; electronically published by American Naval Records Society, Bolton Landing, New York, 2011.

Gamble, John M. Journal paraphrased by David Porter, *Journal of a Cruise Made to the Pacific Ocean,* Vol. II, second edition. New York: Wiley and Halsted, 1822, pp. 178-231.

James, William. *A Full and Correct Account of the Chief Naval Occurrences of the Late War between Great Britain and the United States of America.* London: T. Egerton, 1817.

Johnston, Samuel Burr. *Letters Written During a Residence of Three Years in Chili.* Erie, PA: R. I. Curtis, 1816.

Parton, Dorothy M. *The Diplomatic Career Of Joel Roberts Poinsett.* Doctoral dissertation, Catholic University of America, 1934.

Porter, David. *Journal of a Cruise Made to the Pacific Ocean.* Philadelphia: Bradford and Inskeep, 1815.

Porter, David Dixon. *Memoir of Commodore David Porter, of the United States Navy.* Albany, NY: J. Munsell, 1875.

Rosales, Vicente Perez. *Times Gone By.* Oxford, England: Oxford University Press, 2003.

Chapter 13

Bainbridge, William. Quoted by Long, David F. *Nothing Too Daring: A Biography of Commodore David Porter, 1780–1843*. Annapolis: Naval Institute Press, 1970.

Carrera, José Miguel. *Diario Militar del Jeneral Don José Miguel Carrera* in *Collecion de Historiadores I de Documentos relativos de la Independencia de Chile*. Tomo I. Santiago de Chile: Imprenta Cervantes, 1900.

Columbian, The. Reprinted in *National Intelligencer*, July 22, 1814, in William S. Dudley and Michael J. Crawford, eds., *The Naval War of 1812: A Documentary History*. Washington, DC: Naval Historical Center, Department of the Navy, 1985; electronically published by American Naval Records Society, Bolton Landing, New York, 2011.

Farragut, David Glasgow. "Some Reminiscences of Early Life," in William S. Dudley and Michael J. Crawford, eds., *The Naval War of 1812: A Documentary History*. Washington, DC: Naval Historical Center, Department of the Navy, 1985; electronically published by American Naval Records Society, Bolton Landing, New York, 2011.

Feltus, William M. Diary entry, in William S. Dudley and Michael J. Crawford, eds., *The Naval War of 1812: A Documentary History*. Washington, DC: Naval Historical Center, Department of the Navy, 1985; electronically published by American Naval Records Society, Bolton Landing, New York, 2011.

Gamble, John M. *The Memorial of Lt. John M. Gamble, of the U. S. Marine Corps, to Congress 1828*. New York: George F. Hopkins & Son, 1828.

Hillyar, James. Letter to David Porter, April 4, 1814, in William S. Dudley and Michael J. Crawford, eds., *The Naval War of 1812: A Documentary History*. Washington, DC: Naval Historical Center, Department of the Navy, 1985; electronically published by American Naval Records Society, Bolton Landing, New York, 2011.

Irving, Washington. "Biographical Memoir of Captain David Porter," *Analectic Magazine*, 1814, Vol. IV, New Series. Philadelphia: Moses Thomas.

James, William. *A Full and Correct Account of the Chief Naval Occurrences of the Late War between Great Britain and the United States of America*. London: T. Egerton, 1817.

Jones, William. "Letter from Secretary of the Navy transmitting official account of the capture of the British sloop of war *Reindeer* by U.S. sloop of war *Wasp* on June 28 instant" October 17, 1814, U.S. Navy Department, S33266. Washington, DC: Roger C. Weightman, 1814.

Porter, David. *Journal of a Cruise Made to the Pacific Ocean.* Philadelphia: Bradford and Inskeep, 1815.

Chapter 14

Carrera, José Miguel. *Diario Militar del Jeneral Don José Miguel Carrera* in *Collecion de Historiadores I de Documentos relativos de la Independencia de Chile.* Tomo I. Santiago de Chile: Imprenta Cervantes, 1900.

Galdames, Luis. *Estudio de Historia de Chile,* Santiago: Editorial Universitaria, 1906.

Gamble, John M. *The Memorial of Lt. John M. Gamble, of the U.S. Marine Corps, to Congress 1828.* New York: George F. Hopkins & Son, 1828.

Porter, David. *Journal of a Cruise Made to the Pacific Ocean.* Philadelphia: Bradford and Inskeep, 1815.

Yates, William, in appendix to Graham, Maria. *Journal of a Residence in Chile during the Year 1822.* London: Longman, Hurst, et al., 1824.

Chapter 15

"A. B.," in *Philadelphia Gazette,* quoted in *Salem (Massachusetts) Gazette,* April 4, 1815.

Irving, Washington. Quoted in *Albany Gazette,* November 24, 1814.

James, William. *The Naval History of Great Britain.* London: Richard Bentley, 1837.

James, William. *A Full and Correct Account of the Chief Naval Occurrences of the Late War between Great Britain and the United States of America.* London: T. Egerton, 1817.

Jones, William. Letter to John Rodgers, August 23, 1814, in William S. Dudley and Michael J. Crawford, eds., *The Naval War of 1812: A Documentary History.* Washington, DC: Naval Historical Center, Department of the Navy, 1985; electronically published by American Naval Records Society, Bolton Landing, New York, 2011.

Jones, William. Letter to David Porter, August 19, 1814, in William S. Dudley and Michael J. Crawford, eds., *The Naval War of 1812: A Documentary History.* Washington, DC: Naval Historical Center, Department of the Navy, 1985; electronically published by American Naval Records Society, Bolton Landing, New York, 2011.

"Las Casas" (pen name of unknown writer) in *Albany (New York) Gazette*, November 24, 1814.

Long, David F. *Nothing Too Daring: A Biography of Commodore David Porter, 1780–1843*. Annapolis: Naval Institute Press, 1970.

Miley, Enoch M. et al. Letter to David Porter, July 20, 1814, in William S. Dudley and Michael J. Crawford, eds., *The Naval War of 1812: A Documentary History*. Washington, DC: Naval Historical Center, Department of the Navy, 1985; electronically published by American Naval Records Society, Bolton Landing, New York, 2011.

Porter, David. Letter to James Madison, January 12, 1815, in William S. Dudley and Michael J. Crawford, eds., *The Naval War of 1812: A Documentary History*. Washington, DC: Naval Historical Center, Department of the Navy, 1985; electronically published by American Naval Records Society, Bolton Landing, New York, 2011.

Porter, David. *Journal of a Cruise Made to the Pacific Ocean*. Philadelphia: Bradford & Inskeep, 1815.

Salem *Gazette*, quoted in Georgetown (Washington, DC) *Federal Republican*, December 23, 1814.

Simms, Charles. Letter to Nancy Simms, September 3, 1814, in William S. Dudley and Michael J. Crawford, eds., *The Naval War of 1812: A Documentary History*. Washington, DC: Naval Historical Center, Department of the Navy, 1985; electronically published by American Naval Records Society, Bolton Landing, New York, 2011.

Chapter 16

"A. B.," in *Philadelphia Gazette*, quoted in *Salem (Massachusetts) Gazette*, April 4, 1815.

Booth, Robert. *Death of an Empire*. New York: Thomas Dunne Books, 2011.

Chandler, Charles Lyon. "Admiral Charles Whiting Wooster in Chile." *Annual Report of the American Historical Association For The Year 1916*. Washington, DC: 1919, pp. 447–456.

Collier, Simon. *Ideas and Politics of Chilean Independence, 1808–1833*. Cambridge, England: Cambridge University Press, 1967.

The Gentlemen's Magazine, Sylvanus Urban ed., Vol. XX New Series, July–December 1843, London: William Pickering.

Graham, Maria. *Journal of a Residence in Chile During the Year 1822*. London, Longman, Hurst, et al, 1824.

"Lautaro," letter No. 2 to Henry Clay, Richmond *Enquirer*, reprinted in *Daily National Intelligencer* (Washington, DC), October 2, 1817.

Melville, Herman. *Typee*. New York: Wiley and Putnam, 1846.

Poinsett, Joel Roberts. Letter, October 31, 1817, cited by Henry B. Cox. "Reasons for JRP's Refusal of a Second Mission to SA," *Hispanic American Historical Review*, Vol. 43, No. 3, August 1963.

Poinsett, Joel Roberts. "Report to Secretary of State John Quincy Adams on the Condition of South America," *Annals of Congress, Debates and Proceedings 1789–1824, Vol. 33, 16 November 1818–17 February 1819*, online at Library of Congress website.

"Report from Buenos Aires," February 22, 1817, copied in *American Beacon* (Norfolk, Virginia), May 19, 1817.

Stevenson, Robert Louis. *In the South Seas*. London: Chatto and Windus, 1908.

Twohill, Nicholas. "The British World and Its Role in the Relationship between New Zealand and the Southern Cone Countries of South America, 1820–1914." *Historia*, Vol. 43, No.1, June 2010. Santiago. Online.

Yates, William. Appendix in Graham, Maria. *Journal of a Residence in Chile during the Year 1822*. London: Longman, Hurst, et al, 1824.

Index

A

Abascal, José Fernando de
   American vessels and, 56, 61, 66, 75
   Dixon and, 86, 87
   Gainza and, 136, 137
   Hillyar and, 131–132
   independence movement and, 44,
      50–51
   invasion by, 60, 74
   Porter and, 84
   role of, 3
   royalists and, 53
Adams, David P., 26, 83, 89, 106
Adams, Henry, 154n, 156
Adams, John Quincy, 16, 207, 213
Adeline, 205
Albatros, 115, 160
Alert, 22, 172
Alexander, Czar, 15, 16, 61
Alexandria, 187–190
America, 201
Anderson, Evelina, 8
Anson, Lord George, 35–36, 98
Arteaga, 176
Artigas, José Gervasio, 194, 206
Astor, John Jacob, 85n, 210
Astoria, 85n
Atalanta, 196
Atlantic, 68, 81, 82, 83, 84
Atlas, 68
Aurora de Chile, 45–46, 50
Avon, 196

B

Bainbridge, William, 6, 22, 24–25, 32,
   35, 52, 81, 130–131, 174

Baker (marooned sailor), 103
Balcarce, Marcos, 93, 94, 183
Banda Oriental, 194
Barba, José Vicente, 72, 73
Barbary States, 6
Barclay, 64, 65, 66, 67, 81, 84, 88–89
Barnewall, Edward, 58n, 71, 72, 73, 132,
   156, 159, 186, 190
Barney, Joshua, 187
Baxter, Captain, 81
Beaver, 210
Belcher, Thomas, 160, 163, 164
Benavente, Diego, 59, 61, 177, 184
Blakeley, Johnston, 97, 170–171, 196
Blanco, 153, 179
Bland, Francis, 145
Board of Navy Commissioners, 201
Bolivar, Simon, 210
Bostwick, Melancthon W., 26
Bowman, Captain, 81
Boxer, 97
Brudenell, William, 115, 160, 165, 166
Bunker, Eber, 199
Burbidge, William H., 49n
Burrows, Willian, 97

C

Caledonia, 222
Call, William, 157
Cape Horn, 35–39
Carrera, Ignacio, 46, 176
Carrera, José Miguel
   after defeat, 182–184
   after war, 175–176
   background of, 43
   banishment of, 159

capture of, 206
at Chillan, 76, 93
Cienfuegos and, 94
at Concepcion, 75
defeat of, 166-169
in exile, 211-212
expulsion of, 136
freeing of, 169
independence movement and, 43-46,
   49-50, 56-57
Lastra and, 53
military resources and, 176-177
O'Higgins and, 136-137, 178
ousting of Lastra by, 176
Poinsett and, 194
popularity of, 42
Porter and, 55, 59, 84
in prison, 132, 138, 153, 167, 168,
   208
Rancagua and, 180-183
role of, 2-3
Rozas and, 47-48
Sanchez-Pareja forces and, 74
strategy and, 70, 71
at Talca, 69, 71
in United States, 203, 204-205
war preparations and, 60-62
Carrera, Juan José, 43, 46, 47, 56, 93,
   132, 136-137, 138, 176, 180, 183-
   184, 208
Carrera, Luis (Lucho), 43, 56, 58-59,
   70, 74, 76, 132, 136-137, 167, 169,
   175-178, 180-181, 184, 208
Casas, Las, 192-193
Catherine, 83, 92, 134
Centurion, 36
Charles, 64
Charlton, 89, 90
Cherub, 87-88, 92, 126-127, 133-134,
   140, 142-143, 146-147, 149, 168,
   178-180, 195
Chesapeake, 191
Chilean constitution, 49
Chilean independence movement
   Carrera and, 43-46, 49-50, 56-57
   end of, 167
Chillan, battle at, 76
Cienfuegos, José Ignacio, 93-94

Clapp, Benjamin, 160, 161, 163, 164,
   165-166, 195
Clarke, Midshipman, 31
Clay, Henry, 10, 204, 205, 207-208
Cleveland, Richard J., 210
Clifton, 205, 206
Cochrane, Admiral Lord, 210, 211
Coddington, 165-166
Coffin, Isaac, 160, 161-162
Colnett, 91
Colt, 58n, 61, 71, 159, 196
Columbia, 185
Columbus, Christopher, 112
Comet, 92
Constantinople and Its Environs (Porter), 221
constitution of Chile, 49
Cook, Captain, 8, 9, 79, 98, 100, 108,
   160, 192
Cowan, John S., 83
Cowell, John Glover, 26-27, 39, 40, 67,
   83, 91, 148, 150, 155, 191n
Creighton, John O., 187, 188-189
Creoles
   American relations with, 45
   declaration of independence by, 17
   Poinsett's encouragement of, 19-20
   Porter's assessment of, 57
Crowninshield, Benjamin W., 201, 202
Curson, Samuel, 74

D

Darwin, Charles, 79, 221
Davey, 205
Decatur, Stephen, 22, 187, 193
Dinamore, Samuel, 26n
disease and illness, 27, 37
Dixon, Manley, 85-88, 195
Downes, John
   Cape Horn and, 39
   command of, 84, 95
   departure of on *Essex*, 26
   Hector and, 83-84
   Hillyar battle and, 147
   on *Macedonian*, 210
   Nereyda and, 65
   at Nukuhiva, 107, 110-111
   retention of, 83
   return of, 92

return to United States and, 172
at Santa Catarina, 33
selling prizes, 88–89
in Sumatra, 217n
Taipi battle and, 117–118, 119
in Valparaiso, 2, 52, 127
see also Essex Junior
Dusenbury, Samuel, 71
Dwight, Timothy, 13

E

Edward, 64n, 89, 90
Elizabeth, 31
Enana, 103–107, 109–113, 114–125, 166, 218–220
Enterprize, 97
Epervier, 170
Essex
arrival of in Valparaiso, 1–2
breaking of, 141
crew of, 25–27
description of, 27–28
first cruise of, 22
illustration of, 146
Lastra on, 53
Porter's taking command of, 10–11
repairs to, 107, 112–113, 122
Wasp compared to, 96
Essex Junior
command of, 84
crossing Pacific, 95
escape of, 172–173
Johnston and, 159
at Nukuhiva, 107
Porter's defeat and, 152, 156, 157n, 168
return to United States and, 169, 171
sale of, 186
Taipi battle and, 117
at Valparaiso, 88, 127, 129–130, 133, 141
whalers and, 98

F

Fama, 71, 72
Farragut, David Glasgow "Gatty," 25, 88–89, 106, 135, 144, 145, 147–148, 150, 155, 172–173, 222

Farragut, George, 8
Farragut, James Glasgow, 8
Feltus, William M., 29, 34, 81, 84, 160, 161, 163, 164, 165, 166
Fernando VII, 51, 53, 85, 86, 96, 132, 137–138, 158, 167, 204
Finch, William, 26, 31
Folger, Seth, 64n
Folger, Solomon, 68, 72, 90
Formas, Captain, 138, 142, 156, 177
Fort Madison, 105, 115–116, 159
Fraser, John Went, 188–189
Freemasonry, 215
Freire, Ramon, 210
Frolic, 169

G

Gainza, Gabino, 136, 137, 158, 167, 168, 177
Gallatin, Albert, 16, 17–18
Gamble, John Marshall, 25, 34–35, 82, 89, 91, 123, 157, 159–166, 178–180, 195–196
Gardner, Grafton, 64, 66
Gattanewa, 104–105, 106–107, 109, 110–111, 114–115, 117, 121, 160, 166
George, 63
Georgiana, 81, 83, 90, 92
Gerry, Elbridge, 187
Ghent, Treaty of, 197–198
Gibbs, Thomas, 166
Good Hope, 195–196
Gordon, J. A., 188, 189–190
Greenwich, 82, 84, 89, 95, 159, 162–166
Gross, Samuel, 35
Guerriere, 22

H

Hambleton, Samuel, 25n
Hamilton, Paul, 9–10, 11, 23–24, 84, 154–155
Hapa'a, 104, 107–108, 109–111, 116, 117, 118–119, 121, 160–161, 166, 201
Hawaii, 108, 160, 179
Hazen, Benjamin, 150
Hector, 83, 92, 134, 152
Henriquez, Camilo, 46, 50
Hillyar, James

Abascal and, 131–132
after victory, 166–169
assignment of, 84–85
battle with Porter and, 144
chase and, 141–142, 143
decoy and, 140
Dixon and, 87–88
Gainza and, 158
Lastra and, 131, 132–133
Poinsett and, 156
Porter and, 7, 133–136, 138–139
Porter's blaming of, 154
Porter's surrender and, 150–152, 153
portrait of, 86
in retirement, 222–223
role of, 3
at Valparaiso, 126–131
HMS *Java*, 81
Hoevel, Matthew, 45, 51
Hoffman, Richard, 34, 37, 148, 150, 186, 190
Hope, 51, 100
Hornet, 22, 35, 52
Hull, Isaac, 22, 53, 130–131
Hunt, Captain, 160

I

impressment, 10, 19
Infante, José Miguel, 177
Ingraham, Joseph, 100
Ingram, William, 126–127, 128, 129, 134–135, 143, 144, 151, 155
Irassari, 176, 177
Irvine, Baptis, 204–205
Irving, Washington, 8, 173, 174, 191–192
Isaac Todd, 88
Iturbide, Agustin de, 213

J

Jackson, Andrew, 193, 198, 216, 220
Jackson, General, 95
Jefferson, Thomas, 6, 9, 10
Johnston, Samuel B., 50, 60, 71, 72–73, 132, 142, 144, 148, 156, 158–159, 167
Jones, William, 84, 95–96, 153–154, 171, 174, 185, 186, 187, 188, 191, 193

Journal and Remarks 1832–1835 (Darwin), 221
Journal of a Cruise made to the Pacifick Ocean (Porter), 199–201, 221
Joy, Obed, 68

K

King, John, 72, 73, 123, 161
Klaer, William, 27, 31

L

Laborde, Admiral, 215
Lake Erie, Battle of, 96
Larrain, Father Joaquin, 93, 177
Larrain family, 43–44, 49, 93, 138, 194
Lastra, Francisco de la
Barnewall and, 72
blaming of, 156
British and, 158–159
Carreras and, 175, 176
as governor of Valparaiso, 138
Hillyar and, 131, 132–133
imprisonment of, 176
lack of U.S. support for, 86
nationalist navy and, 70, 71, 73
Poinsett and, 156
Porter and, 52–53, 57, 59, 60, 131, 134
Lawrence, 96
Lawrence, James, 22, 25, 32, 52, 130–131, 169, 191
Lindsey, Joseph, 191n
Lircay, Treaty of, 167, 176
Livingston, Robert, 14–15
Louis Philippe, 218
Lowry, Robert, 17
Lyman, James R., 168, 196

M

MacDonogh, Giles, 191
Macedonian, 210
Mackenna, Juan, 43–44, 46–47, 70–71, 74, 76, 93–94, 136–137, 159, 167, 169, 176–177, 182, 184
Madison, James
British and, 187
Carrera and, 203
Florida and, 17

impressment and, 10
lack of support for, 23
New Orleans and, 198
Poinsett and, 16, 18, 19, 42, 51
Porter and, 174, 191, 193, 199, 201
reelection of, 92
war effort and, 95
Maipu, 208-209
Manners, William, 170
Marco, Casimiro, 205
Marin, Gaspar, 43
maritime commerce
Britain and France and, 10
Britain's dominance over, 7-8
privateers and, 11-12
Marquesas, 99-102
Mary Ann, 92, 107
Maury, John M., 103, 107, 140
McKnight, Stephen Decatur, 26, 68, 82, 83, 128, 129, 148-149, 168, 196
Melville, Herman, 218-219
Milay, Enoch Morgan, 26n, 148n, 186
Miller, Robert, 26
Miranda, Francisco, 17, 46
Mollen, Jan Gabriel, 196
Monroe, James, 19, 61, 76-77, 189, 193, 203-204, 207, 213
Monson, Massena, 58n
Montagu, 33, 35
Monteaguda, 208
Montezuma, 81, 84, 92
Mouina, 109-111, 114, 118, 120, 160, 166, 201, 219

N

Napoleon, 6, 10, 14, 15, 16, 21, 85, 96-97, 197-198
Narcissus, 172
Nash, Captain, 171, 172
National Portrait Gallery, 217
Necker, Jacques, 15
Neptune, 29-30
Nereyda, 65-66, 67, 73, 84
neutrality, 6, 10, 130, 152
New Orleans, Battle of, 198
New Zealander, 89, 92, 95, 123, 159, 160, 161

Niagara, 96
Nimrod, 65, 66-67, 67
Nocton, 30-31, 35
North Point, Battle of, 191
Nukuhiva, 102-113, 114-125, 159-166, 191-192, 218-220
nullification movement, 216

O

O'Brien, George, 126
Odenheimer, William H., 83
O'Higgins, Bernardo
background of, 46-47
Carrera and, 70, 72, 93, 94, 136-137, 175
Clay and, 204, 207
Concepcion and, 69-70
Gainza and, 168, 169
Hillyar and, 132
Infante and, 177
L. Carrera and, 177-178
Lastra and, 86
Lircay treaty and, 167
patriots and, 62
Poinsett and, 49, 140-141
Rancagua and, 180-183
Rozas and, 47
with San Martin, 205-206, 208, 209-210, 211
at Talcahuano, 75-76
Oliver Ellsworth, 196
Ordonez, 209
Osorio, Mariano, 177, 178, 180-182, 193, 203, 206, 208-209

P

Pareja, General, 69-71, 74, 76
Patriot, 205
Paulding, James K., 173, 201
Peacock, 169-170
Pearl, 71, 72-73
Perla, La, 71-73, 73, 132
Perry, Captain, 65
Perry, Oliver Hazard, 96, 188, 190
Pettenger, John, 165, 166
Philadelphia, 6

Phoebe, 88, 92, 126–131, 133–136, 140, 142–147, 149–153, 156, 168, 173, 222

Pinckney, Charles, 15

Piteenee, 104–105, 106

Pitts, Captain, 81

Platt, Charles, 188

Poinsett, Joel Roberts
  on Argentina, 193–194
  arrival of in Chile, 42
  background of, 13–16
  in Buenos Aires, 18–20
  Carrera and, 45, 61, 93, 177, 203–204
  on Chile, 46, 194–195
  Chilean constitution and, 49
  in Congress, 213
  description of, 3
  Dixon and, 85–86
  expulsion of, 156
  Gallatin and, 17–18
  Hillyar and, 87, 132
  intelligence from, 92
  joining army of Chile, 61–62
  lack of U.S. support for, 51
  Monroe and, 207
  new Chilean government and, 48–50
  nullification movement and, 216
  Porter and, 138–139, 140–141, 142, 214, 215
  Porter's arrival and, 2, 55–57
  Porter's loss and, 152–153
  portrait of, 44
  return to United States of, 196–197
  Sanchez-Pareja forces and, 74
  as secretary of war, 216–217
  self-assessment of, 76–77
  strategy and, 70, 71, 74–75, 76
  at Talca, 69
  at Talcahuano, 75
  in Valparaiso, 59–60

Policy, 81, 88, 92, 98

Porter, David Dixon, 222

Porter, David, Jr.
  after defeat, 168, 169
  after surrender, 153–154
  after war, 199–202
  in Alexandria, 188–189

arrival of in Pacific, 40–41
arrival of in Valparaiso, 1–2, 51, 52
background of, 5–9
Bainbridge and, 22
at ball, 57–58, 60
blaming of others by, 154–155
Cape Horn and, 35–39
Caribbean plan and, 191, 193
Carrera and, 56–57, 204–205, 206–207
command of *Essex* and, 10–11
Cowell and, 26–27
crew and, 28–29, 91–92
criticisms of, 192–193
death and burial of, 221–222
description of, 3
distribution of spoils by, 90
Dixon and, 87
escape attempt by, 142–144
escape from Nash by, 172
failures of, 156–157, 185–186
first cruise on *Essex* and, 22
at Galapagos, 78–81, 89, 91
Hamilton and, 23–24
Hillyar and, 88, 92, 126–131, 133–136, 138–139, 140
Hillyar battle and, 144–149
in Istanbul, 220–221
justifications of, 66–67
Lastra and, 52–53
at Marquesas, 99–102
marriage of, 8
in Mexico, 214–215
Nereyda and, 65–66
new ship and, 185, 187
at Nukuhiva, 102–113, 114–125
Poinsett and, 55–57, 138–139
portrait of, 24
on privateers, 11
rendezvous attempts by, 28–32
on repairs, 113
reprisal for, 73–74
return to United States and, 173–174
at Santa Catarina, 33–35
self-assessment of, 98–99
start of war and, 22–25
surrender of, 150–152

Taipi battle and, 114-122
at Tumez, 83
at Valparaiso, 126
whalers and, 63-65, 78-82
at White House Point, 189-190
Worth and, 63
Portus, J. M., 177-178, 181
Posadas, 193
Potrillo, El, 71, 72, 73, 132
Pratt, 189
Preble, Edward, 28
President, 68, 72
Pringle, Mary Izard, 216
privateers
maritime commerce and, 11-12,
21-22
role of, 169
Provost, General, 191
Puerryedon, Juan Martin, 204, 206, 207
Puga, Juan, 70-71

R

Racoon, 85n, 87, 88, 92, 167-168
rafts, 68-69
Ramsey, Doctor, 195
Rancagua, 180-183
Randall, Gideon, 64, 67, 88-89
Reindeer, 170
Revenge, 222
Rivera, 176
Roberts, Josiah, 100
Robinson, John, 161, 162
Rodgers, John, 22, 187, 188, 190
Rodriguez, Manuel, 59, 184, 208, 209-
210
Rose, 83-84
Ross, George, 115, 160, 165, 166
Ross, Henry, 70-71
Ross, Robert, 187
Rozas, Juan Martinez, 43, 44, 46, 47, 62
Ruff, Henry, 145
Russell, Thomas, 26n, 148n
Rynard, James, 80, 91-92

S

San José de la Fama, 59
San Martin, José Francisco de, 93, 138,

177, 182-183, 194, 205-206, 208,
209, 211
Sanchez, Juan Francisco, 74, 76, 94
sanitation, 28
Santa Ana, General, 215
Santa Catarina, 33-35
Saturn, 171, 172
Seahorse, 188, 189
Seringapatam, 63-64, 67, 89, 91, 95, 159,
161-164, 186, 198-199
Shaler, William, 9, 17, 213
Shaw, John R., 26, 34-35, 83, 139
Shuttleworth, John, 82, 84
Simms, Clark, 188, 189
Sinclair, William, 26n
Sir Andrew Hammond, 91-92, 95, 159,
161-166, 179, 195
Skinner, John S., 204, 207
slavery, 47
Smith, Robert, 17
Smith, Samuel, 188, 191
Smithsonian Institution, 217
Spafford, James, 68
Staël, Madame de, 15
Standard, 66
Stanley, Martin, 163-164
Stansbury, Richard, 164
Stavers, William, 64n, 89-90
Stevenson, Robert Louis, 219-220
Sumter, Thomas, Jr., 16, 195
Sweeney, Edward, 35
Swook, Peter, 162

T

Taipi, 114-125, 160-161, 192, 200, 201,
218-219
Talcahuano, 40, 59, 61, 68, 70-72, 74-
76, 75, 81-82, 92, 177, 186
tattoos, 101-102
Tavee, 121
Temaa Tipee, 114
Terra del Fuego, 37
Thomas, John, 166
Thomas, Joseph, 26, 148n
Ticonderoga, 191n
Tingey, Captain, 187
Torpoint, 222-223

Tucker, Captain Thomas Tudor, 88, 126, 140, 141, 143, 168, 178, 179–180
Tyler, John, 222
Typee (Melville), 218

U

United States
  after revolution, 6
  declaration of war by, 21, 50
  war effort and, 95–96
Uribe, Julian, 184
U.S.S. *Constitution*, 22, 28, 35, 52–53, 81

V

Van Buren, Martin, 216
Vitoria, Battle of, 96
Voyage of the Beagle (Darwin), 221

W

Wadden, Benjamin, 26n, 148n
Walker, 64, 65
Warren, 72, 73
Warrington, Lewis, 169–170

Washington Islands, 99–100
Wasp, 29, 96, 97, 169, 170, 196
Welch, John, 162
Wellesley, General Arthur (Wellington), 21, 85, 96, 158, 167, 198
West, Paul, 64, 65, 66, 67
whalers/whaling, 9, 34, 63–69, 75
White, Robert, 160, 164
White House Point, 189–190
Wilkes, Charles, 217
Wilmer, James P., 26, 34–35, 83, 127, 145
Wilson (marooned sailor), 103–104, 107, 117, 119, 123, 124, 160, 165, 166
Wilson, James, 26, 90
Winder, William, 187
Witter, John, 161
Worth, Benjamin, 63–64, 67, 165–166
Worth, William, 164
Wyer, Obed, 68, 81–82, 84

Y

Yates, William, 211, 212

Robert Booth (Marblehead, MA) grew up on salt water as a lobsterman, yacht racer, and sailing instructor. He is an authority on New England's historic architecture and maritime culture and curator *emeritus* of the Pickering House (1664) of Salem. In 2005 he helped to rescue America's last surviving Revolutionary War privateering base, which was moved from Marblehead to Salem's federal park devoted to seafaring. He works as executive director of the Center for Clinical Social Work, a national association for members of the largest mental health-care profession in the country. Among his publications are the guidebook *Boston's Freedom Trail*, still in print after thirty years; a chapter in the 2004 anthology *Salem: Place, Myth and Memory*; the book *Death of an Empire: The Rise and Murderous Fall of Salem, America's Richest City* (Thomas Dunne Books, NY, 2011), and the upcoming *The Women of Marblehead*, a feminist history of the town in the nineteenth century.